ARE WE SCREWED?

ARE WE SCREWED ?

HOW A NEW GENERATION IS FIGHTING TO SURVIVE CLIMATE CHANGE

GEOFF DEMBICKI

B L O O M S B U R Y

NEW YORK · LONDON · OXFORD · NEW DELHI · SYDNEY

Bloomsbury USA
An imprint of Bloomsbury Publishing Plc

1385 Broadway	50 Bedford Square
New York	London
NY 10018	WC1B 3DP
USA	UK

www.bloomsbury.com

BLOOMSBURY and the Diana logo are trademarks of Bloomsbury Publishing Plc

First published 2017

ISBN: HB: 978-1-63286-481-9
ePub: 978-1-63286-482-6
TPB: 978-1-63557-078-6

Library of Congress Cataloging-in-Publication Data is available.

2 4 6 8 10 9 7 5 3 1

Typeset by RefineCatch Limited, Bungay, Suffolk
Printed and bound in the U.S.A. by Berryville Graphics Inc., Berryville, Virginia

To find out more about our authors and books visit www.bloomsbury.com. Here you will find extracts, author interviews, details of forthcoming events and the option to sign up for our newsletters.

Bloomsbury books may be purchased for business or promotional use. For information on bulk purchases please contact Macmillan Corporate and Premium Sales Department at specialmarkets@macmillan.com.

For Kara

Contents

Introduction

WHEN I WAS AT the Paris climate talks in late 2015, I witnessed something that totally opened up my mind. It happened at an event called Young and Future Generations Day. The purpose of the event was to celebrate the achievements of people my age. It was packed with people under thirty-five. They'd come from the United States, Australia, China, India, South Africa, Brazil, Britain, and just about every country in between. There were reporters and camera crews and security all over the place. You needed a special UN badge to get into the converted airport where the event was being held. Outside, thousands of police and soldiers guarded against a terrorist attack like the one that had killed 130 people in Paris three weeks earlier. Inside, leaders from all the world's nations were trying to figure out how to keep civilization from collapsing.

Like all the young people seated around me, I had a special stake in the outcome of the COP21 negotiations. Ever since I was a toddler, world leaders had been meeting to discuss my future—whether I would have a safe, stable, and prosperous world to grow old in, or one defined by extinction, disaster, and ruin. What progress they had made toward the first option was terrifyingly slow. Before the Paris talks even began, climate scientists were predicting that 2015 was going to be the hottest year in recorded history. If leaders from nearly two hundred countries couldn't broker a deal in the French capital capable of cooling the planet, it would be me and everyone else in my generation who felt the impacts. Most of the leaders in Paris were in their forties, fifties, and sixties. They wouldn't be around when every coastal city was underwater.

But many of the people at Young and Future Generations Day could be. Most of us were in our twenties or early thirties. As "Millennials" we were the most closely studied age cohort in history. Yet rarely did the advertisers and politicians and pollsters and columnists who made sweeping generalizations about people my age ask what it was like to live with the awareness that human civilization could come undone in our lifetimes. It seemed that people of older generations were much more interested in speaking to us—or about us—than in listening to what we had to say. The UN climate change chief at the Paris COP21 talks was no exception. In her opening speech at Young and Future Generations Day, Christiana Figueres told the room to be "very proud of yourselves" for taking part in this year's climate negotiations. When she was finished speaking, she got up and walked out of the room. Nearly all the security and camera crews and reporters left with her.

For the most part, it was just people my age remaining. A delegate in her mid-twenties, Anjali Appadurai, took the mic. "I am disappointed that Christiana left the room before the youth had the chance to speak," she said. If the UN climate change chief had stayed, Anjali explained, she would have heard from a generation that has a completely different view of the world than the leaders negotiating its future. Figueres would've heard from people whose survival is literally threatened by climate change, who know that a better world is possible but see it blocked by the "deeply flawed" structures of our current one. "A new paradigm that is not based upon extraction from the Earth and oppression of one another does live in this generation," Anjali declared.

All around me young people were nodding their heads in agreement. And when Anjali finished speaking, the room erupted in cheers and applause. Dozens of people gave her a standing ovation. I realized in that moment that Anjali was speaking to an anxiety lodged deep in my generation's subconscious—one at the very center of what was being negotiated in Paris. Since our formative years we'd lived through one global disruption after the next. We'd been ripped from our place and history by neoliberalism, duped into disastrous conflicts by the Wars on

Terror and Drugs, and stunted by the Wall Street crash. Nobody needed to convince us to distrust our political and economic system. The evidence was everywhere.

But the most damning piece of it was accumulating in our atmosphere. In the lead-up to the Paris talks, the former NASA climatologist James Hansen warned that if we did not immediately send global emissions on a downward trajectory—a feat that would require us to completely transform society—humankind could within the next fifty years face a multimeter sea level rise that would threaten "the fabric of civilization."[1] The surest way of avoiding such a scenario is to keep over 80 percent of the world's oil, coal, and gas reserves in the ground. Yet in 2012 the fossil fuel industry spent $674 billion finding and developing new reserves.[2] Over the past decade it's spent billions more to influence politics in its favor. In the United States, oil companies and their allies have spent over $500 million lobbying Washington since President Obama's Clean Power Plan was proposed.[3] And the billionaire Koch brothers, much of whose fortune comes from fossil fuels, announced they would spend $889 million influencing the 2016 election (a figure that was later scaled back).[4]

To the people my age at Young and Future Generations Day, this was evidence of a political and economic system that didn't care about our survival. And after spending our entire lives inside that system, we were starting to reject it. More and more of us were becoming convinced that capitalism needed to ditch its focus on short-term profits; that our national identities were less important than our global ones; and that politics was way too obsessed with left versus right. This generational values shift posed a radical challenge to the world we currently live in. It was the "new paradigm" that Anjali was describing in Paris. Yet as I'd seen when Figueres walked out of the room, few people in positions of power seemed to be taking it—or us—all that seriously.

It wouldn't be long before they were forced to. I now knew from firsthand experience that under the right conditions, my generation is capable of rapid and transformational change. Before Paris, I'd been to Silicon Valley, Canada's tar sands, Washington, D.C., Wall Street, and many places in between. Along the way I saw powerful glimpses of the future that people my age are creating. I saw it in a young homesteader fending for himself in the Pacific Coast rain forest. A Brooklyn artist unwittingly terrifying the oil industry. A Middlebury graduate helping to force Obama's hand on climate change. A Vancouver activist risking his reputation and career to topple a petrostate. A Harvard sophomore taking on a $5 trillion industry. A scientist running across Norway's rapidly melting Arctic. An indigenous filmmaker challenging the worldview of Silicon Valley. A Muslim feminist fomenting a political revolution in Iowa.

Each time people my age came together to create a better future—when, for instance, we transformed a fringe socialist politician named Bernie Sanders into a serious contender for U.S. president—elders dismissed our radical worldview as a passing phase. But the Millennials I met while researching this book proved that worldview has in fact been developing and evolving for years, and that its impacts will persist long into the future. Like many others my age, these young people are fed up with a status quo that refuses to take their survival seriously. And they were told over and over again by people in power that it is naïve and impractical to demand one that does. What I learned from hearing their stories was that those people in power are completely wrong. Our political and economic leaders think things will stay the way they are now forever. Like all the others seated beside me in Paris, though, I knew that the system we live in is more fragile than it appears. I knew that when people of my generation work together to confront it, the impacts are profound and immediate. But I also knew that time is ticking down. The planet is getting hotter every day. And with the election of Donald Trump to the White House, we don't have much time left to prove it.

PART I

Rejecting the Status Quo

1

Alone on a Little Island

IN 2003 PETER JANES said goodbye to our political and economic system—or tried to, at least. He started by saying goodbye to his under-graduate degree in anthropology and environmental studies at the University of Victoria. Next, he said goodbye to the sleepy British Columbia capital of Victoria on Canada's west coast, where he'd pursued it. Then he packed his bags for the rain forest. Ever since Peter could remember, he'd felt a sense of deep unease about the future. Where our political and economic leaders talked of endless growth and profits, he could see only an unfolding catastrophe. Across the world, forests were shrinking, glaciers were melting, oceans were acidifying, and plants and animals were dying off. And up above it all was the existential tick-tock of our overheating atmosphere. How much carbon dioxide could we pump into it before human life was completely fried?

The warning signs were becoming more obvious all the time. In 2003 a European heat wave warmer than anything the continent had experienced since at least the 1500s killed an estimated 35,000 people.[1] A massive Australian drought caused billions of dollars in economic losses. Japanese researchers recorded accelerated rates of sea level rise. And across North America winters were getting shorter, annual temperatures were getting warmer, and extreme weather was becoming more common. Researchers noted that if these trends continue, a future "Illinois summer may well feel like one in east Texas today."[2] By then, the world's leading authority on rising global temperatures, the Intergovernmental Panel on Climate Change, had already noted that "there is new and stronger evidence that most of the warming observed over the last 50 years is attributable to human activities."[3]

The fossil fuel industry had known this fact for decades. Scientists working for ExxonMobil warned the company in 1977 that "mankind is influencing the global climate . . . through carbon dioxide release from the burning of fossil fuels."[4] Yet instead of taking that planetary threat seriously and trying to shift the company away from oil, Exxon spent tens of millions of dollars over the next decades on studies and reports denying that its core business was linked to climate change. It was soon joined by the billionaire Koch brothers, much of whose fortune comes from fossil fuels, who in 1997 began giving upward of $88 million through their charitable foundations to conservative groups questioning the very science of climate change.[5] Our economic system chose short-term profits over long-term human survival.

And our political system was doing the same. The U.S. president at the time of Peter's decision, George W. Bush, presided over an administration with deep ties to the oil industry. His family had run oil companies for the past fifty years. His vice president, Dick Cheney, was the former CEO at the oil services company Halliburton. His national security adviser, Condoleezza Rice, had been a Chevron board member. "No administration has ever been more in bed with the energy industry," *Salon* reported at the time.[6] So it was no wonder that Bush opposed the international Kyoto Protocol, pushed to open up the Arctic Wildlife Refuge to oil drilling, and, just like Exxon and the Koch brothers, openly questioned the accepted science behind global warming, claiming that "there is a debate over whether it's manmade or naturally caused."[7] (Donald Trump later one-upped him by calling it a "hoax.")

Peter wanted no part of this madness. He decided to create a new way of life in the Canadian wilderness that would take his future seriously. "I wanted to be more responsible to myself and other people and try to physically make the world a better place," he said.[8] His plan was to find a piece of land in the woods, educate himself about the trees and plants and soil, grow his own food, slaughter his own animals, forge his own tools, build his own home, and generate his own electricity. Peter had only a rudimentary understanding of how to do any of this—if even that. But he figured he'd learn what he needed along the way: "I felt like becoming self-sufficient in the country was a response to the general destruction of the world I was witnessing."

He looked all over for the right piece of land. After months of searching for someplace affordable, he ended up on Denman Island, in the northernmost reaches of a Gulf Island archipelago that stretches south into U.S. waters. "It was pretty random in a way," he said. "I didn't know anything about Denman. I came here blind, so to speak." It's a small place, only about twelve miles long and three wide, bordered on the east by the Georgia Strait and on the west by Vancouver Island. Deer and pheasants tramp through its lush rain forest of Douglas fir and western red cedar. Bald eagles soar high above. Killer whales glide by the coast. The forty acres of land for sale in the interior were relatively inexpensive: "It seemed like the perfect place."

With financial help from his parents, Peter bought the property. "There's no way I'd have been able to do this without them," he admitted. He was in his early twenties. He was terrified about the future but also excited by its possibilities. He was going to build an education center in the woods where people would come to learn how to survive in the outdoors. The center would also instill in them the values of a new political and economic system. It would be a place where the survival of the planet and its people was taken just as seriously as profits; where people saw themselves as part of a global whole; where decision making was based on collective progress instead of on narrow self-interest. But first Peter needed to get himself established. He needed nourishment, shelter, and electricity. There was lots of hard work ahead.

It helped that the property on Denman came with two trailers. Peter and a girlfriend who he's no longer with sold the newer one—"a big ugly white vinyl double-wide," as he described it—for some badly needed cash. With the assistance of family and friends, they started building some chicken coops and planting a small vegetable garden. "None of us really knew what we were doing," Peter said. "We were doing little things without much of a strategic plan." It was an exciting time for him. Each action, no matter how small, pointed toward the day when he would no longer be complicit in a political and economic system bent on destroying the planet, a day when he could prove to himself that alternatives were possible. "It was definitely an ideal," he explained, "but we were doing everything we could" to achieve it.

Peter spent the coming years trying to achieve that ideal. He made a greater effort than most people would be ever able to make to live in harmony with nature. But during that time the impacts of climate change just kept getting worse and worse. California suffered its worst drought in a millennium. Arctic sea ice was melting faster and faster. In the spring of 2016 record hot temperatures in the ocean caused massive swathes of the Great Barrier Reef to bleach white. "This is the most devastating, gut-wrenching fuck up," the University of Queensland professor Justin Marshall explained.[9] And yet our political and economic system was growing ever more resistant to change. In 2013 and 2014 alone, fossil fuel companies like Exxon spent an estimated $350 million to lobby Congress against any restrictions to its business model.[10] "All oil companies have an invest-to-grow model," explained HSBC analyst Paul Spedding. "They believe the best possible thing they can do is to continue to invest in fossil fuels."[11]

At the macro level it was clearer than ever to Peter that our status quo cares little about his survival. But at the micro level he was discovering just how hard it is to build an alternative to it. Peter had faced steep challenges each step of the way. After over a decade, he seemed no closer to fixing them. His need to make money got in the way of his ideals. His daily grind made it hard to think wider than his surroundings. His independent existence offered few chances to create a wider social impact. He wondered what it added up to, and if a safer future for his generation was even possible. "I can't universalize our experience, but it takes a really long time to build alternative systems," he said. Yet by rejecting our status quo, he'd taken a crucial first step toward achieving that future—one more powerful than he realized.

AMONG THE FIRST PROMINENT people to raise the alarm about climate change was a mild-mannered NASA scientist from Iowa. In the 1970s James Hansen studied what was happening to all the carbon we were pumping into the atmosphere by burning fossil fuels. What he found was shocking. The carbon was accumulating and trapping the sun's heat. If the trend continued, he predicted, humankind could by 2100 increase the global temperature by 2.5 degrees Celsius. The Reagan administration cut funding to Hansen's research. But he kept refining his data and predictions, and in June 1988 he testified before the U.S. Senate about his research. It had been a record hot summer. Hansen was visibly sweating. "It's time to stop waffling so much and say that the evidence is pretty strong that the greenhouse effect is here," he explained to the room.[12]

In July 2015 Hansen made another shocking prediction. During the intervening decades he'd written dozens of papers about climate change and given countless interviews about its implications. He'd become one of the world's most prominent climate scientists. People across the planet paid attention when he and sixteen other co-authors put out a new paper drawing attention to a little-known internal current in the Atlantic Ocean that helps moderate global weather. As melting ice from Greenland weakens that ocean current, they calculated, it's causing heat to build up rapidly at the North and South poles. As a result, massive ice sheets in Greenland and Antarctica could melt ten times faster than previously thought.

Hansen's paper was not without controversy. He considered its findings to be so important to the upcoming climate talks in Paris that he and his co-authors put it online before it could undergo a rigorous scientific review. "As such, the paper went through an unusually public review process," wrote Robinson Meyer in the *Atlantic*.[13] It was covered in major outlets like the *New Yorker, Rolling Stone*, and the *New York Times*. Within days of its release, several climate scientists had made substantive critiques. "The paper is being revealed as much more of a rough sketch, a provocation, than a thorough, deeply grounded new thesis," Andrew Revkin wrote in the *Times*.[14] But after eight months of intense scientific peer review, it was finally published in the international journal *Atmospheric Chemistry and Physics*.

Its key findings were mostly unchanged. Ruth Mottram, a climate scientist who was originally skeptical of Hansen's paper, told *Slate* the final version was "considerably improved." She said the scenario it described was "implausible though perhaps not impossible" but added that it was "frankly terrifying." Another scientist, Richard Alley, who studies polar regions, said the paper "usefully reminds us that large and rapid changes are possible."[15] If Hansen and his colleagues were correct about Antarctica and Greenland's faster rate of melting, it could cause the oceans to rise by several meters—or over ten feet—within 50 to 150 years. At that level every coastal city on the planet could become uninhabitable: New York, Los Angeles, Shanghai, Sydney, Mumbai, Cape Town, London, Rio de Janeiro. "Have we passed a point of no return? I doubt it, but it's conceivable," Hansen explained in a statement after his paper's release. "But if we wait until the real world reveals itself clearly, it may be too late to avoid sea-level rise of several meters and loss of all coastal cities."[16]

The scenario described in Hansen's paper was so dystopian that many reporters compared it to the 2004 science fiction thriller *The Day After Tomorrow*. "We had all better hope these scientists are wrong about the planet's future," the *Washington Post* declared.[17] If Hansen and his co-authors are correct, it's hard to wrap your mind around the implications. Their paper was published as countries all across Europe struggled to handle a flood of refugees from Syria's civil war. Over three-quarters of the world's large cities are on coastline. The global impacts Hansen described would make the Syrian crisis look quaint by comparison. "Social disruption and economic consequences of such large sea level rise could be devastating," he speculated. "It is not difficult to imagine that conflicts arising from forced migrations and economic collapse might make the planet ungovernable, threatening the fabric of civilization."[18]

Hansen's warning had an especially scary significance for Peter—and for the entire generation he belongs to. Peter was born in the year 1980, a time of special interest to demographic researchers. Sometime in the late 1970s and early '80s—the year is open to debate—the cohort we've come to think of as Generation X stopped growing and a new demographic began. Boomerangs. Generation Y. Or the name most commonly bestowed on the generation of people who came of age as the twentieth century turned into the twenty-first: Millennials. Its estimated 2.5 billion members make it the world's largest living genera-tion. And the 75 million of those living in the United States not long ago passed America's Baby Boomers to claim the title. Since Millennials from other countries "are going to keep immigrating to the U.S. in the coming years," noted a 2016 story on *Vox*, "that means millennial dominance could last a long time."

But as that story's writer Libby Nelson went on to point out, the very concept of a generation is in some ways flawed. "It assumes that people born around the same time share a variety of traits and values," she wrote. "Even though the sample size those assumptions are based on is often much smaller than the entire age cohort."[19] There is one sweeping generalization about Millennials that is difficult to dispute, however. The evidence to support it is contained in Hansen's most recent study. If his findings are accurate, it could mean that the doomsday scenario he described could happen as early as 2065. Most Boomers won't be around by then. Even the youngest Gen Xers will be pushing into their nineties. But older Millennials like Peter will be in their mid-eighties. And the youngest Millennials may not even be retired.

You can certainly quibble with Hansen's timeline, as well as many of the scientific assumptions behind it. He's admitted himself that the ice sheet models he used "are still very primitive."[20] And 2065 is no doubt a worst-case scenario. But what his study reminded the world is that climate change is not an abstract scientific issue. It could in very real ways physically impact an entire generation. "What we're threat-ening to do to the future of young people is . . . irreversible, irreparable harm," Hansen said in March 2016. "We have reached a point where this is really urgent. We can't continue on this path of just hoping that emissions will go down, we're going to actually have to take the actions."[21] Because if we don't, people like Peter and myself and everyone else across the world in our generation could witness the impacts in our lifetime.

The good news is the future Hansen described is not inevitable. There's still time to avoid it. But it requires rapid changes to our polit-ical and economic system. It means that over the coming decades all the world's nations must work together to reduce carbon emissions to effectively zero. If we are successful, we still have a shot at keeping all the world's coastal cities above the oceans. If we fail, the global impacts could be felt for literally the next ten thousand years. That was the conclusion reached by a 2016 study in the prestigious scientific journal *Nature Climate Change*: that decisions we make over the next twenty or thirty years—decades when Millennials will be ascending to positions of power in society—will define the future of civilization. "No generation has ever had such an opportunity to help or harm so many hundreds of generations coming after it," said study co-author Benjamin Strauss. "We have the chance to build a legacy as the most hated or the greatest generation for 10,000 years."[22]

For the moment we seem headed toward the former. Climate scientists revealed in 2016 that February of that year was the most unusually warm month in history. It shattered the record set only one month earlier, in January. Eric Holthaus described it on *Slate* as "a major milestone moment for humanity and our relationship to our planet."[23] It strongly suggested that 2016 would be the hottest year ever. Across the world it was hard to deny the impacts. An unprecedented drought on the Marshall Islands caused the government to declare a state of emergency. France's winter was among the mildest ever recorded. Arctic sea ice shrank by about a million square kilometers from its winter average. Massive forest fires blazed out of control across Indonesia. To David Vaughan of the British Antarctic Survey, the message was clear: "This is an absolute warning of the dangers that lie ahead."[24]

ANYTIME I TOLD SOMEONE my age I was writing a book about climate change, I would get the same response. It would be some kind of variation on "Well, I recycle and I try to bike when I can and buy organic food but it doesn't seem to make that much of a difference." This is why I so badly wanted to meet Peter and learn his story. In some ways he had taken this logic of personal responsibility for climate change to its furthest possible extreme. By attempting to cut all his ties to our political and economic system, he had in effect tested the ability of one person on his or her own to make a wider difference. I wanted to know what he had learned along the way and what lessons it contained for our generation's wider struggle for a safer future.

But to actually meet Peter in person at his farm on Denman Island, I had a long journey ahead of me. From my small apartment in Vancouver, I would be taking four buses and two ferries in the pouring December rain. The seven-hour journey to the isolated Pacific coast island where Peter had spent more than a decade building a new life in the rain forest gave me lots of time to think. It gave me lots of time to ponder some confusing research that I'd been reading.

Based on Hansen's study, you would think that Millennials cared way more about climate change than their parents or grandparents. Global warming poses a much more direct threat to our future, after all, and we only have a few decades left to do anything about it. But I'd been seeing some evidence suggesting the opposite: that people my age didn't think the issue was all that urgent. A 2015 study from Harvard's Institute of Politics was particularly perplexing. It asked more than three thousand Americans between age 18 and 29 about many topics. But its questions on climate change produced some unexpected results. When asked about the science behind the rise in global temperatures, only 55 percent of the survey's respondents agreed that "global warming is a proven fact and is mostly caused by emissions from cars and industrial facilities such as power plants and factories." Climate writer Chris Mooney reported on the survey for the *Washington Post*. "That majority—55 percent—is not much bigger than the majority of Americans as a whole who feel the same way," he wrote. "So contrary to our common expectations, it doesn't seem . . . that young people today are very far out ahead of their parents when it comes to accepting the science of climate change."[25]

This was a counterintuitive finding, and not a universal one. Part of the reason I found it so confusing was that other surveys of Millennials seemed to contradict it. Four years earlier the Pew Research Center asked 4,400 U.S. adults across all age groups for their opinions on global warming. About 64 percent of those my age agreed there's solid evidence the Earth is getting warmer, compared to 59 percent of Gen Xers and 55 percent of Boomers. And Pew found that Millennials "are almost twice as likely" as people above age 65 "to say that global warming is caused mostly by human activity."[26] Pew noticed a similar generation gap several years later when it surveyed about 45,400 people in forty countries. More than 50 percent of Americans between 18 and 29 saw global warming as "a very serious problem," its survey suggested, compared to just 38 percent of people above over 50.[27]

But I still kept thinking about the Harvard survey. I couldn't get the voice of doubt that its findings had created for me out of my head. The problem with comparing one set of survey results to another is that there isn't any way to prove one is more definitive than the other. The conclusion reached by a respected institution like Pew made sense to me: people my age faced a greater threat from climate change than our parents, so we cared more about it. But who was to say that the opposite conclusion reached by Harvard was less legitimate?

I decided to look deeper into the Harvard survey. The report summarizing all its findings was forty-one pages long. Maybe there was something I'd overlooked. A few lines down from the question about climate science I saw an interesting data point. Researchers had asked the survey's young respondents what they thought was an appropriate response to global warming. Over two-thirds of them agreed with the statement that "the United States should take action to address climate change, regardless of whether or not other nations have agreed to it."[28] That didn't seem to make any sense. Hadn't only 55 percent of young people said that they accepted the mainstream science of climate change? Why were people who were unsure about the exact cause of global warming in favor of action to prevent it?

In fact, the international survey on climate change from Pew I referred to earlier contained a similar finding. Six in ten of its Millennial respondents agreed that the atmosphere is getting hotter because of human activity. But in the United States at least, 85 percent of young people supported the idea that America should participate in an agreement to limit humankind's carbon emissions. This was quite a bit higher, as it turned out, than the 60 percent of older Americans who held the same opinion.[29] The more I thought about it, the more it began to make sense. Since you don't need to be certain about the science of climate change to think it is worth addressing, scientific questions aren't the best predictor of people's attitudes. Researchers should ask about solutions to the crisis rather than its causes.

When University of Texas researchers did just that in 2014 they found evidence of a dramatic generational divide. Their survey asked more than 2,100 U.S. adults to give opinions on various solutions to climate change. Two-thirds of its Millennial respondents said they supported efforts to cut carbon and increase the use of renewable energy, while only half of people 65 or older held a similar view. And about 56 percent of young people said they'd pay higher prices to reduce environmental harm, as opposed to 20 percent of older respondents. "It certainly is a striking difference," explained Sheril Kirshenbaum, the survey's lead researcher. "That's well beyond the margin of error."[30] To her it was evidence "we're seeing a widening gulf among older and younger Americans" on climate change.[31] Many other major surveys, including ones from ABC News and research firms like Greenberg Quinlan Rosner, reached a similar conclusion. "The polling evidence on this score is copious," wrote David Roberts on *Vox.* "Millennials are enthusiastic about the need for carbon regulations and the promise of clean energy."[32] More so, it seemed, than their elders.

But there was still something nagging me about that Harvard study, something I couldn't quite wrap my mind around. There was plenty of evidence people my age favor strong climate action more than older generations. That made sense to me. If studies like Hansen's are correct, our future survival is at stake. Yet the Harvard study suggested that our support for a safer and more stable future on this planet isn't very passionate. Less than one-third of its Millennial respondents agreed with the statement that "government should do more to curb climate change, even at the expense of economic growth." That number hardly suggested a sense of urgency. How could you explain it?

I kept turning it over and over in my head. I couldn't figure it out. Finally, I decided to go through the Harvard survey report once again. And when I did, I saw something I hadn't noticed before. It was true that a depressingly small number of Millennials seemed willing to address climate change "at the expense of economic growth." But the most common response to the statement wasn't in favor or against. Forty-four percent of respondents said that they "neither agree nor disagree."[33] This was interesting. What it suggested to me was that the question itself was confusing to people my age. Perhaps the reason nearly half of the respondents couldn't give a clear answer is that to them it didn't make sense to pit climate action against economic growth. They didn't see those two options as mutually exclusive. They didn't see them as options at all.

I wasn't the only one to reach this conclusion. Several prominent polling firms had found evidence to support it. A survey of over two thousand people between the ages of 18 and 31 done by Greenberg Quinlan Rosner Research found that 77 percent of young people agreed with the statement that it's "possible to combat climate change and have a strong economy; don't have to choose."[34] Further polling on this issue among Millennials by Hart Research got a similar response. "Expanding clean energy is seen [by young people] as a multifaceted solution," the polling firm said in a summary report. "It will create jobs, grow our economy, and reduce our dependence on foreign oil, while still addressing the problem of climate change." There was another intriguing finding in that same report. Though Millennials overall tended to support strong climate action, the ones who already had an active interest in the issue— people who, for instance, would share a climate news article on Facebook or Twitter—were very, very passionate about the issue. "A whopping 84% say that expanding renewables and creating clean-energy jobs is an extremely important priority for them," Hart Research explained. It was "by far the top-testing issue among this group," trumping unrelated issues like student debt.[35]

Given their passion for a less destructive status quo, it wasn't surprising that many young people had a deeply negative view of the political and economic leaders standing in its way. Further polling from Hart Research found that a majority of 18-to-34-year-olds distrusted large oil companies, while 72 percent worried that fossil fuel companies have way too much influence over our government.[36] That was backed up by another poll done in 2014 by Democracy Corps suggesting that young people trust fossil fuel companies much less than environmental groups. "Millennials' hostility to corruption, dislike of oil companies, and concern about the influence they exert over our political system," explained a report from the advocacy group NextGen Climate, "suggest the potential for significant backlash against politicians who favor fossil fuel companies over climate solutions."[37]

If that potential for backlash existed—a wave of politically active young people that could sweep those politicians out of office—then how come so few of our leaders seemed to take it seriously? By the time I'd arrived on the small West Coast island where Peter had spent much of his adult life rejecting their system, I had a good guess as to why. Today's leaders, as the Harvard study had made clear, assume that the future will be no different than the past. They are "accustomed to a very particular, narrow approach to measuring environmental awareness," explained Daniel Weinberger, a young researcher at the New York–based Roosevelt Institute.[38] They assume that climate change is primarily an abstract scientific issue, and that any solutions to it must come at the expense of economic growth. But this is not how most people of my and Peter's generation see it. To us, climate change presents clear and compelling moral evidence that our political and economic system is broken. It contains an opportunity to create a radically better one.

SHORTLY AFTER ARRIVING ON Denman, I met Peter inside the island's only café, a cozy hideaway looking out onto farmhouses and thick coastal forest. I almost didn't recognize him. In a photo I'd seen online, he was wielding a pointed hoe. He'd had a thick beard and the no-nonsense stare of someone accustomed to lots of hard labor. But in person Peter was clean-shaven. He looked younger than I expected. He had a self-effacing, if not exactly gregarious, demeanor. "How was your trip over?" he asked. We got a table at the back, and I asked him to tell me his story from the very beginning. We were joined midway through the conversation by his partner, Magdalene Joly.

There is no denying that Peter's way of life would be considered extreme by most people—even people of his Millennial generation. Few of us would ever consider giving up the conveniences of our modern lifestyles in order to fend for ourselves in the wilderness. We couldn't stomach the idea of slaughtering animals. We wouldn't have the patience to grow crops, the strength to cut down trees, the skills to build a house out of them. We wouldn't know the first place to start. Peter was well aware of this. "I wouldn't recommend that anyone starts from scratch [like me]," he said. "In that sense I don't think we're a model." But his decision to reject our industrial world sprang from anxieties that transcended the particulars of his day-to-day existence—as did the values of the new way of life he attempted to build.

The decision that started all of it can't be traced back to a single epiphany. There was no "aha" moment, no straw that broke the camel's back—none of the clichés we associate with life-changing moments. Peter's decision came from something deeper. It arose from a gnawing sense that our status quo is leading his generation to destruction, and a feeling that a degree in anthropology and environmental studies at the University of Victoria wouldn't provide him the chance to do something about it. "My university experience taught me that I didn't really want to be part of that whole world," he said. "I went through academia pretty unsatisfied with its lack of real world application." For inspiration, he instead looked to writers like Wendell Berry, who spent his life critiquing assumptions many of us take for granted.

In the 1960s Berry gave up a teaching and writing career in New York to start a small farm at Lanes Landing, Kentucky. For the next half century he drew from his experiences there in novels, poems, and works of nonfiction to critique our modern society. Berry believed that the separation between money and values imposed by our capitalist system is destroying people's relationship to the natural world—and to each other. He wrote with scorn about the shallow incentives that system uses to buy people's acceptance: "the quick profit, the annual raise, vacation with pay."[39] He advocated for the creation of an alternative model that values survival as much as profits. Berry's work made Peter want "to be more responsible to myself and other people and try to physically make the world a better place."

It was around this time that Peter decided to embark on a "crazy walk" all the way across Vancouver Island. He started at Cape Scott, on the island's northern tip, and trekked by himself more than three hundred miles to Ten Mile Point in Victoria, on its southeast. It took him seventy-seven days. "On a typical day I got up at 7 A.M., ate oatmeal and drank tea, which was my biggest comfort," he told a student newspaper. "Then it was an 8 to 10 hour walking day, then dinner, and I was in bed by 7 or 8 P.M."[40] He followed old logging roads. He bushwhacked. He climbed mountains. He saw bears every day. He hung out with lots of activists along the way and took part in their long, passionate debates about fossil fuels, globalization, water pollution, climate change—"you name it." But something didn't feel quite right.

Peter began to notice disconnects between the relatively comfortable lifestyles of some of those activists and the global injustices that they spent hours railing against: "They were drinking black tea with white sugar and living in houses with propane furnaces." To most people, that wouldn't have seemed like a big deal. But Peter saw it as symbolic of a wider challenge: "It was a big catalyst for me that it doesn't make sense to be upset about all this stuff but then be supporting it." He was convinced that little could be achieved by "just complaining about things and going about life as usual." If you wanted to change our modern way of life, you had to find ways to operate outside of it. You had to be prepared, as he put it, to "internalize that responsibility to actually do something different."

Peter figured the best way to start was by following Berry's lead. If he could learn how to survive without all the physical comforts that our society provided, then he'd be proving—at least to himself—that alternatives were possible. That was the theory anyway. He arrived on Denman Island in 2003 determined to test it out. He brought a stack of books about permaculture—the design of food systems that adhere to nature's cycles rather than flout them—and drew from those books to plant fruit trees and vegetables. He bought a flock of chickens. Soon he was raising sheep. In the city you don't have to think about where your meat comes from. You simply pick the nicest cut from behind the butcher's glass. But it's different when you have to butcher an animal that you've housed and fed and cared for.

Peter can still vividly recall the first sheep he slaughtered. "I'm a bit of a bull, a hardheaded person, so I don't get as upset about stuff," he says. Yet he recalls feeling "pretty emotional" preparing for the kill. "We invested a lot of meaning in it. It was a big deal at the time." He tried to make the process as humane as possible. He separated the sheep he planned to shoot from all the others, and placed them in a corral so they wouldn't be spooked by the gunshot. Peter fed the doomed sheep a helping of grain. He pulled the trigger. Afterward he hung the sheep's carcass on a hook. It started bleeding onto the feed pile. Just then the other sheep escaped. They ran to the feed pile and began munching obliviously. "We're trying to minimize the trauma, and here they are eating the bloody grain of their buddy," he said. "I don't mean to sound callous, though, because if anything, I've gotten more sensitive."

Peter was learning how to provide for himself. He could now butcher a sheep. He could propagate plants. But there was one very important skill that he'd overlooked: making money. The farm earned almost none at all during the early days. Nor was it productive enough to nourish him. In the meantime he needed to buy food and tools. "You've really got to think about how you're going to make a living," he said, "and what your employability is because almost all of your city skills are useless." Just over a thousand people lived on Denman Island. Jobs were scarce. And the type of work that was available to him was "much more manual and menial and doesn't pay all that well." Growing weed was an option, but he decided against it.

Instead Peter took the odd labor job whenever he could, "rednecky kind of stuff" like construction and chain-sawing and firewood chopping. He had done plenty of physical labor before. "I mean, I'd worked on landscape crews and golf courses like most young people do," he said. Yet there only were so many hours in a day. Surviving outside our system was going to be a much bigger challenge than he'd anticipated: "Whether it's nut trees that actually bear nuts or houses that have hot water from your woodstove, it's all really expensive and it takes time." His goal had been to reject a status quo that valued money over his survival. But he hadn't counted on needing so much money to survive.

Before Peter arrived on Denman, he knew that many people before him had attempted something similar. In the late 1960s and early '70s, anywhere from 10,000 to 100,000 Americans fled the Vietnam War draft by moving up into Canada. One historian called it "the largest politically motivated migration from the United States" since the American Revolution.[41] Many of its members believed that our political and economic system threatened their survival—it was trying to send them off to war, after all. And like Peter, some of them responded to that threat by setting up communes in the Canadian wilderness. They were joined in spirit by countless others across the United States and Europe whose experiments in back-to-the-land living in many ways laid the foundation for the modern environmental movement. But by the time Peter set out on his own, most of the physical remains of their alternative system had been reclaimed by the forest.

Among the pioneers was Jim Bohlen, a Bronx-born engineer who moved his family to Vancouver in 1967 so his stepson couldn't be drafted to fight in Vietnam. Bohlen later joined a small group of antiwar and environmental activists who attempted to sail a halibut fishing boat named *Greenpeace* to a nuclear test site in Alaska. Their voyage would become the genesis for a global activist group with over three million members in forty countries. Bohlen and his wife at one point in their lives spent nearly ten years trying to build a self-sustaining farm community on Denman Island. They fervently believed that "the war to preserve the Earth's ecosystems must continue, everywhere," as Bohlen once explained. "Globally, locally, and within one's self."[42]

Peter was aware of draft dodgers such as Bohlen. He agrees that our political and economic system is too narrowly focused on short-term gain. That it refuses to acknowledge its wider long-term impacts. And that any alternative system must at its core instill in people a larger global awareness. Unlike the draft dodgers, though, he hadn't fled into the wilderness as part of a wider social movement, at least not one that he was aware of. His journey was a solitary one. And it would have stayed that way too if he hadn't met Magdalene Joly one day in a mutual friend's backyard. Magdalene still lived in the city of Victoria at the time. She'd gone to music school to study jazz but dropped out after only a few months—"I realized, 'What am I doing?'" she recalled—and spent more and more of her time out on Denman Island.

Like Peter, who is about a year older than she, Magdalene thought constantly about the global implications of her actions. "I grew up in a superaware family, so I knew what environmental degradation meant from a young age," she said. She believes that our society makes it harder to have that awareness. We are told all the time to focus on our narrow self-interest and not to worry about the bigger picture. Magdalene thinks you can resist this inertia by becoming more rooted in the natural world. Only then can you understand humankind's impact on it. When she was nineteen or twenty, she began to work on urban farms in Victoria. Growing fresh food in accordance with nature's rhythms provided some bearings on a system that felt adrift and disconnected. "We're in this hyperindustrialized place as a society where our relationships are not in any way dictated by a sense of place," she explained.

Magdalene found herself drawn to Peter's idealism. She admired his rejection of the status quo and his stubborn efforts to create alternatives. He had taught himself from scratch how to mill wood, propagate plants, build a house, and do electrical work. "He can basically do anything," she said. Not long after their introduction, Magdalene and her child, Raphael, moved in with Peter. She brought to the farm a formidable skill set. She was a trained herbalist and nutritionist. She baked steaming loaves of bread and made many types of herbal medicines and teas. What her family didn't use they sold in local markets and cafés. In a system obsessed with short-term gain, she loved the challenges of staying put, of keeping animals alive, the taste of freshly picked kale. "The nature of society's problems lies in being alienated from the land," she said.

Being attached to your surroundings forces you to be more responsible to them. "The urban emphasis on what you put in your body is only the one selfish end of all of that," Peter said. "It's also about looking after your environment and stewarding species of plants and animals and actually having a multigenerational relationship with them." It can be a lot of work. "When you put the garbage behind the house, nobody comes and takes it away," he said. That's up to you. And if you are too busy or too lazy or too tired after working all day to move the garbage yourself, it accumulates. "There's stumps and there's animal poos and ruts in the ground and broken-down trucks that city people don't have lots of tolerance for."

The more they grew attached to their surroundings, the less time they had to take part in the outside world. They were always busy. "I'm running around all the time just trying to keep everything going," Magdalene said. She and Peter were in effect trying to build a new political and economic system from scratch. They had little in the way of history to draw from, and no sense they were carrying on traditions handed down for centuries. "We've only been here a few years," she said. "We don't have elders saying, 'This is what it was like when I was a kid.'" The only history they had to draw from were the thousands of draft dodgers who'd also tried to build a new system in the wilderness. But Peter and Magdalene knew how that story ended. "They all got older and stopped," Peter said. "I don't want that to happen, but who knows."

Doubts started to creep in. If climate scientists like Hansen are correct that every coastal city on Earth could be underwater by 2065, then is it morally okay to spend your days growing carrots? "While we're trying to do that work, the rest of the world is getting torn apart," Magdalene said. "I'm so busy running my farm that I'm not, for instance, putting time into stopping a huge coal mine." Magdalene is tormented by trade-offs like that. "I wish we had ten more generations' worth of time to heal our deep wounds that are caused by living in this culture," she said. "But I sometimes worry that we really don't, and then I start to feel like 'What am I doing living on this little island?'" She and Peter came here to live a more globally aware life than society allows. Yet they were consumed by their immediate surroundings.

WHEN PETER TOOK OFF to the wilderness in 2003, there really wasn't much that an individual like him could do to reverse the destruction of our planet. But as time passed, new options seemed to appear everywhere. Sales of energy-efficient lightbulbs doubled and tripled every year. So did hybrid vehicles. Cities all over North America installed bike lanes. Whole Foods expanded aggressively. Gardens grew up from old industrial land in cities like Vancouver, Brooklyn, London, and Mexico City. Farmer's markets underwent a dramatic resurgence. Self-sufficiency gurus like Marcin Jakubowski gave TED Talks describing their vision of a do-it-yourself economy. "On some campuses," the *New Yorker* reported, "a junior year spent weeding an asparagus bed has become as popular as studying abroad."[43]

This was in some ways a validation of Peter's entire project: that if enough people decided on their own to seek out alternatives to our status quo, then the collective impact would surely become visible. It was true that none of these larger trends made much of a material impact on Peter and Magdalene. But slowly their skills and hard work mounted. Money started coming in. One of the first sources was a small edibles nursery that Peter built adjacent to their house. Inside he propagated plant species that he found across Denman or ordered from catalogs or online. Over time he began to sell seedlings—for Meyer lemons, Chinotto sour oranges, Italian prune plums, yuzu mandarins, autumn olives, gooseberries, kiwis, persimmons, quinces, and many others—in small towns across Vancouver Island. He set up an online store not long afterward. "That was the first actual farm income," Peter said.

Peter also found time to make his own hand tools. "I built the forge just out of junk," he said. A bit of scrap metal, an antique anvil and blower, and some tools from friends were all it took. He found designs he liked online and modified them to suit the needs of a small farmer like himself. "I've always sort of played at it," he said. "But I just started selling them in the last few years." He created the Gulf Island Deer Skinner. He forged Hori Horis—a sharp-edged knife with a saw down one side that's used for digging and mixing soil—with carbon steel reclaimed from old farm implements. He made Deer Leather Belt Sheaths from deer that he hunted on Denman. "You won't find these sheaths anywhere else," he boasted.

When Peter is deep at work on some new project, Magdalene often becomes the main breadwinner. She plants a huge garden. She bakes bread to sell at cafés. She caters local events with food grown on the farm. From May to November she runs a community-supported agriculture program. In the spring a number of local families purchase a weekly box likely to be bursting with fresh radishes, turnips, cilantro, spinach, garlic tops, and baby beets. By fall they may be receiving squash, chard, hazelnuts, apples, and nettle pesto. Both she and Peter have learned to adjust their lives to nature's rhythms. "If you live totally disconnected from the land, it's always the same," Magdalene said. "You always go to same coffee shop and buy the same food." On Denman their diet and daily routines changed with the seasons.

To a large extent, they eat whatever was available. "It's hard to generalize because it's so seasonal," Peter said. "You'll end up with a whole lot of one thing at any given time." Fresh eggs are pretty much a constant. But from March to November, he and Magdalene barely need to buy any fruits and vegetables. In early spring they are deluged with greens. Then come berries and apples and tomatoes. The late summer is when much of the harvesting is done. It is when Magdalene makes the most amount of money. "So there's like this frenetic amount of activity," she said. By mid-fall things start to calm down a little. That's when Peter does a lot of plant propagating in preparation for next spring. They can fruit for the winter and store boxes of apples and potatoes in a root cellar. There are lots of mushrooms to eat. Peter also goes hunting on Denman. "We have two to three deer a year that we process," Magdalene said. "Sometimes we make this incredible fermented sausage."

At first the winter can be a relief. "When you go through that intensity of activity [in summer and fall] you think, 'Oh man, it's going to be really nice to have time when there's less to do,'" Magdalene said. It's a period for inner pursuits: to read, play music, make art, and just not do anything. But winter is also when the least money comes in. All that free time leads to a lot of reflection. "Sometimes it can be hard," she said.

For someone as deeply aware of the planet's problems as Magdalene, it can be intensely depressing to imagine the potential scale of destruction caused by climate change. Toiling in the rain forest lets her and Peter feel like a better future is possible. "The impact it has on us psychologically and spiritually and emotionally" to be out here "is really meaningful." Yet it can also feel profoundly isolating. Even on Denman Island, where most people knew each other and share similar values, Magdalene hardly ever sees her friends or neighbors. "We're all just so busy," she lamented. "Everyone is living on their own piece of land, building houses, growing gardens."

As time went by, she and Peter began to wonder what exactly they were accomplishing. They came to this small island because they believe our industrial system threatens their survival. By opting out of that system, they hoped in some small way that their individual actions would make the world a better place. Yet the further that they fled the status quo, the more tied to it they felt. The rice they eat is grown on plantations in India and shipped across the Pacific on diesel-burning tankers. The fuel for their pick-up truck comes from one of the world's most environmentally damaging oil industries: the Alberta tar sands. The feed for their animals is produced on large industrial farms. But cutting out any of those things isn't easy. "As soon as you stopped buying feed for the animals, you'd hardly get any eggs," Magdalene explained.

And any time they spent growing their own feed would leave them with fewer resources to produce their own fruits and vegetables. Those types of trade-offs are endless. "Self-sufficiency is almost impossible without a whole community doing it," Peter slowly began to realize. "You need a division of labor between properties and families." Magdalene agreed. She began to wonder whether "it's really that strategic to be two individuals trying to do all this stuff." For any of it to persist in the long run, you need the assurance that children and grandchildren and whoever comes after you will build upon all your work. "It's a multigenerational project," Magdalene said.

And supposing all that could somehow be figured out, what wider impact would it achieve? Even if a group of families working together on Denman managed to cut all their ties to our political and economic system, the power of the oil companies and the politicians that they funded "would just continue on," Magdalene said. "We are going to keep experiencing more intensity of climate change." She and Peter found it harder to sustain the idealism that brought them here to begin with. "I feel profoundly cynical about the future of our society," Peter said, "because I now know by direct experience how hard it is to shift away from the momentum that our society has." An individual can get the process started, but only a collective can finish it.

BY THIS POINT IN my conversation with Peter and Magdalene, it was early evening. They asked if I wanted to join them for dinner at their farm. As we walked out of the café into the starless night, I felt a sense of calm come over me that was lacking in my urban existence. I saw treetops swaying in the wind. Felt the soft patter of rain. Smelled damp smoke in the woods. I had to remind myself that for more than a decade Peter and Magdalene have been fighting here for their future survival. As climate scientist Hansen warns, after all, without profound changes to the way we structure our society, "continued high emissions will make multi-meter sea level rise practically unavoidable and likely to occur this century."[44] Jason Box, a respected glaciologist who looked over Hansen's paper and concluded that its findings were plausible, puts our crisis into starker terms. Unless we change our status quo immediately, he says, "we're fucked."[45]

As we squeezed into their pickup truck and drove toward the island's interior, I couldn't help but think how hopeless it all seems. Peter and Magdalene have made a greater effort than someone like me would ever be capable—to reject the reigning ideology of our society and build a more stable and less destructive alternative to it. Yet after all their time on Denman Island, their goal seems no closer to actually being achieved. If the two of them are unable to convince themselves that a different status quo is possible, and if their efforts to leave our system have only made them feel more tightly bound to it, then what hope is there for the rest of us? What reason do members of my generation have to feel that we are anything but completely, utterly screwed?

But as we neared their farm, something unexpected flickered inside me. The more I thought about it, the more I started to see just how crucial a first step Peter and Magdalene have taken. I realized that what I was feeling was hope. Out here in the rain forest, they have confronted three of the most deep-seated arguments against systemic change. They've had to reconcile their ideals with their need to earn money. Square their immediate surroundings with the world outside of them. Find in their individualism a path to wider social impact. They haven't solved these challenges. But they haven't totally failed either. What I saw in their journey is a different future than the one we're told is inevitable.

One of the many topics I discussed with Peter was the electric grid. Back in 2003 this was a huge issue for him. He wanted to generate his power from small solar panels and not be dependent on fossil fuels. But the property came hooked up to a utility that occasionally burns them. "It's such a turn-off for me," he says. "I have plans to go off it, but it's expensive and we don't have a lot of money." On a micro level this would seem to validate one of the key macro-arguments that our economic and political leaders use to justify the status quo: that changing it is too costly. It's the rationale that Rex Tillerson, the ExxonMobil CEO appointed secretary of state by Donald Trump, uses to explain why we shouldn't limit fossil fuels. Keeping the oil that's causing climate change in the ground would make life more expensive for billions of people. "What good is it to save the planet if humanity suffers?" argues the former leader of one of the planet's richest corporations.

To Tillerson, fighting climate change is uneconomical. It goes against the principles of free-market capitalism. "And I think there are much more pressing priorities that we as a human race and society need to deal with," he argues.[46] In his worldview short-term profits must trump long-term survival. This is still widely accepted in our society.

But Peter and Magdalene showed me that it doesn't have to be. Out on their property, I couldn't help but marvel at the two-story house Peter built with wood from the surrounding rain forest. Inside, I watched young Raphael bounce around the living room as Peter and Magdalene got dinner ready on a wood-burning stove: goat they'd recently killed and kale from outside their front door. By Tillerson's logic, Peter and Magdalene's decision to live in the woods makes no economic sense. But tonight their existence felt safe and secure and prosperous.

After dinner I asked Peter a question that I'd been thinking about for some time. Before I came out to Denman Island, I'd read about a global movement based on the paradigm of "degrowth," which seems to share many of his and Magdalene's ideals. Its adherents, who can be found across Europe, America, and Asia, believe "we need a more modest and sane alternative to the constant pressures of expansion that are destroying the ecological basis of our existence," according to one account.[47] Does Peter see himself as part of this movement? "I've never heard of it," he says. He questioned the premise of my question: "Claiming to be building self-sufficiency and being for degrowth is an oxymoron." A global awareness brought him to Denman in the first place, but he had trouble identifying with like-minded people elsewhere.

This is exactly the sort of disconnect our leaders use to justify the status quo: that we have to look after the people within our own narrow borders before we can think about the world outside of them. One of the clearest articulations of it came from Republican presidential candidate contender Marco Rubio. In the fall of 2015 he was asked if he would support stronger actions to reduce America's contribution to climate change. Rubio said there was no way. "We're not going to make America a harder place to create jobs in order to pursue policies that will do absolutely nothing, nothing to change our climate," he insisted. "America is not a planet."[48] Trump, who made "America First" his inaugural slogan, doesn't think so either.

The implication was that a threat to global survival is inherently less important than the national interest. And for that reason your sense of identity should end at the borders you reside in. When I met Magdalene the next morning at the café and hostel where I spent the night, she explained that she and Peter are doing all they can to reject that reasoning. Right now they are consumed by their surroundings. But the goal is to someday "be engaged on multiple fronts," she said. To grow carrots, say, and fight new coal plants, "so we can see [our actions] in a bigger context." We drove back to her farm. She told me someone in Scandinavia recently e-mailed to buy one of Peter's homemade tools. It blew Raphael's mind. "He said, 'I feel really inspired by what you and Peter are doing,'" Magdalene said. "That does penetrate." In that moment Raphael connected her and Peter's existence to a world much larger than their surroundings.

When we got out of the truck, several chickens squawked at our feet. Magdalene squished through the mud in rubber boots to where she was growing kale that tasted sweet and nutty. "The frost does wonders for it," she says. Those are the types of things that make what they are doing feel worthwhile. But Magdalene sometimes worries that she is too "insularly focused . . . on my own little life." In a more connected society, she imagines the food she and Peter are growing would feed a whole community of artists and scientists and engineers and laborers and whoever else—each doing their part to build a better future on this planet. She hopes "that people can move out of their individual lives and be able to support each other." But for now their independent existence makes it difficult to have a wider social impact.

It is in the best interest of our political and economic system to keep things that way. You don't have to be an oil executive or Republican candidate to agree. Even our status quo's more moderate defenders distrust the type of transformational change demanded by people of my and Peter and Magdalene's generation. Those defenders, whether they intend to or not, undermine the collective voice of regular people. When college students began urging schools to drop fossil fuel investments from their portfolios (a campaign we'll examine in depth later), the Harvard professor Robert Stavins argued that "the movement is fundamentally misguided." Working with like-minded people to fight a system that doesn't value your survival "may feel good," but it would "have relatively little real-world impact."

To political and economic elites like Stavins, "climate change is fundamentally a scientific, economic, and political challenge."[49] Solving it is a job for the experts like him. And for those who tinker around the edges of the status quo. Not for a movement of regular people who want to overthrow it. Every hour that Peter and Magdalene spend out on their farm, they are rejecting that logic. Even while doing the type of mundane tasks—feeding goats, corralling chickens, checking on new batches of microgreens—that take up much of their days. To Peter, it makes no sense to wait for someone more powerful than him to assure his survival. Especially when evidence suggests that will never happen. To create real change, you have to "internalize that responsibility to actually do something different," he says. The status quo will never be transformed until enough of us believe it can be.

The cabin where he and Magdalene live had been consuming much of Peter's time. On the day I visited its front landing, living room, and kitchen were mostly complete, but the upstairs still needed work. "I like to think that when our house is finished we'll be able to relax more," he said once we were inside. "But I don't know." Peter has invested so much of his life in the farm, he now finds it difficult to leave even for short periods of time. "I get anxiety being away," he admits. "The general rule is that something always goes missing or dies." I looked out the window at the geese and the chickens and the kale and everything else that is the result of a decision more than a decade earlier to live more responsibly than our society allows. "In hindsight," Peter explains, "it's a tall order. In that sense I don't think we're a model except of idealism."

But as I later waited at the ferry berth for the boat that would take me off Denman Island, I realized that I totally disagree. Years and years of public opinion research suggest that a large majority of people my age share Peter and Magdalene's anxieties about the future. We feel a gnawing sense that the people in charge of our society don't care about our survival. Yet every time we think about challenging the status quo, we have to deal with a Tillerson or Rubio or Stavins telling us that systemic change isn't possible. Peter and Magdalene have struggled for more than a decade to prove them wrong. In many ways they are still struggling. What they showed me, though, is that the first step toward change is to recognize the arguments sustaining it—and to try in your own small way to go beyond them. In the Trump era, this doesn't have to be a futile and lonely gesture. As we'll see in Chapter 2, when enough young people take that first step, the impact can be profound and immediate.

2

Capitalism's Worst Nightmare

OIL AND GAS COMPANIES are terrified of people like Bradley Johnson.* They consider him one of the greatest long-term threats to their industry. He looms over their future growth and profit margins. He's a crisis that just cannot seem to be solved. And the strangest thing is that Bradley is for the most part oblivious to the threat he poses. His day-to-day existence has very little to do with oil and gas. Bradley is a conceptual artist living in New York. He's not earning very much money. "I have to work really hard to just survive," he says. Bradley makes art that he calls "formal, humorous, and experimental."[1] It's abstract and apolitical. He worries about climate change but not enough to attend a rally or demonstration. He doesn't go out of his way to talk shit about oil and gas. But a decision he made in his twenties is causing the industry to question its own existence.

For the significance of his decision to make sense, you first have to understand the context it was made in. Since the day Bradley was born in the early 1980s, his life had revolved around oil and gas. His grandpa was a crane operator from Canada's east coast who regularly criss-crossed the country for work. "Wherever there was some kind of job or a refinery, he'd go there and drive trucks and operate a crane," Bradley said. He'd bring the whole family with him. When Bradley was a child, they settled out west in Fort McMurray. The town is eight hundred miles

---

* Not his real name. Due to the sensitive nature of climate politics in Fort McMurray, particularly in the wake of the 2016 wildfire, Bradley, and the other names associated with his story, are pseudonyms—unless otherwise noted.

north of Butte, Montana. It's surrounded by Alberta's boreal forest at the confluence of two mighty rivers—the Athabasca and the Clearwater. Fort McMurray feels like an outpost at the edge of civilization. Yet it's at the center of the world's third-largest proven oil reserves: the tar sands.

People aren't drawn to Fort McMurray for the culture. They don't come for the history or the architecture or the food or the museums. They pretty much come for one thing only: a fat paycheck. Bradley's family was no exception: "They moved here for work, because of the oil industry, which is the case for eighty percent of the people who live here." The work is intense. It can require twelve-hour shifts for weeks straight in weather as cold as negative fifty-nine degrees Fahrenheit. But the payoff for the average truck driver or engineer or electrician is a salary in the six figures. Fort McMurray is what happens when you strip down our economic system to its pure undistilled essence. During the 2008 oil boom, its nickname was "Fort McMoney."

Bradley knew from an early age that he had trouble fitting in. "I've definitely always felt like an outsider in Fort Mac," he said. Through elementary and junior high and high school, it seemed like his classmates shared an unspoken understanding. "They could all get each other's jokes," he said. "I did not click, and people could sense it for sure." But one thing they all agreed on was that in the pantheon of places to live, Fort McMurray definitely wasn't at the top. "There was never a feeling of love for that place," he said. In a town so single-mindedly devoted to making money, it could be difficult to find a meaning beyond it. Still, it was the only way of life that Bradley had ever known. And plenty of people, including members of his own family, did see something more to the town. "Growing up I felt like 'Am I going to buy into working at the oil refinery or get the fuck out?'"

A job in the oil industry here is about as extreme as they come. The oil that surrounds Fort McMurray is not the smooth-flowing stuff that can be sucked from the ground with a conventional derrick. It comes in the form of bitumen, a tarry substance with the viscosity of a hockey puck. One way to get at it is to tear down the boreal forest and mine the bitumen in vast open pits. Over the past fifteen or so years, an area more than eleven times larger than Manhattan has been transformed into strip mines. And stored across them is enough toxic waste to fill more than a third of a million Olympic swimming pools. When the American photographer Alex MacLean came here on assignment in 2014, he found it hard to take it all in: "The scale of the oil sands area and the devastation to the landscape was overwhelming."[2]

The other way to extract the bitumen is to lay a grid of pipes across the landscape and melt it to a flowable state with injections of high-powered steam. This has the advantage of not demolishing the boreal forest. But in other ways it's much worse for our planet. All the industrial might needed to steam bitumen from the Earth and cook impurities out of it in an upgrader means that each barrel of tar sands oil is about 14 percent worse for the climate than a barrel of regular oil. By mining and steaming, the industry produced 2.2 million barrels of oil every day in 2014 and shipped much of it to the United States. In an era when we badly need to cut our use of fossil fuels, the ones we use are getting worse. To James Hansen, whose doomsday research on climate change we discussed in Chapter 1, this was nuts. "Going after tar sands," he says, "is the sign of a terribly crazed addict."[3]

It's also the sign of an economic system that values short-term profits over the survival of people like Bradley. Several years ago Greenpeace compiled a list of the fourteen riskiest fossil fuel expansions on the planet. They were oil, coal, and gas projects that threatened to take our climate past a "point of no return." The list included a massive expansion of coal exports from Australia, Indonesia, and the United States; offshore drilling for oil in Brazil and the Arctic; and a tripling of production in Canada's tar sands. "These projects have the potential to ensure the world is irretrievably on course to suffer extreme weather events, increased conflict, reduced availability of food and water, and potentially catastrophic disruption," the report claimed.[4]

When Bradley was growing up in Fort McMurray, these weren't the types of things that many people talked about. It's not like nobody cared about the town's impact on climate change. But in a place set up for the purpose of maximizing wealth, the wider consequences were irrelevant to most people. "There was no urgency to it," he said. "In the culture of Fort Mac there wasn't a bigger mindset that even thought of those questions." Yet as Bradley finished high school he wasn't thinking much about climate change either. He had a more immediate question on his mind: "What the fuck are you going to do with yourself?" The easiest thing would be to stay in Fort McMurray. He could get a job in the tar sands just like his grandpa and stepdad and earn lots of money. He knew his job would lack wider meaning. "But it's going to give me enough money to do what I want," he figured.

Yet Bradley had an inkling that another life was possible. He had always been fascinated by the way things looked. He loved big weird spectacles, the kind of stuff that makes you stop and say, "Can you believe what we're looking at here?" But the idea of transforming that fascination into creative energy, of actually making his own visuals, was daunting. "I really did think like so many people that you're either gifted at being an artist or not, and I'm not because I don't know how to find evidence of that," he said. That all began to change after a high school art teacher taught him how to draw. "She hammered it into me that it's a skill like any other—you just have to practice." He began to draw everything in sight. At home he copied album covers into a notebook. After a while he started to get pretty good. So good, actually, that his teacher got him to enter a local art competition. The prize was reduced tuition at an art school in Fort McMurray. Bradley won, and "it shocked the shit out of me."

For the next few years he struggled to decide which of these two life options he should pursue. He could accept the status quo and dedicate his life to making lots of money. Or he could reject it and search for a wider meaning. What he didn't realize was that at that very moment millions of others in his generation were struggling with the same dilemma—and that like him, they would select the second option. He didn't know that by doing this they were posing a long-term threat to the future of the oil and gas industry, that the combined impact of their actions would within a few years put more than $100 billion of projects at risk (as well as the fossil fuel agenda of Donald Trump), and that it would ultimately call into question the operating principles of our economic system. But the industry did. And it had a word to describe what was happening: *terrifying*.

THE ENTIRE TAR SANDS industry can be traced back to a single self-effacing scientist named Karl Clark. In the late 1920s he figured out the chemical process that eight decades later would transform Canada into the largest supplier of oil to the United States. Clark is now regarded as a hero. He's been inducted into the Canadian Petroleum Hall of Fame. There's a school named after him in Fort McMurray. At the town's inaugural We Love Oil Sands Dinner in 2013, one local painted a live portrait of Clark in front of hundreds of people. *Alberta Venture* magazine deemed him the sixteenth greatest Albertan of the past century, just behind Wayne Gretzky.[5] But all the accolades and official histories omit a crucial detail about his life. In Clark's final years, he came to a heartbreaking realization about our economic system.

Clark was born near Toronto in 1888. Though he grew up in an academic family—his dad was a language professor at McMaster University—there was little evidence in his early years that he'd aspire to much of anything. Clark got bad grades in high school. He was "an indifferent student," according to one account. At one point he decided to drop out, but "his father would not hear of this and insisted that Karl remain in school."[6] The one subject he did excel at was chemistry. He went on to earn a Ph.D. in it from the University of Illinois. Clark would sometimes unwind after a stressful day by playing music. He loved the clarinet. It "provided him with many hours of relaxation," his daughter Mary Clark Sheppard later explained.[7]

But Clark was happiest away from the industrialized world. Throughout his adolescence he'd spend two months every summer at his family's cabin in rural Ontario. There he learned how to survive in the wilderness: how to start a fire, build a shelter, portage a canoe. During his university years, he put those skills to use in his summer job as a fire ranger in Algonquin Park. The park was filled with so many lakes that walking among all the fire towers was difficult. Clark would paddle his canoe as far as he could go, hoist it onto his shoulders, and carry it until he hit the next lake. He often stopped along the way to watch birds and squirrels. He had "a great love of the outdoors and the wildlife it supported," Sheppard wrote.[8]

When the First World War started, Clark was disqualified from the army because of his bad eyesight. He took a job with the Geological Survey of Canada instead. His assignment was to find a road-making material that would be durable enough to survive the extreme Canadian weather. He drove all over the country in a Model T Ford. During one of his field trips, he learned about the Fort McMurray region. The town was just a tiny trading post at the time. There was so much tarry sand in the vicinity that it literally oozed out of riverbanks. Nobody knew what to do with it. Clark figured it could be used to waterproof prairie roads, but first he'd have to find a way to extract the actual oil from the sand around it.

Solving that problem became Clark's life's work. Back in Ottawa, he began tinkering with small samples of tar sands. And after some promising results, he was invited to pursue his research full time at the University of Alberta. He was given a lab in the basement of the university's mechanical building, as well as six tons of tar sands from northern Alberta to experiment with. He put it through all kinds of tests. At one point he cooked it inside his family's washing machine. During the early 1920s he started to make some real progress. He found that the chemical bonds holding the oil and sand together could be loosened with a combination of scalding hot water and chemicals. In 1928 he filed a patent for the process. Two years later his research moved to a separation plant near Fort McMurray. By that point it was clear that tar sands had much more value as an oil source than as a road covering.

The basic process for extracting the oil worked fine in small samples, but it took several more decades before it was ready for a commercial scale. This period was among the happiest in Clark's life. In the summer he and his wife would take their children to a lakeside cottage outside Edmonton, where Clark taught them about the canoe and other outdoor survival skills he'd learned as a child. He also made frequent research trips all over the Fort McMurray region. Long canoe journeys down the Athabasca River evoked happy memories from his youth. He loved the solitude of the boreal forest, the way it looked when the leaves were changing color. He declared the Clearwater River "one of the beauty spots of the north."[9]

By the 1950s the technology Clark had spent more than three decades perfecting was showing real commercial promise. The business world took notice. In 1954 a group of Toronto investors created a company called the Great Canadian Oil Sands and later hired Clark as a consultant. It took over a decade of setbacks and delays before they were able to build a large-scale facility outside Fort McMurray. Clark was there on Tar Island the day construction began. He'd spent much of his life working toward this day, yet he was traumatized by what he witnessed. "Giant backhoes tore into the ground to drain the muskeg, while rampaging bulldozers pushed away the overburden," as the historian Alastair Sweeny recounted.[10]

An immense sadness fell over Clark in that moment. In the years to come he never recovered. "It affected him deeply," his daughter later recalled. "It broke his heart to see the devastation done to his beloved landscape." He was in his late seventies by that point. He'd begun to struggle with cancer. When it got worse, he went for treatment in Britain. And not long before he died in 1966, he told his daughter that he "had no wish to return [to Fort McMurray] since he wanted to remember the country as he had known and loved it for so many years."[11] Clark never questioned our economic system. In many ways he had dedicated his whole life to helping it thrive. But as the bulldozers tore up Tar Island, he realized that its drive for profits would destroy anything standing in the way. All the system cared about was money.

The landscape would be unrecognizable now. When the first oil sands plant began operating in 1967, nine months after his death, it could process only 32,000 barrels of oil per day. It consisted of just one open-pit mine. By 2004, improvements to the extraction technology, along with a sudden rise in the global price of oil, allowed the number of barrels to reach one million. A decade later production had more than doubled. The industry is trying to double it again by 2020. "Were he living today, Clark might well be in a state of perpetual grief," argues the journalist Andrew Nikiforuk. "Much of the forest that served as his laboratory and tramping ground has been leveled."[12] As every major oil company in the world—including Exxon, Chevron, Shell, BP, Statoil, Total, Petronas, and Koch Industries—scrambled for a piece of the action, the boreal forest has been bulldozed, strip-mined, and littered with vast toxic lakes.

The oil they have extracted from this dystopian landscape is among the worst for our climate in the entire world. It's more polluting than the fracking operations in North Dakota that vent natural gas in hundred-foot walls of flame. The industry's carbon emissions are greater than New Zealand's and Kenya's combined. In an era when we desperately need to cut our reliance on fossil fuels, places like the tar sands are sending our addiction into overdrive. "Higher CO_2 emissions, higher concentrations [in the atmosphere] and greater warming that our children and grandchildren have to deal with," is how one climate modeler described it.[13]

None of this would have been conceivable to the soft-spoken scientist who enjoyed few things more in life than paddling quietly past an untouched forest. "He would be astonished," Clark's daughter is convinced.[14] The official histories of Clark choose not to speculate. His entry on the Canadian Petroleum Hall of Fame website simply ends with a date on a timeline: "1965 Witnessed sod turning at [first oil sands] Plant."[15] It leaves Clark standing in mute admiration of our economic system. But his daughter knows that the story doesn't end there. If her dad were alive, she argues, "I feel sure he would be doing whatever he could to urge government and industry to work together . . . to find a solution to the environmental challenges of the oil sands."[16] He'd be trying to create an economic system that cared about more than just profits.

ON A BLAZING HOT summer day I embarked on the same journey to Fort McMurray that Clark had made countless times. But instead of driving a Model T Ford, I was crammed onto a Greyhound bus with dozens of male oil workers. As I looked around the bus at the muscled dudes cracking jokes and passing around a bottle of whiskey, I realized there were few people my age among them. Most seemed to be at least a generation older. This was not an isolated observation. For years the Hays group had been tracking the demographics of oil and gas workers. What it found is "terrifying" for the industry.[17] At a time when oil companies are desperate for young workers, the percentage of Millennials in their workforces is steadily declining. If this can't be reversed, over $100 billion worth of new projects are at risk.

In some ways this crisis has been building since the late 1980s. A downturn in oil prices that continued throughout the 1990s caused oil companies to fire thousands of workers and stop hiring new ones. And by the time oil prices spiked in the 2000s, their workforces were demographically lopsided. Much of the technical expertise that those companies needed to operate and expand was concentrated among Baby Boomers. As those Boomers neared retirement, companies realized there weren't enough Gen Xers to replace them. In theory the industry could solve this issue by hiring large numbers of Millennials. But try as it might, oil companies in the United States and Canada just could not get young people to work for them—at least not in the numbers needed to replace all the Boomers who'll be leaving in the next decade.

By 2013, the industry began to really worry. "The looming shortage was seen by many as the biggest single threat to increasing oil and gas supplies in the second half of the current decade and into the 2020s," a Reuters story read.[18] Worldwide about one-third of oil and gas workers were Millennials, but 2013 research from groups like Hays suggested only one-fifth of North America's oil and gas workforce was comprised of people my age. And two years later things hadn't improved. "The United States has a very pronounced problem," Hays analyst Jim Fearon explained. He warned that there was only "a five- to ten-year window" left to do something about it.[19]

Fearon was making similar warnings in Canada. The percentage of young skilled workers in places like the tar sands was just 19 percent, compared to over 37 percent aged 50 or older. Companies "need to be thinking about how they're going to be attracting increasing volumes of fresh talent," he said.[20] Yet it was about the worst possible time for them to do so. In 2014 global oil prices began an eighteen-month freefall to below $40 per barrel, the lowest they'd been in a decade. The result was crushing. Close to 200,000 oil and gas-related jobs were lost across Canada and the United States. Hiring new and inexperienced workers became less of a priority. By 2016, the number of Millennials in Canada's oil and gas workforce had dropped from 19 percent to 14 percent.[21] "There is a storm gathering within the industry," Hays managing director John Faraguna explained.[22]

From my Greyhound, I watched as the strip malls and late-hour liquor stores of Edmonton's outskirts gave way to vast fields of canola. The laughter and chatter of the oil workers surrounding me died down. For the most part, all I could hear was the low drone of the highway. If oil and gas companies didn't start to attract huge numbers of people my age, the impacts would soon be existential. *Bloomberg* had in 2013 estimated that in the United States alone, more than $100 billion worth of new oil and gas projects were threatened by the looming labor shortage. "We have to find new solutions," argued a vice-president at ConocoPhillips.[23] An article on *OilGrowth* was even blunter: "Millennials will either make or break the oil and gas industry."[24]

On the surface none of this seemed to make much economic sense. Many people in my generation were still reeling from the 2008 recession. They were struggling to find decent entry-level jobs. Even during the oil price downturn, the industry could offer six-figure salaries. All the oil companies were desperate for young workers. So how come so many Millennials refused to work for them? The polling I discussed in Chapter 1 seemed to offer a clue. It implies that people my age are more passionate about fixing the climate than older generations. That we are terrified of a future where every coastal city is underwater—and that we distrust the political and economic leaders who seem bent on ensuring it. Is this why Millennials are shunning oil and gas?

Some people within the industry certainly think so. "This generation sees our industry as a dirty relic of the past, exploiting a resource that could run out before their career does," argues Jason Rubli, a former Houston-based consultant for the industry group Molten. Many young people also believe that fossil fuel companies are blocking our transition to a cleaner future "through force of their hold on the market," he says. All this won't be easy to reverse, as "this perception has been growing for decades," and "repairing the negative perception Millennials have of the oil and gas industry is a long term effort." But he warns that if it isn't undertaken immediately, the financial impact could be "disastrous."[25]

Other industry observers downplay the challenge. They question how many Millennials actually hold these negative perceptions about oil and gas. A writer for *OilPrice*, Andrew Topf, suggests that the problem is mostly confined to urban hipsters. "Bearded, environmentally-conscious men in their 20s no longer consider 'roughneck' to be a viable summer job, let alone a gateway into a petroleum engineering career," Topf wrote in 2014. "Truth is, most would rather swill coffee at Starbucks than work in an industry many in their generation blames for ruining the planet." These hipsters threaten the industry's ability "to remain productive and profitable," he argued. But if the industry improved its outreach to the nonhipster majority, "it could make significant progress in closing skills and labor gaps."[26]

Maybe he has a point. The oil workers filing off the Greyhound for our fifteen-minute break in Grassland certainly weren't sipping single-origin coffee and pontificating about climate change. They were more of the Coors and ATV types. Yet the hipster argument doesn't really hold up under scrutiny. Years of research suggest that young people's distrust of oil and gas is far more widespread. Back in 2011, PricewaterhouseCoopers polled four thousand young people across seventy countries. It found that 58 percent of these Millennials "would avoid working in a particular sector solely because they believe it had a negative image." Of all the sectors where young graduates could work, "oil and gas was seen as the most unappealing globally."[27]

The American Petroleum Institute (API) reached a similar conclusion. Not long ago it held several focus groups with Millennials to determine their views on oil and gas. It discovered that a "majority had negative view of the industry," a summary of the findings read. Young people don't want to be associated "with an industry that has negative perceptions/public image." API figured that it wouldn't be too hard to change those perceptions. Once companies informed skeptical young people about the "positive aspects of the industry," it argued, those young people would be "more likely to enter the industry."[28] Yet even Millennials now employed in oil and gas are unsure. "The way the industry is currently positioned," writes the young consultant Illya Skripnikov, "does not align with the views of many people my age."[29]

As the Greyhound left Grassland behind and entered the boreal forest, I pondered what those views represented. Why do so many young people distrust oil and gas? Many people my age are clearly loath to work for companies that value short-term financial returns over their generation's future well-being. But I sensed in our rejection of oil and gas a deeper meaning. What clued me in was a story I'd read recently about Wall Street. Its large investment banks are facing a similar demographic challenge to oil and gas companies. They can't find young workers. "Wall Street is in crisis mode," argues *New York* magazine writer Kevin Roose. "Banks aren't attracting the kinds of high-achieving students they want to attract." Not even entry-level salary raises are helping. "Young people want to feel virtuous about their jobs," Roose adds, "and Wall Street still can't offer that, no matter how much it pays them."[30]

It seems that young people are rejecting Wall Street for the same underlying reason that they are rejecting oil and gas. They don't want to work in industries that care only about making money. Researchers have noticed this developing for years. A 2012 poll of 1,250 insurance industry workers done for LifeCourse Associates, for instance, found that nearly two-thirds of Millennial respondents want their employer to create a positive social impact, as opposed to 50 percent of older generations. Studies like these contain a warning for our economic leaders. "The surest way to ensure the failure of a firm's economic performance in the Millennial era that is now emerging," write Morley Winograd and Michael Hais of the Brookings Institution, "is to focus solely on profits."[31]

They believe that this generational shift will soon present a radical challenge to our society. And further research suggests that it won't be confined to North America. A 2015 survey of more than 7,800 Millennials in twenty-nine countries done by Deloitte found that "business needs a reset." Three-quarters of young respondents said our economic system is "not focused enough on helping to improve society."[32] In a survey from the year before, Deloitte asked young people in North America, Asia, Europe, and Latin America what challenges businesses should be confronting. At the top of the list were resource scarcity and climate change. A majority of Millennials think our economic system should do more to address them. These young people want to work "for organizations that benefit society," the survey concluded.[33]

The flip side is also true: we are rejecting a system that doesn't. That was the conclusion reached by the Harvard Institute of Politics. A 2016 survey of 18-to-29-year-olds suggests that a majority of young Americans—51 percent—are deeply skeptical of free-market capitalism. They believe that our economic system in its current form is amoral and unfair. That it is actively preventing our shift to a safer and more equitable future. "Let's face it," argues Robin Scher on the progressive site *Alternet*, "young Americans are fed up with the economic status quo."[34] Even mainstream media agrees. The *Washington Post* described the findings as an "apparent rejection of the basic principles of the U.S. economy."[35]

From my Greyhound window, I could see we were entering Fort McMurray's outskirts. The thick boreal forest was giving way to McDonald's and Burger King and car dealerships and beige warehouses. The shortage of people my age in oil and gas was starting to make more sense to me. For as long as my generation has been alive, we've been told by our economic and political leaders that money is the primary driver of all human activity, and that profit-seeking merely reflects this fact of human nature. But it seems that millions of Millennials have come to the same realization Karl Clark reached in the 1960s: that there was more to life than making the most money possible and not thinking about the consequences.

WHEN BRADLEY JOHNSON GRADUATED from high school in Fort McMurray, he was unsure what to do with himself. Part of him desperately wanted to leave a city that treats money as life's ultimate pursuit, one where newcomers and transients show up to make quick cash in the tar sands and then take off for something better. "What is the culture of Fort Mac?" Bradley sometimes wondered. "It's more like a situation than a culture." But Fort McMurray was also home. He had friends there. Many of his family members tried hard to establish roots. They took pride in the town. "They wanted nothing more than to have a deeper rooted community," he said. So with high school now behind him, he debated if he would join them. "I felt like 'Am I going to leave or stay? Am I going to buy into working at the oil refinery or get the fuck out?'" he said. Most people his age were asking themselves the same question.

After some reflection, Bradley decided to stay—at least for a little while. He briefly thought about pursuing art. The competition that he'd won in grade twelve, the one his art teacher had encouraged him to enter, made him eligible for the art program at Keyano College in Fort McMurray. He knew he was good at drawing, but he had trouble seeing himself as an artist. And the idea of spending any more time in a class-room was a turnoff. "I decided I wasn't going to postsecondary," he said. "I thought it was all bullshit." Instead he decided to travel. He wanted to see what the world was like outside Fort McMurray. But for that to happen, he needed money. So he did the same thing as many of his former classmates: he went looking for a high-paying job in the tar sands.

People have this idea that you just show up at the tar sands and get handed a job. But it wasn't that easy for a young unskilled laborer like Bradley. At the time, his stepfather was working for an oil and gas contracting firm that hired students for the summer. His stepfather made arrangements for Bradley to come in for a job interview. "It was sketchy," he said. "My stepfather's boss was really weird." Bradley showed up at the job site one morning for the interview. "The guy's name was Randy," he said. Randy was nowhere to be seen. "I just sat there in the lunchroom, this dusty, grimy trailer room, and waited and waited," he said. Hours went by. "Then Randy finally came and sat down and said, 'I can't start you today, but come back the week after next, and you can start,'" Bradley said. "I'm thinking I'm definitely not getting the job."

Sure enough, he called up the contracting company two weeks later, only to find out that Randy was gone on vacation. "I really needed a job, though," he said. "I wanted to make money so I could take off." He recalled a conversation he'd had with another worker at the contracting company. Many of the employees lived in fear of Randy. They thought they'd lose their job if they ever crossed him. Bradley had an idea: "If I just go out there while Randy is on vacation and tell everyone that he told me to come in, everybody is just going to go along with it." Bradley had nothing to lose by trying. "If I get there and they say 'No, you're full of shit,' then I'll just go home, and I'm back where I'm at," he said. "But if it works, I'll have a job for the summer."

On his first day at work, some people were skeptical. Bradley kept insisting he'd been hired by Randy. Nobody wanted to fire him and later find out that he was telling the truth. "They're going to be in trouble," he said. "Randy's going to be pissed." That's how he got his first job in the tar sands. The work was terrible. For most of it he was based inside an oil plant. He had to go into every weird nook with a three-inch fire hose. It was very hot, and bitumen coated everything. "I just had to spray this stuff off the catwalks and railings, vainly cleaning up around the shop," he said. "There were like three other summer students, and we did work that was created only for us."

It was a pretty masculine environment. "Lots of posturing, and a lot of straight faces," Bradley explained. There were all types of guys working in the tar sands: funny guys, serious guys, smart guys, sensitive guys. "But when you're a summer student you get pushed in with people doing unskilled labor, or just barely skilled labor," he said. "Those folks tend to be like grunts." Many of them met the criteria of "stereotypical meatheads." They were the type who'd drink all night and show up bleary-eyed for their shift the next morning. Now and then Bradley ran into a friend from high school. "We'd give each other knowing looks like 'Here we are for the next twelve hours,'" he said.

Most people got through those twelve hours by lowering their heads and doing the job required and blocking out their surroundings. But for Bradley that was sometimes difficult to do. He had always been sensitive to weird visual spectacles, and the tar sands were full of them. There were black strip mines stretching off to infinity, bursts of flame a hundred feet tall. It could often be overwhelming for him. "I remember plenty of times where I would get this ecstatic kind of joy or sublime trembling from what I was looking at," he explained. "Just pausing for a second and placing myself in context at the moment and then in the landscape and just keep zooming out on myself and just keep thinking 'What the fuck am I doing right now in the world?'"

Sometimes such feelings could be triggered by a specific piece of equipment. After the boreal forest has been cut down and the over-burden is stripped away, giant industrial shovels scoop up what's left into heavy hauler trucks that are bigger than houses. Those trucks then drive their loads of tar sands and boulders and whatever else to a machine called a crusher. "The crushers are basically these pits that the heavy haulers dump their loads into," Bradley says. "This thing looks like a giant leech or something with these huge teeth that are crushing up gigantic rocks and pulverizing them in seconds." It's so loud that you have to wear two sets of earplugs to even get near the crusher. To Bradley, the entire spectacle was totally mind-blowing.

In a few months he saved up enough money to leave Fort McMurray. "I went and traveled for a year," he said. "I thought, 'I'm never coming back.'" But he grew restless near the end, and a little bored. He couldn't travel forever. "I have to do something," he thought. The idea of coming back home and starting a career in the tar sands wasn't appealing. There was that scholarship, though, the one he'd won in high school to study art at Keyano College. It was still available. He knew there wasn't much money in pursuing art, and he didn't consider himself an artist. Yet he loved drawing, and he had a strong visual eye. After much delib-eration, he decided to enroll. "I was really insecure," he said. "Like, 'They're going to find me out as soon as I get there, and they're going to realize I'm not a fucking artist.'"

IN A TOWN DEVOTED to oil and the quick profits that can be made from it, people weren't exactly clamoring to get into Fort McMurray's art school. There were only about four other people in Bradley's class. Yet one of the teachers had spent much of the 1980s working at a highly respected printmaking studio in New York. "They'd invite cutting-edge artists to their shop and bend over backward to create prints for them," Bradley said. His teacher had worked directly with artists like Frank

Stella, David Hockney, and Roy Lichtenstein. "You name it, a ton of people," he said. "He was showing us things you'd be seeing if you did a first-year drawing class at [New York's] Cooper Union."

Bradley was never completely sure how an artist and teacher of this stature ended up at a tiny college in northern Alberta. He was just grateful for the exposure to a world much bigger and full of more possibilities than the one he'd grown up in. He learned about Jonathan Borofsky writing numbers on paper to infinity. He learned about the drawings Willem de Kooning did with his eyes closed. "It blew my mind," he said. Unlike the world of oil and gas, the art world wasn't resigned to a single version of reality. It actively sought new perspectives. Some artists were getting filthy rich. But mostly meaning seemed to take precedence over money. "I can get into this," Bradley thought. "I want to work with my own ideas and be my own boss." It was the exact opposite of any lifestyle in the tar sands.

Bradley was energized and excited. "I was voracious as a student," he said. He dug in hard for two years and got really good grades. "I was killing it there," he said. "That inflated my ego." After graduating, he decided to apply at the most prestigious art school he could imagine attending: the Alberta College of Art and Design. It was in Calgary, Canada's equivalent to Houston—a sprawling prairie city of about a million people where the oil companies making billions of dollars from the tar sands have offices in skyscrapers overlooking the Bow River. Bradley moved there in the summer. Compared to Fort McMurray it felt like a metropolis. "I was like 'Oh my God, holy fuck, they have a railcar system,'" he said.

Bradley was so confident he'd be accepted by Alberta College that he didn't bother applying to other programs. He even enrolled in summer session classes so that he'd be able to spend more time in the studio the following spring. "Then I get a rejection letter in the middle of it," Bradley said. "I'm totally incredulous." After he finished freaking out, he got a job driving a junk-collecting truck in Calgary. He also got a studio downtown. "I would just collect junk all day and go to my studio at night and make a ton of work," he said. He slowly rebuilt his portfolio and reapplied to Alberta College the following year. This time he wasn't taking chances. He also applied to art schools in Vancouver and Toronto. He got accepted at every one.

He decided to enroll at the Emily Carr University of Art + Design in Vancouver. It had a decent reputation in North America. Douglas Coupland, the novelist and artist famous for coining the term "Generation X," had gone there. "I was definitely feeling the scope of my world get bigger," he said. Vancouver is similar in size and culture to Seattle. It has a large Chinese population. "I felt like I was in a huge city," Bradley said. "I thought I would have to learn Mandarin." Once again he dug into his studies. He did well at Emily Carr, and after he graduated, a professor helped connect him to a small gallery. Bradley was printing large images and having them laminated onto honeycomb aluminum. "The work I was making cost a lot to produce," he said. He was also struggling to repay his student loans. If he was going to be an artist, he needed some cash. "So I went back to Fort McMurray," he said.

Bradley stayed for more than a year, working in the tar sands as a serviceman. His job was to drive a big rig transport truck stocked with diesel, engine coolant, truck grease, hydraulic fluid, or anything else an oil operation in the middle of nowhere might require. "I would drive that thing around and go and service and top up fluids on all the heavy haulers and the dozers and the other equipment," he said. Often he had to work the night shift: "You're driving around in pitch black on basically dirt roads." The companies would install mobile light towers at work sites. "Like those things that police put up," he said. "Permanently dramatic lighting everywhere." In his truck he could spot them far off in the distance.

On one of his first night shifts, he had to go assist another service truck that had hit a dip in the road and flipped onto its side. It was the middle of winter and cold, about negative twenty degrees. "These really bright spotlights are reflecting off the snow," he said. "It was gorgeous in a funny way." The flipped service truck was spewing diesel from its tank all over the road. The driver stood next to it casually smoking a cigarette. Bradley turned to a mechanic who'd driven out with him. "What is he doing? He needs to put that out immediately," Bradley demanded. The mechanic laughed. He assured Bradley that diesel has totally different properties than gasoline. It wouldn't explode. You could even put out your smoke in it. "So no fear at all," Bradley said. "But I've seen movies—I know what comes next. He flips the cigarette, and we all blow up."

Another time Bradley pulled up beside a large industrial vehicle known as a dozer idling beside the road. "The driver was sitting in his cab, maybe he was sleeping," he said. The whole scene was lit by one of those mobile towers. Suddenly he saw a coyote: "It's just sitting there staring at the dozer and waiting for a snack to come out the window." For the most part, he hated working in the tar sands. Still, in moments like that, he felt something "profound and evocative and dramatic, if you could call it that," he said. "There's only one way to see something like this, and it's to be either me or the other guy."

None of these scenes ever directly influenced his art: "I wasn't at all thinking that I'm going to get photographs of this or document this or make some sort of statement about it." Something about being so close to the tar sands made him feel detached from them. He knew that his job was damaging to the natural world, but it could be hard to make the knowledge feel real. On the winter night when Bradley watched diesel pour out of the overturned truck, he wasn't "thinking about the fact that it's diesel and what the chemical is and whether it's hurting the environment or any stuff like that." At the end of the day, all he really cared about was when his shift ended and how much he'd get paid. A year like this was all he could handle. "I freaked out," he said, and moved back to Vancouver.

Bradley realized he just wasn't cut out to work in a place that cared only about money. What he truly valued in life had a wider meaning, but for the next two years he was unsure how to pursue it. He was working in coffee shops and making art in his spare time. "I was really just afloat," he said. But slowly it dawned on him that if he really was going to live for more than just a paycheck, he had to commit fully to doing something different. And so he started applying to grad schools in the United States. At the very least he could become a professor and inspire a new generation of students, the way his own art teacher had inspired him back in Fort McMurray. He got accepted at Yale and NYU. He chose Yale and packed his bags.

IN THE FALL OF 2014 Matthew Booth* set out from Los Angeles for the shale oil fields of North Dakota. He was joined by his good friend Austin Lynch and three others. "We were in a huge van with so much film equipment," Matthew said. They were on their way to America's version of Fort McMurray, a town called Williston at the epicenter of the U.S. fracking boom. Five years earlier few Americans could've located it on a map. But when improvements to fracking technology made billions of barrels of shale oil feasible to extract, the town's population tripled to 36,000. People arrived "hoping to earn fat paychecks working long hours on an oil rig," a story in the *International Business Times* read.[36] They dreamed of a place where "the money flowed as quickly as the oil gushed."

Matthew Booth and Bradley Johnson were good friends. They'd known each other nearly a decade. They met in Vancouver and applied for grad school at the same time and both got into Yale. After graduating, they moved to New York together and helped found an artists' studio in Brooklyn's Gowanus neighborhood. So many years now separated Bradley from his life as a tar sands worker that he rarely ever thought about it. So it was with some amusement that he learned of his friend's plan to travel to North Dakota and film the oil worker "man-camps" around Williston. The footage would be for an experimental film exploring "politically and socially charged domestic situations" in five locations, Matthew explained. They'd also be visiting a Gulf Coast shrimping boat, a Virginia commune, an Oregon women's penitentiary, and a modernist Los Angeles home. Bradley wished his filmmaker friend good luck.

Matthew and Lynch and the rest of the team arrived in North Dakota at night. The scenery was "initially pretty uninspiring," Matthew said. "Like you might imagine, very flat." What did grab their attention were the hundred-foot towers of flames across the horizon. Like the tar sands, the oil contained in the Bakken Shale formation that runs through

---

* Real name.

North Dakota is hard to extract. It's literally encased in shale rock. Companies drill holes deep into the ground and "frack" the rock with millions of gallons of chemicals and water. The methane gas that also comes out of the ground is burned off into the atmosphere. At night the flames light up the undersides of clouds. "It looked like something out of science fiction," Matthew said.

All that venting is terrible for the climate. The methane gas it releases has a long-lasting impact. Over twenty years it results in eighty-six times more global warming than carbon dioxide. Since the fracking boom took off over the last decade in North Dakota (and in Pennsylvania, where the technology is used to extract natural gas), America's methane emissions have spiked 30 percent, according to a Harvard study. "The increase almost certainly must be coming from the fracking," explained Cornell University methane researcher Robert Howarth.[37] Fracking, along with tar sands, is among the fourteen fossil fuel expansions across the world that Greenpeace calculates could lead our planet past "the point of no return" on climate change.[38]

Matthew, Lynch, and their team spent three weeks shooting footage in and around Williston. They filmed inside the vast modular camps set up to house thousands of transient workers. "It felt like a moon base," Matthew said. They also spent lots of time hanging out in bars. Few of the mostly male workers throwing back shots and pints after their twelve-hour shifts had much love for their jobs or for North Dakota. Their attitude was "get in, get the money and leave," he said. "Everyone has an exit strategy." The tone of the film was apolitical. Matthew and Lynch wanted to understand the psychology of the man-camps. "I don't think anyone is getting off on exploiting the land," he said. The problem was that no one thought about the consequences of their paycheck. There was simply no incentive to do so. "That was the biggest takeaway for me," Matthew explained. "It's hard to fault an individual acting within a system that's fucked."

Each day that Bradley spent making art in New York he was rejecting that system. Even if none of the art that he created at his studio explicitly conveyed that message. Bradley's work was for the most part abstract and apolitical. It drew from a wide variety of forms:

paintings, books, sculptures, and computer software. For one project Bradley convinced a car service company called Empress Car and Limo in Brooklyn's Park Slope to let him "do a show in their not-so-often occupied storefront," he said. The show's centerpiece was an abstract white structure of rigid angles and curves that was exposed to passersby on Fourth Avenue. Bradley and his partner made a cryptic website with early-Internet graphics. They called the project Empress Fine Art.

But the fact remained that his day-to-day existence in New York was guided by the pursuit of something larger than just a paycheck. "You don't get into this line of work for the financial stability," he said. The point was to open your mind. To find new perspectives on reality. To reframe old problems, and maybe even to solve them. Money was simply a means to those ends—not the other way around. "Part of the reason I'm interested in art is that it appeals to my curiosity," Bradley said. "I have the kind of personality where I really don't like working for someone else unless I really respect them." New York is expensive. So when he wasn't making art he did mindless "Photoshop stuff" for an online retail company. "I have to work really hard to just survive and have the sort of moderately decent lifestyle that I have," he said.

Like many people of his generation, climate change lurked at the back of his mind. He knew it was getting more urgent, and that our political and economic leaders didn't seem to care. "It's there, I think about it," he said. "I do worry." Global warming felt scary and daunting. It was the gnawing feeling of unease that came when his thoughts drifted too far into the future. On the surface Bradley didn't seem to be doing much about it. When four hundred thousand people marched through New York in 2014 to demand that world leaders take action on climate change, for instance, Bradley wasn't among them. "If I worried about climate change 'a lot, a lot' I would have to be an activist or a politician or something," he said. Not an abstract visual artist.

But Bradley's life choices had larger implications for our planet's future than he imagined. By rejecting a career in the tar sands he was also rejecting a way of life that cared more about making money than humankind's future. This wasn't just a temporary phase. The only way Bradley could ever see himself working in the oil and gas industry again was if he could create some kind of wider societal progress. "If I were apt to get involved with the point of view I have now, where would I fit?" he said. "I'm sure there are solutions to a lot of the problems causing us to pollute so badly in that industry. But it doesn't seem like there are people involved in it who give that much of a fuck long term." To people of Bradley's age the industry's values were growing more and more outdated. And if Millennials like him continued to avoid it, the industry itself wouldn't have much of a long-term future.

THE THREE DAYS THAT I spent in Fort McMurray after my five-hour Greyhound trip from Edmonton were surreal. I stayed in a flawless suburban neighborhood with pick-up trucks outside every door. I walked the city's deserted downtown streets. I went to a 7-Eleven where Al Jazeera reporters had been offered crack. I met union reps. I met social workers. I met people struggling to build a community. I joined several dozen elderly tourists on a guided tour of the tar sands. I had my mind blown by the toxic lakes, the flame-spitting refinery towers, the sheer scale of it all. This part of the book was going to be about my experiences. But as I started to write it something big happened. Something that made me see Bradley's story in a whole new light.

On May 2, 2016, a wildfire in the forest southwest of Fort McMurray suddenly exploded and moved toward the city so fast that it barely had time to prepare. "When I got in the shower earlier today the sky was blue. When I got out, the sky was black," one resident explained.[39] By the early afternoon, people living in Fort McMurray's southern neighborhoods were fleeing walls of orange flame that looked like something out of Armageddon. Massive plumes of smoke billowed out of control. Several hours later an evacuation order was issued for all eighty thousand of the town's residents. The highway to Edmonton was blocked by flames. People went north instead. More than sixteen hundred homes and businesses were burned down. Two people died in a fiery explosion as they tried to escape.

Fires happen all the time in the boreal forest. But this one was so bad partly due to climate change. Higher global temperatures suck moisture out of forests, making them drier and more prone to burn. They've lengthened the Earth's fire season. They also increase the frequency of lightning. Climate change wasn't directly responsible for the Fort McMurray wildfire. A dry and mild winter caused by an El Niño weather system contributed, as did a shift of winds once the fire started burning. Yet scientists who've studied wildfires estimate that the area burned in Canada has doubled since 1979. "We attribute the increase in wildfires and their severity and intensity to human-caused climate change," said University of Alberta scientist Mark Flannigan. "Many of us saw a Fort McMurray–like situation coming, but none of us expected anything as horrific as what has happened."[40]

But as the days went by, it seemed that anyone who linked this sober scientific conclusion to the wildfire was immediately criticized. After the leader of Canada's Green Party remarked that the disaster "is very related to the global climate crisis," she was quickly reprimanded by Prime Minister Justin Trudeau. "Pointing at any one incident and saying: 'This is because of that,' is neither helpful, nor entirely accurate," he said.[41] The *Climate Central* journalist Brian Kahn said he received a "shocking" amount of hate mail after writing about the wildfire's connection to climate change.[42] And readers called a story by *Slate*'s Eric Holthaus "disgusting" and "insensitive," accusing him of pushing a "political agenda."[43]

That wrath was also reflected in Canada's conservative media. An op-ed in the *Calgary Sun* offered "one giant middle finger" to the "opportunistic cowards" who engage in "told-you-so mockery about climate change."[44] *National Post* columnist Kevin Libin attacked the "climate alarmists [who] want you to believe that if it weren't for the carbon emissions created by oil, the people of Fort McMurray would not be facing this crisis."[45] The more I read about the wildfire, the more I understood that the debate wasn't about science at all. It was about the future of our economic system and the way we live inside it. And I realized my generation was already deciding the outcome.

If you accept that Fort McMurray's wildfire is linked to climate change, then you have to accept that the 2.2 million barrels of tar sands being pumped out of the region each day—much of that to the United States—are partly to blame. You have to accept the fact that this is making the world more dangerous and that the immense profits that oil and gas create come with negative consequences. Many people, particularly among older generations, are not prepared to do that. They prefer to see the wildfire as an unpredictable accident devoid of any wider significance. "No real scientist believes that wildfires can be completely prevented," Libin wrote. "[They] have been routinely sweeping across vast swathes of Albertan forest long before the first settler arrived." In his opinion, large oil companies like Exxon have zero responsibility. "There would be forest fires, even without oil," he argued.[46]

By this logic, there was no need to question the economic system propped up by such companies. After all, it was doing exactly what it was set up to do: create massive amounts of profit. The *Globe and Mail* columnist Gary Mason urged anyone thinking too hard about the wildfire's link to climate change—as well as the fossil fuels causing it—to "consider for a moment the enormous wealth that the oil sands have generated over the years, a fortune that has been shared with the country . . . Lord knows, Fort McMurray has helped many of us."[47] An op-ed that later appeared in the *Toronto Sun* was even blunter. "Arguing the Fort McMurray fire was caused by man-made climate change and is payback for the oil sands is idiotic," it declared. "Activists should get down on their knees and thank Gaia that Canada has the oil sands."[48]

If the wildfire didn't present an indictment of our economic system, if it was a reminder of how good things are, then it could be used to justify the expansion of that system. Just three days after the wildfire started, that's exactly what happened. Political leaders from Alberta and British Columbia began arguing that the best way to recover from the economic loss the wildfire had inflicted—a 1.5 percent drop to Canada's GDP caused by a slowdown in tar sands—was to build more pipelines and produce more fossil fuels to fill them. "We are going to keep moving to get our [oil] to [west coast] tidewater," said Alberta's deputy premier Sarah Hoffman. "We're not going to apologize for that."[49] It was insane. A natural disaster that was exacerbated by climate change was now being used to expand the very activity causing climate change in the first place.

The wildfire debate clearly had little to do with science. It was a clash between two competing sets of values. Whether they intended to or not, the commentators who downplayed—or outright denied—the link between the disaster and climate change were defending the right to pursue financial returns without worrying about the consequences. Those who pointed out that such consequences existed, meanwhile, were providing evidence that this way of doing things badly needed to change. "What's happening now is undeniably a tragedy," the young Canadian writer Nicholas Ellan wrote in response to the wildfire. But its relationship to climate change is a "critical, and arguably existential, discussion."[50]

On *Slate*, Eric Holthaus completely agreed. "Talking about climate change during an ongoing disaster like Fort McMurray is absolutely necessary," he insisted. "Adding scientific context helps inform our response and helps us figure out how something so horrific could have happened." It does something else too. It forces us to have a conversation about what kind of world we want to live in. During an era "where all weather events bear at least a slight human finger-print," the way we choose to structure our society has profound consequences for human survival. Fort McMurray's fire showed us what was at stake. "We need to talk about what we want to do with that information," he wrote. "There's no better time to have that conversation . . . [than] when we can see what exactly inaction might continue to cause."[51]

It seemed anytime someone tried to have that conversation, though, they were shouted down. They were called "insensitive." They were blaming the victims. They were given the "middle finger salute." Some people undoubtedly deserved it. Former politician Tom Moffat, for instance, was forced to apologize after tweeting that the wildfire was "karmic" payback for a city founded on fossil fuels. Yet most people who made the link to climate change had nothing but sympathy for Fort McMurray's citizens. Their true target was the wider economic structure that the town's citizens—and all of us—belong to. "We are all consumers of oil, not to mention coal and natural gas, which means that we've all contributed to the latest inferno," wrote the *New Yorker*'s Elizabeth Kolbert. "We need to own up to our responsibility, and then we need to do something about it."[52]

What I learned from Fort McMurray's wildfire was that our political and economic leaders are not prepared to do that. They would rather continue on as usual than acknowledge that a system that values profits over everything else has no long-term future on this planet. They used one of the most devastating wildfires in North American history, one linked in significant ways to climate change, as a pretext to expand fossil fuels instead of questioning our reliance on them. They were the same leaders who were fracking shale oil fields in North Dakota, expanding coal exports from the United States, Australia, and Indonesia, drilling off the Brazilian coast, and filling the administration of Donald Trump. They threaten to take us past the point of no return on climate change. They threaten humankind's very existence.

Yet the entire logic of their strategy is being undermined by a former tar sands worker now making conceptual art in New York. The oil and gas industry is terrified of young people like Bradley Johnson because if Millennials continue to reject careers in oil and gas, the industry is not going to be able to replace all the Baby Boomers set to retire in the next five to ten years. Fort McMurray will be rebuilt. Tar sands production will resume. The price of oil may even climb back to hugely profitable levels. But the generational values shift that people like Bradley represent will continue to loom over everything. It threatens more than $100 billion in new oil and gas projects. It poses an existential quandary to the entire industry.

More than that, it calls into question a basic assumption of our economic system. Members of my generation grew up in a society that treats money as life's highest pursuit. But as millions of people my age got older and had to choose the sort of lives they want to live, they have rejected that logic. Like Karl Clark, they realize that the blind pursuit of profits leaves little room for anything else. That it's an amoral impulse. That our lives and society should have a wider meaning than simply achieving the biggest bank balance. And that we should be doing all we can to pursue it.

Which got me thinking. If people like Bradley Johnson can rattle the foundation of our status quo without even really intending to, then what will happen when people my age directly confront it? As I'll explain in the next chapter, a confrontation like that can influence the world's most powerful leader.

3

Citizens of Planet Earth

THE YOUNG ACTIVIST WHO helped force President Barack Obama's hand on climate change never felt like his identity mapped neatly onto the country he was born in. Growing up, Phil Aroneanu always had the sense that he carried some kind of hidden awareness. Most of the people he knew in the upper-middle-class suburb of New York where he grew up were quote unquote "American." Their first language was English. Phil, who spoke Romanian at home with his immigrant parents, did his best to be just like them. But he always suspected that his true self was anchored in something larger than his immediate surroundings. "I felt like I had this sort of secret," he explained. "I had to hide it a little bit to blend in."[1] As he got older, the borders separating him from the rest of the world began to feel more and more arbitrary. And he eventually came to realize that if you act as if they don't exist, you can influence the decisions of powerful leaders.

When Phil's parents emigrated from Romania, all they wanted was a nice quiet life in the suburbs. In the context of his family's history, that was a radical proposition. Phil's great-great-grandfather led the Romanian socialist party until his execution in the early 1900s. A generation later many of Phil's Jewish ancestors died in the Holocaust. Those who survived grew up under the brutal dictatorship of Nicolae Ceauşescu. "A bunch of my ancestors who I never met were sent to the gulag because they were the wrong kind of communist," Phil said. So when his parents were lucky enough to escape to the United States in their mid-twenties, their primary goal was stability. They "worked hard to give my sister and me a good life," he said. "My upbringing was much saner than any of my ancestors'."

But in some ways the world that Phil grew up in was much more tumultuous and disorienting than anything his ancestors had experienced. Like millions of other people born in the 1980s, Phil became a teenager during an era of deep and rapid globalization. Throughout the 1990s an explosion of free trade and commerce turned him and his generation into global consumers. The Internet grew from 16 million users in 1995 to over 360 million in 2000. And the September 11 terrorist attacks showed that events on one side of the planet could have terrifying consequences on the other. Of all the turbulent changes caused by globalization, however, none had as large an impact on Phil's teenage identity as climate change.

Phil was fifteen when "a wacky physics teacher" in his high school explained that the routines he took for granted—flicking on the lights in the morning, getting a ride to school, heating up a snack in the microwave before dinner, watching TV before bed—were setting in motion a chain of events that could someday flood all the world's coastal cities, drive a quarter of the Earth's species extinct, and send human civilization into complete disarray. "When I learned about climate change, I was like 'Holy shit, this thing is not just about the climate, it's about everything we care about on Earth,'" Phil recalled. "It's sort of unexplainable, but it just hit me that this was something I'd be working on for the rest of my life."

As a teenager, he knew he was more likely to feel the full impact of climate change in his lifetime than his parents or grandparents. "Young people are at the front lines of this," he said. "We're literally fighting for our lives." That realization affected his entire worldview. It made him question the stable life in the suburbs that his parents had tried to build for him—as well as the status quo that it supported. There must be something wrong with mainstream society, he figured, if it was destabilizing the atmosphere that thousands of years of human civilization had depended on. As he got older, Phil decided to devote himself to radical social change. "It seemed to be exactly the opposite of what my parents wanted," he said.

In his early twenties Phil found a community that shared his views at Middlebury College. As part of his undergraduate degrees in sociology and anthropology, he took a seminar taught by the economics professor Jon Isham called "Building a New Climate Movement." Its premise was that the only way humankind could create the far-reaching economic and political changes needed to address climate change was if a massive social movement of regular people demanded them. They spent months studying the civil rights movement, how it was run, why it succeeded, and if its lessons could still be applied. Phil was fascinated. He and six friends from the class began meeting to discuss how they could put the ideas from the class into action. They formed the Sunday Night Group and set a goal, which they later met, of pressuring Middlebury to go carbon neutral. "It wasn't official," he said. "But we managed to mobilize hundreds of students."

Around this time they started working with a scholar-in-residence at Middlebury, Bill McKibben. In the late 1980s he'd written the best seller *The End of Nature*, which was among the first books to explain the looming crisis of climate change to a general readership. But in the years since then McKibben had become increasingly frustrated that our politicians and business leaders didn't seem interested in doing anything to solve it. Like Isham, he believed that the pressure for solutions needed to come from a movement of regular people. But as McKibben and Phil and the others in the Sunday Night Club would come to realize, that movement would need to be unlike any other in history. To reflect the global scale of climate change, it would have to transcend every national border on the planet.

That was a daunting proposition for seven undergrad students and their adviser. No less so because the state where Middlebury is located, Vermont, is among the most politically and environmentally progressive in the country. Phil wasn't at all sure whether people in the rest of America—let alone the entire world—cared about climate change as much as they did. "We really didn't know if there was a movement out there," he said.

To figure out if there was, they formed the organization 350.org. And as they set about building the planet's first truly global social movement on climate change, Phil realized that the tension he'd always felt between his immediate surroundings and the world outside was shared more widely among people his age than he'd suspected. Under the right conditions it could be channeled in new and exciting and transformative ways. By the time he reached his early thirties, it would influence the decision making of the world's most powerful nation.

To UNDERSTAND THE GLOBAL identity on climate change that Phil and the others at 350.org set out to build, it helps to meet one of the people now in charge of growing and maintaining it. Allyse Heartwell was born on the Hawaiian island of Oahu and raised in the Honolulu suburbs. "I was a pretty outdoorsy kid," she said. "My parents took me hiking a lot, and we lived in a house that was right on the beach." She spent much of her childhood out in the azure-blue Pacific, poking at tide pools, picking up crabs, swimming behind sea turtles. "It's kind of weird to call it 'special' because that's the childhood everyone deserves," she said. "I can say I'm very lucky in that regard. I got to have a lot of nature in my life."² Hawaii is much more than just home to her. It's where she feels most rooted as a human being.

After finishing high school, she decided to go to college in the most exotic place she could think of: Rhode Island. "All the ivy and old brick and whatnot," she said. "We don't really have multicentury-old buildings in Hawaii. It seemed very romantic to me." During her four years at Brown University, Allyse took a lot of courses in environmental studies. One day she had a realization that changed her life. "I was sitting in the windowsill of my college dorm, and it was spring, and the plum trees were flowering," she said. As she looked out the window, she pictured ocean water flooding Hawaii. She saw rain forests and coral reefs becoming lifeless. "There are places and ecosystems that I love deeply that are actively in danger," she realized. "And why would I do anything else with my life other than try to protect them?"

She moved to San Francisco after college and began working for a nonprofit focused on local economic resilience. In her spare time she volunteered on an urban farm. She read a lot of Internet articles about the challenges facing human civilization. She soon became obsessed with the idea that our global supply of oil is running dry—and that we need to build a more resilient economic system capable of operating without it. Allyse read sites like *Energy Bulletin* and *Oil Drum* every day. Though she didn't consider herself an activist, she joined a Bay Area group trying to raise awareness of peak oil. "I don't think that it's likely that we're going to make smart choices in the next 10 or 20 years," Allyse told *Salon* at the time, but "I would be kicking myself if I didn't do something."[3]

She would later apply the same logic to climate change. As massive new sources of oil were opened up in Canada's tar sands and in U.S. shale deposits, the concept of peak oil became less relevant. But if anything, our need to move away from fossil fuels was more urgent than ever. "This historical moment is such that one cannot confront the facts of climate change—to say nothing of the worst-case predictions—without being deeply, existentially afraid," she wrote.[4] She figured it was better to do something tangible about those fears than suppress them. When the position of digital campaigner opened up at 350.org's Oakland offices in 2011, Allyse decided to apply for it. She wanted to join the "fight for a livable planet" and be part of a "powerful and beautiful" global movement.

Allyse Heartwell appears to share that desire with many people her age. For over a decade the veteran political pollster John Zogby has done extensive public opinion research on the values held by U.S. Millennials. He has concluded that this generation has a more global perspective than others before it. Its members, he argues, are more empathic toward other cultures. They're more likely to care about global problems. They see national borders as a veneer, and they think solutions to society's ills should transcend them. In short, Zogby's ten years of polling suggest that members of Allyse's generation "express opinions reflecting a larger vision of the world than their elders."[5] They see themselves as part of a "global society."

That's not totally surprising for a generation that can barely imagine what life was like without the Internet. In 2014 the Pew Research Center set out to quantify the generational divide between these so-called digital natives and their parents and grandparents. A major survey of thousands of Americans suggests that the average Millennial has 250 "friends" on Facebook, compared to 200 for Gen Xers and 98 for Baby Boomers. Millennial respondents are twice as likely to say they've shared a selfie online as Gen Xers, and ten times as likely as Boomers. Statistics like this, silly as they may seem, were evidence to Pew researchers that young people had "taken the lead in seizing on the new platforms of the digital era."[6]

But people often forget that the Internet is only a tool. What's more telling is how the tool is actually used. From an early age, people of Allyse Heartwell's generation used the Internet to experience events on the other side of the planet in real time. It compresses physical boundaries. And in doing so it makes issues such as climate change, ones that you don't necessarily experience firsthand, feel closer. "This increased access to information has created a heightened awareness of the world's challenges, often leading to a deeper commitment to social and economic justice," argues Howard Dean, whose campaign for the Democrat presidential nomination in 2000 was among the first of any U.S. candidate to effectively utilize the Internet. "This is the first generation that embraces the notion of 'shared fate.' They understand the connection each has to the other across the globe."[7]

In particular, they understand how that connection is threatened by climate change. Unlike older generations, argues the North Carolina–based psychotherapist Chris Saade, "who can put their heads in the sand about what we have been doing to our planet, [young people] are very aware of what's going on . . . Because of the web, it's not hidden any more."[8] This appears to have had a formative impact on the worldview of Millennials. In 2007 the education company BrainPOP asked one thousand U.S. middle school students, who are now in their mid-twenties, to rank their greatest fears for the future. Nearly 60 percent said they feared climate change more than terrorism, car crashes, or cancer. "We were not surprised in our survey to discover that children are really worried about global warming," BrainPOP said. "We have received thousands of e-mails from children expressing their fears."[9]

As those children entered adulthood, they put less emphasis on national borders than their parents and grandparents. In years of polling, Zogby Analytics found that almost one in three Millennial respondents "prefer to be called 'citizens of the planet Earth'—more than any other age cohort."[10] A major 2014 study conducted by the American National Election Study reached a similar conclusion: 70 percent of Boomer respondents felt their U.S. identity to be extremely important, compared to 60 percent of Gen Xers and only 45 percent of Millennials.[11] There are of course many complex reasons for this shift. But it suggested that young people feel greater attachment to the planet than to the country they were born in.

And they're more likely to support policies protecting the planet. In 2015 the Pew Research Center conducted a massive global survey—over 45,000 interviews in forty countries—on attitudes toward climate change. It found that 85 percent of 18-to-29-year-olds in the United States supported an international treaty to limit carbon emissions, compared to only 60 percent of people over 50. "Young Americans are generally more concerned than their elders about climate change," a report on the data concluded. Similar age gaps were detected in Europe, Asia, and Australia. "This might be expected," the report explained, "since the younger generation may see itself as most likely to have to live with the consequences of global warming."[12]

That is effectively what 350.org discovered when it began reaching out to young people across the world. Millennials were more likely to see themselves as global citizens than their parents. They were more connected online. They knew climate change threatened their survival, and they wanted their leaders to do something about it. But the energy produced by these tectonic generational shifts didn't have an outlet, and so 350.org set out to provide it. It wanted to remind young people across the world that they share a global identity. When Allyse Heartwell joined the group, she was tasked with the daily work of helping maintain it. As a campaigner at 350.org, and later as the group's digital director, she would oversee the website updates, the e-mails, and the social media blasts that remind someone in Bangladesh that they're fighting the same struggle as someone in the United States. The true innovation of 350.org was to "expand people's sense of self," she said. And as the story of a tar sands pipeline known as Keystone XL would later prove, it was the group's greatest source of power.

THE IDEA THAT YOUR identity transcends national borders sounds like a unique product of the digital era. But for centuries it's been ingrained in the worldview of North America's original inhabitants. Before European settlers arrived in the mid-1600s, millions of indigenous peoples lived a seminomadic existence—that is, their settlements migrated along with the wildlife that they hunted. And though different regions were home to different tribes, there was nothing comparable to the rigidly defined borders that exist today. That all changed as European settlers pushed west across the continent and confined what indigenous people weren't killed by disease or armed conquest to a series of ever-shrinking reservations separated from each other by the forty-ninth parallel. Yet their modern descendants never forgot the borders that were imposed on them. And in September 2011 I sat in on an emergency meeting of indigenous people in the basement of a South Dakota tribal casino who thought that by fighting a tar sands pipeline from Canada to Texas they could help redress this legacy of oppression.

When the oil and gas corporation TransCanada first applied for a permit to build the Keystone XL pipeline in 2008, it never could have predicted the size and intensity of the public opposition that would arise against it. The first phase of the project, a pipeline from Canada's tar sands to Illinois that was known simply as Keystone, was approved by the U.S. State Department with little public scrutiny. Initially the project's second phase, a 1,661-mile pipeline from Canada's tar sands to a string of refineries along the Texas Gulf Coast, seemed no different. But starting in 2010 a coalition of ranchers, environmental groups, and indigenous leaders began warning about the impact of an oil spill from Keystone XL as it crossed prime agricultural land and drinking water supplies in the Midwest.[13]

As that opposition grew stronger and better organized throughout the summer of 2011, I reached out to the Indigenous Environmental

Network, and in early September its lead pipeline campaigner, Marty
Cobenais, asked if I had any interest in attending a high-level strategy
meeting of indigenous leaders from the United States and Canada. For
two days they would huddle in South Dakota's Rosebud Casino to draft
a Mother Earth Accord explaining the true impact of TransCanada's
proposal. If they could get the accord adopted by the National Congress
of American Indians, the biggest Native lobby group in the United
States, it could be presented to President Obama at the White House's
annual Tribal Nations Conference in December. "With an accord at
that level," Cobenais explained to me, "we believe the administration
would have a hard time saying yes to this pipeline."[14] I quickly booked
my flight.

People were coming to the meeting from all over the place. One
leader was flying in from Canada's frigid Great Bear Lake near the
Arctic Circle; another was flying from Frog Lake in central Alberta; a
husband and wife were driving east on Highway 18 from the Pine Ridge
Indian Reservation; and several more driving west from Minnesota on
Interstate 90. I flew into Sioux Falls on a crisp and sunny autumn afternoon. Seen from my airplane window, South Dakota reminded me of a
tile bathroom floor. Earthy rectangles of green, brown, yellow, and red
were lined up in geometric precision. The view on the ground, after I
landed at the Sioux Falls Regional Airport, reinforced that image. In my
rental car I drove past endless fields of corn, wheat, soybeans, and
sunflowers. The smell of manure was everywhere.

Along the way I flipped from one radio station to the next: KBHB
810 AM Five State Ranch Radio; the daily Farm and Ranch Review on
KWYR Country 1260; and KILI Radio 90.1, Voice of the Lakota
Nation. South Dakota is home to one of the largest indigenous populations in the United States, with over 71,000 Lakota, Dakota, and Nakota
peoples spread over eight reservations. The proposed Keystone XL
route wouldn't enter any indigenous reserves as it traversed South
Dakota, but it would go under tributaries of the Missouri River flowing
alongside tribal territory. University of Nebraska engineering professor
John Stansbury had calculated that an oil spill could release a toxic
chemical plume "possibly stretching for 450 miles."[15]

The pipeline also had a wider historical significance. The flat and austere countryside that I drove past on my way to the Rosebud Casino had been contested ever since settlers began pushing west in the 1800s. A compromise was reached in 1851, when Lakota leaders signed the first Treaty of Fort Laramie with Washington, giving them control over tens of millions of acres across the Great Plains. But decades of encroachment and war eventually shrank those borders to a few impoverished reservations. Many Lakota people think the full 1851 territory is still rightfully theirs. And it wasn't lost on them that Keystone XL would cut through it. Leaders like Rosebud tribal chief John Spotted Tail believed that in fighting the pipeline, they could "take a stand against the nearly 200 years of judicial injustice inflicted upon Indian tribes."

In the distance I saw a small jumble of beige buildings. As I approached, I could read the casino's official slogan: "A little bit of Vegas on the prairie." Inside the casino I was pointed to a small room in the basement. I'd arrived a bit early, and attendance was so far modest. Scanning the room, I saw white farmers in flannel and blue jeans, leaders from the Rosebud tribal council, a few residents of South Dakota's Pine Ridge Indian Reservation, some antipipeline activists from Nebraska, and Cobenais, the meeting's organizer. I poured some coffee into a Styrofoam cup and took a seat at the back. Slowly the room filled out. Alex White Plume, a fifty-nine-year-old from Pine Ridge, kicked things off by delivering an opening prayer in the Lakota language.

After he was finished, White Plume looked at the white farmers with a mischievous smile. "Excuse me if I just spoke too fast for you to understand," he said. The whole room erupted in laughter. But the mood grew serious when Cobenais projected an aerial photo of Canada's tar sands—the same area that I'd visited in Chapter 2—onto the basement wall. In the photo you could see miles of strip-mined darkness where the thick boreal forest used to be. The bitumen that was extracted from these mines would pass less than seventy miles from the Rosebud Casino as it was pumped through Keystone XL to refineries in Texas. "Jesus," one of the farmers muttered. White Plume added: "Something bad is coming to our nation and to our land."[16]

Four hours into the Rosebud Casino meeting, the Canadian delegation arrived. It included Dene Nation leader Bill Erasmus, from Great
Bear Lake in Canada's North West Territories, which is downriver
from the tar sands; and George Stanley, a tribal leader from Alberta's
Frog Lake, which is located right in the heart of the Cold Lake tar
sands deposit. In some ways this meeting was Erasmus's idea. A few
weeks earlier he had come to an important realization about the indigenous opposition to Keystone XL. "Our peoples in Canada and the
United States have been working in isolation," he explained to me. "I
became intrigued by the idea of bringing us together."[17]

Many North American indigenous communities do not recognize
the forty-ninth parallel. Like the borders encircling their reservations,
they see it as an artifice imposed by European settlers. Rather than
identify as Canadian or American, aboriginals from both sides of the
border prefer to think of themselves as a continental peoples. Yet local
priorities and distance often thwart cross-border cooperation. The plan
at today's meeting was to draw from their shared sense of identity to
create a two- to three-page Mother Earth Accord opposing Keystone
XL. Erasmus and Stanley, who sat on Canada's Assembly of First
Nations, hoped to get the accord adopted by the wider leadership.
Cobenais, in turn, would help push it to the National Congress of
American Indians. Both groups wanted to present the accord directly to
President Obama and Hillary Clinton, who was then secretary of state,
later in December.

By now we'd been in the meeting for nine hours. Marty Cobenais
decided to call it a day. Everyone else was staying at the casino's Quality
Inn, so I got a room there as well. The receptionist gave me a ten-dollar
credit for the slot machines down the hall. Later that evening I drifted
asleep to a glowing TV screen and the howl of prairie wind.

The meeting was slow to start the next day. After a breakfast of
doughnuts and orange juice, I joined Alex White Plume outside as
he smoked a hand-rolled cigarette. "The ones with filters give you
bad breath," he explained. Dark clouds spat rain onto the casino's
parking lot. White Plume revealed a surprising fact: he claimed to be
descended from the same tribal band as Crazy Horse, the Lakota

warrior who in 1874 wiped out General Custer's cavalry regiment at Little Big Horn.

Given his ancestral history, White Plume saw the Keystone XL pipeline as more than just a threat to South Dakota's natural environment. In some ways he saw it as a test of his people's commitment to their surroundings and history—the latest chapter in a centuries-old struggle to protect their land and identity from the impositions of an unjust political and economic system. "When the settlers came and killed off all our buffalo, they wiped out an ecosystem that we depended on," White Plume said. "And now they're trying to bring dirty oil through our country." He paused for a second, and then laughed slowly and sadly. Back inside the casino, Chief John Spotted Tail expressed a similar sentiment. "Our ancestors protected the land when they were alive," he said at the meeting. "Our belief is that we need to do the same."[18]

For the remainder of the day, Erasmus and Stanley and Cobenais and Spotted Tail and everyone else at the meeting worked as fast as they could to finalize the Mother Earth Accord. While they drafted new clauses and crossed out old ones, I took a walk through the fields surrounding the casino. And by the time I returned, it was nearly finished. A draft copy affirmed the obligation of Native communities in the United States and Canada "to protect and preserve for our descendants, the inherent sovereign rights of our Indigenous Nations," and it warned of the potential for Keystone XL to "impact sacred sites and ancestral burial grounds, and treaty rights throughout traditional territories." The accord concluded by calling on President Obama and Secretary Clinton to "reject the Presidential Permit for the Keystone XL pipeline."

I had a flight to catch so I left the meeting before it was finished. Months later it would be adopted by the National Congress of American Indians. And when the accord finally made it to Obama, it had thousands of signatories. But as I drove north through the Rosebud Reservation and then east on I-90 past fields of corn and wheat, all I could think of was White Plume's sad laughter in the casino parking lot. To him as well as the other indigenous leaders, Keystone XL was about more than a steel pipe. It represented an economic and political system that cared little for the survival of his people or the planet. And in his fight against the pipeline, White Plume drew from a shared identity that transcended borders.

Such ideas would later become central to 350.org's campaign against Keystone XL. Few could have guessed it then, but they eventually would help get the pipeline rejected.

WHEN PHIL ARONEANU WAS at Middlebury College, he and the six other students who'd formed the Sunday Night Group kept running into the same problem anytime they debated what possible difference they could make on climate change. The issue was so huge and daunting and scary that most regular people assumed their actions couldn't possibly make a meaningful difference. So they turned inward. They blocked it out. But their adviser McKibben came up with a potential way to reverse that impulse. If you could expand people's sense of self, he figured, and show them that the anxiety they feel about our civilization's future is shared by their friends and neighbors and fellow citizens, they'd be more likely to believe change is possible. So in 2006 he suggested to the Sunday Night Group that they organize a march across Vermont. Hopefully, McKibben said, they would "make some headlines" and "get people riled up."[19] The result was better than they could have predicted. More than a thousand people hiked for five days from Robert Frost's cabin in central Vermont to the federal building in Burlington.

Still, it was one thing to get people riled up in progressive Vermont. A true test of their ability to build a social movement around climate change would be whether the rest of America cared. "We really didn't know," Phil said. In order to find out, they teamed up with national green groups such as the Natural Resources Defense Council and the Sierra Club and put out the word that they would be hosting a national day of climate-change-themed events in April 2007 called Step It Up. It was based on the decentralized structure of the Internet. Anyone could join. They could set up a march, a bike rally, a public art display—whatever they wanted—and then upload photos or videos of it to the Step It Up site. The result would be a visual archive demonstrating to someone in Alaska, say, that people in Florida and across the United States cared as much about the climate as they did. "We wanted to test the assumption that there are people out there who want to take part in [a movement]," Phil explained.

Their assumption ended up being totally correct. Mountaineers skied Wyoming's melting Dinwoody Glacier. Scuba divers took photos of Key West's endangered coral reefs. Gardeners planted native trees in downtown Oklahoma City. Activists walked the levees of New Orleans's Ninth Ward. In total there were more than fourteen hundred events. More than twenty members of Congress attended rallies. And McKibben was asked to testify before a House committee on climate change three days later. "We weren't professional organizers," Phil said. "It was pretty unbelievable what we were able to do." The seven recent college graduates and their adviser McKibben realized that people all over America were sick of a status quo that didn't take their future survival on this planet seriously. "We realized, 'Wow, there is a movement, they're out there, and all they really needed was permission to do their work,'" Phil said. "We thought, 'What if we could take this global?'"

To do that, their group needed a name. By the time Phil and his six friends made it to that December's international climate talks in Bali, they still hadn't thought of one. The talks themselves were demoralizing to witness. "We're sitting there watching the negotiations unfold painfully slowly," he said. "No one was agreeing to anything." But as it was all about to wrap up, they got an e-mail from McKibben, who explained that the NASA climatologist James Hansen had just a calculated a new threshold for climate change: if concentrations of carbon in the atmosphere exceeded 350 parts per million, every coastal city on Earth could be submerged underwater. McKibben suggested they name the group after Hansen's calculation: 350. At first Phil and the others thought it was weird. But it grew on them. It was culturally neutral. It transcended national borders. "It lent a sense of scale to what we were doing," he said.

The *.org* part came later. When they got home, they were faced with a practical dilemma: how did seven college grads in Vermont build a global movement? "We just decided to divide up the world into seven pieces," Phil said. He was given the Middle East and Africa. "There's no way that one American like me with almost no contacts in the region was going to make this happen," he thought. "So I just started cold-calling environmental and development organizations in literally every country on those continents." He sought out youth leaders. He set up endless Skype sessions. He flew out to conferences. His pitch was simple and compelling, in many ways mirroring the model established by Step It Up. He asked people across the region to join the 350.org mailing list, wait for the group to issue a call to action, set up an event in their area, brand it somehow with "350," and share photos and videos online. This is what the *.org* in 350's name came to stand for. It refered to a social network. And to a global identity.

Tapping into that identity was easier than Phil had expected. He didn't have to convince anyone that climate change is a big deal. The young people he met across Africa and the Middle East felt it every day. "They were like 'yeah, duh,'" he said. They saw it affect the food they grew and the water they drank. "They understand climate change is happening in a way that a lot of Americans don't because we're insulated from what's happening in nature," he said. But those young people lacked an outlet for their anxiety, or the sense their actions could make any sort of difference: "It's hard to feel agency on something as big as climate change if you don't feel part of a movement that's global." Phil provided basic leadership coaching. He provided tips on how to organize events and shoot videos of them. "Some of the people we trained ended up taking part in the Arab Spring," he later claimed.

Meanwhile the other six organizers at 350.org were reaching out to people across North America, South America, India, China, Europe, and Oceania. After two years, 350.org decided to test the power of what it had created. In late October 2009, two months before the international climate negotiations in Copenhagen would start, it put out a call for action. The goal was to show world leaders that young people all over the world wanted a treaty capable of ensuring their survival. "Our hope is that a huge worldwide outpouring on Oct. 24 will set a bar to make any action in Copenhagen powerful," McKibben wrote in an e-mail to supporters.[20]

More than five thousand organizers in 181 countries responded to 350.org's call. *Foreign Policy* described it as "the largest ever global coordinated rally of any kind," while CNN called it "the most widespread day of political action in our planet's history."[21] Phil Aroneanu was twenty-five years old at the time. "It was pretty incredible for a bunch of college kids and a professor," he said.

BUT THE EUPHORIA PHIL felt was short-lived. The world had projected big hopes onto the Copenhagen climate change talks. World leaders, UN officials, activists, and pretty much anyone involved with climate change saw in them the potential to create a historic treaty capable of limiting the global temperature rise to safe levels. Instead, the talks collapsed. Major emitters like the United States and China feuded endlessly. The result was a climate treaty so weak that Al Gore called it "an abysmal failure."[22] More setbacks were soon to come. That April, BP's Deepwater Horizon rig exploded in the Gulf of Mexico and leaked more oil than any other spill in history. An even more demoralizing setback came later that summer, when the Senate defeated a wide-ranging bill to cap U.S. carbon emissions and push America's economy toward clean energy. Green groups had spent over $22 million trying to get it passed. Yet ExxonMobil on its own had spent $27 million lobbying against the bill, and the oil and gas sector as a whole spent more than $175 million. It was "easily an industry record," the watchdog group OpenSecrets noted.[23]

Those events were painful for Phil and the others at 350.org to witness. But they contained a crucial lesson. "We saw the limitations of just doing feel-good days of action," he said. Such actions implied that climate change could be won if enough people became aware of the crisis and demanded that leaders take it seriously. Yet the disasters in Copenhagen, the Gulf of Mexico, and Congress had revealed just how resistant our political and economic system was to truly transformative change. Phil knew the global awareness and energy that 350.org was creating needed to be focused on challenging that system's legitimacy. But where would you even start? "We haven't built the kind of political power that we should," McKibben lamented.[24]

Their network could bring tens of thousands of people into the streets. But behind closed doors, the Exxons of the world could simply block whatever they demanded. So it wasn't enough for them to protest the status quo. They had to threaten it. "We needed to rethink ourselves," Phil said. Nearly a year went by without a feasible option. But in the summer of 2011 NASA climatologist Hansen seemed to provide one. That June he wrote an incendiary critique of TransCanada's Keystone XL project. Opposition to the tar sands pipeline was growing in Canada and across the U.S. Midwest—thanks in part to the people I met at the Rosebud Casino in South Dakota. Few people outside the region were paying much attention, but James Hansen was determined to change that. "If this project gains approval," he warned on his website, "it will become exceedingly difficult to control the tar sands monster." Keystone XL would lock us into decades of reliance on the planet's most polluting oil. It would, he argued, be "game over" for the climate.[25]

This was a very unusual statement to make, especially for a high-profile public figure like Hansen. "Even the most radical climate activists weren't saying stuff like that at the time," Phil said. From a national perspective, Hansen's "game over" argument made little sense. The Keystone XL pipeline would carry 800,000 barrels of tar sands a day to refineries in Texas. There would be a lot of climate-warming carbon in those barrels, equivalent to every car and truck on the road in Canada. But the tar sands industry would expand with or without Keystone, and new pipelines were being built all the time. What made this particular one "game over" for the climate? The University of Alberta economics professor Andrew Leach spoke for a lot of skeptics when he scoffed that Hansen's argument was "laughably out of context." It was the type of thing "most likely to be ignored as alarmist."[26]

But Hansen wasn't looking at Keystone XL from a national perspective. He was looking from a global one. If we burned all the planet's oil, coal, and gas reserves, it would take us well over the safe carbon concentration of 350 parts per million that he'd identified back in 2007. However, if we succeeded in leaving much of that coal in the ground, as well as high-polluting oil sources like the tar sands, "it is conceivable to stabilize [the] climate."[27] What Hansen suggested in his paper was that Keystone XL represented a political and economic system that intended to take us over a dangerous threshold. It wasn't the pipeline itself that would be "game over" for the climate but our status quo. It mirrored the message that 350.org was sending with its days of action: a photo of one person skiing down a glacier, say, wouldn't help fix climate change, but the knowledge that it represented a global movement might.

Hansen's paper caused a debate within 350.org. Should it join the public opposition to Keystone XL? By the narrow definition of people like Leach, Keystone XL was just one more pipeline traversing the United States. The question Phil Aroneanu and the others asked themselves was whether they could convince people to accept Hansen's wider global definition: that the pipeline symbolized a society intent on destroying the planet. Intellectually, it was a lot to ask of people. "I thought it was a bad idea when I first heard about it," Phil said. "We made a big bet basically." But there were advantages to joining the Keystone XL fight. The pipeline was tangible in ways that carbon emissions are not. A single person would decide its fate: President Obama. So if 350.org could pressure Obama to reject it, it would be a financial and moral blow to the fossil fuel industry. It would directly threaten the status quo.

That was a big *if*, of course. America's most influential green groups had spent more than $22 million lobbying to get a climate bill passed through Congress, and still the fossil fuel industry had defeated them. How did seven recent Middlebury grads and their old adviser hope to do any better? What 350.org eventually decided was that it would use a strategy that the green groups had been reluctant to consider: it would try to get its supporters arrested. The radical climate activist Tim DeChristopher had been urging 350.org to do this for years. "He was like 'You guys say you're building a movement, but you're not willing to put your bodies on the line,'" Phil said. "And we'd be like 'Nobody's ready to do that yet.'" But by the summer of 2011 things had

changed. Copenhagen had failed. New climate laws had died. Congress
was hopelessly polarized. The fossil fuel industry was reaping record
profits. Then here came this pipeline. "We were young in age, and we
could take risks," Phil said. "That actually put us in a pretty powerful
position."

In late June 2011, 350.org sent out an invitation to its supporters.
"We want you to consider doing something hard," McKibben, Hansen,
and other prominent activists wrote in an open letter. Later that August,
350.org would be helping lead a two-week demonstration in front of the
White House. The target was Keystone XL, "a 1,500-mile fuse to the
biggest carbon bomb on the continent"—the Canadian tar sands. They
urged people "to come to Washington in the hottest and stickiest weeks
of the summer" to protest the pipeline. But, they warned, it could "get
you arrested." This wasn't just about a piece of steel. Anyone who
attended would be standing up for a fairer and less destructive future.
"It's time to stop letting corporate power make the most important
decisions affecting our planet," the letter read. "We don't have the
money to compete with those corporations, but we do have our
bodies."[28]

By the time the protest began, more than two thousand people had
signed up. What happened on day one set a pattern for the next two
weeks. A group of people sat down in an off-limits area near the White
House, police told them to leave, anyone who didn't was arrested, and a
new group moved in. This wasn't the sort of thing mainstream green
groups were normally comfortable with. For decades they'd written
reports, lobbied politicians, and led letter-writing campaigns. "They'd
never really thrown down publicly in a mass protest kind of way," Phil
said. But midway through the protest the leaders of the Natural
Resources Defense Council, the Environmental Defense Fund, the Sierra
Club, and several others wrote to President Obama to express their soli-
darity. "Many of the organizations we head do not engage in civil
disobedience," they explained. "Regardless . . . we want to let you know
that there is not an inch of daylight between our policy position on the

Keystone Pipeline and those of the very civil protesters being arrested daily outside the White House."[29]

The protest was radicalizing America's green movement, "shifting their strategies," Phil said. It was also pushing Keystone XL onto the national radar. When it first began, few reporters had heard of the pipeline. That's one reason 350.org scheduled the protest in late August, one of the deadest news times of the year. "Congress was on break, so we were the only story in town," said 350.org cofounder and communications director Jamie Henn. "The first few days I did press, and we were ignored by everything but *Democracy Now*." But as the arrests added up—more than 1,250 in total, including actors Mark Ruffalo and Daryl Hannah—so did media coverage. The *New York Times*, *Washington Post*, *USA Today*, CNN, and *Politico* reported on the protest. "We saw how it began to break through," Henn later recalled. "People hadn't seen something like this done before on climate."[30]

Republicans were also beginning to notice. Later that fall, 350.org worked with the Sierra Club to organize a massive follow-up protest. On a chilly November afternoon more than twelve thousand people encircled the White House to protest Keystone XL. The message seemed to resonate. Four days later the U.S. State Department decided to postpone a decision on the pipeline until the 2012 presidential election was over. Republicans were pissed. "That was the point where we were all like 'What's going on?'" a GOP aide later explained to *Politico*. Keystone had gone from "being a quirky Energy and Commerce subcommittee issue to being a full House national issue," said Lee Terry, a Republican House member from Nebraska.[31] It became a staple on Fox News and right-wing radio. In April 2012 Mitt Romney himself took it on. "I will build that pipeline if I have to myself," said the Republican nominee for president.[32]

Keystone XL opponents dared him to try. By the time Allyse joined 350.org as a digital campaigner, their numbers and intensity were surging. "It was clear Keystone XL was animating people," she recalled. In early 2013 Sierra Club leader Michael Brune broke with his group's 120-year ban on civil disobedience in order to get arrested outside the White House. "We need to create political moments that break through the lethargy and the paralysis that is gripping Washington," he said.[33] Days later more than fifty thousand people, many of them in their twenties and early thirties, rallied across the U.S. capital. Even at that point 350.org still considered it "an incredible long shot" that Obama would reject the pipeline, Allyse explained. "But it was an impossible battle that thousands and thousands of our supporters cared deeply about."

Many progressive commentators couldn't understand why. To most media and policy people—and I'll admit that for a time I shared their concerns—Keystone XL was just a pipeline. If it was rejected, others would surely be built. Weren't there better things to get people riled up over? More potentially effective things, like an economy-wide tax on America's carbon emissions? "Greens are wrong to make their political stand on the Keystone pipeline," *Time*'s Bryan Walsh argued.[34] The *New York Times*'s Andrew Revkin deemed it "an unnecessary issue" that let conservatives misrepresent progressives as "anti-jobs." Michael Levi from the Council on Foreign Relations argued that fighting Keystone XL was polarizing U.S. politics to the point where Congress would never pass new climate policies.[35]

To 350.org they were all missing the point. Critics like Walsh and Revkin and Levi were focused on the national implications of a piece of steel, but the people fighting Keystone XL saw it in global terms. To them, the pipeline represented a political and economic system that had no regard for the planet. "It was symbolic of a larger story," Allyse said. The only way they were going to defeat Keystone XL was to convince Obama this larger story was legitimate. So far they hadn't been successful. In March 2012 the president had invoked national security to approve the bottom half of Keystone XL—from Oklahoma to Texas. "We need as much [oil] as possible," Obama said.[36] But a year later, after winning reelection, he signaled that he was coming around to 350.org's view. "The pipeline's impact on our climate will be absolutely critical" to deciding if it gets built, he said.

"That was a turning point," Henn argued. "That said to us, okay, we're on our turf here. It isn't a debate about jobs, about the American economy, about energy independence—it's about climate change."[37]

Keystone XL's youngest opponents were convinced they could win the debate. In March 2014 more than twelve hundred college students and recent grads gathered in Washington, D.C., for a protest march named XL Dissent. The *Nation* later remarked on the "sheer size, intensity, and noise" of their march from Georgetown University to the White House, where nearly four hundred of them were arrested. "The inaction on the part of Obama and the system in general is what's making [this] necessary," explained Tufts University junior Evan Bell.[38] Phil helped train some of the leaders but wasn't directly involved. "Young people really took it to the next level," he said. "They felt very strongly like their lives were going to be on the line because of Keystone."

Since 350.org joined the fight in 2011, more than seven hundred anti-pipeline protests had taken place across the United States. By 2015 it was clear they were having an impact. Obama was sharing his skepticism about Keystone XL openly. At one point he referred to tar sands oil as "extraordinarily dirty." But nothing could have prepared Phil and Allyse and everyone else at 350.org for what happened on November 7. Standing at a podium inside the White House, Obama announced he was officially rejecting the pipeline. Approving it, he said, would undermine America's "global leadership" on climate change.[39]

"I cried so many times that day," Allyse Heartwell recalled. "To actually see that win happen felt extraordinary and hopeful." "It was huge," Phil said. "It basically said that even though the game is rigged, even though the fossil fuel companies can outspend us, we can still beat them." Obama no longer viewed Keystone XL as just a piece of steel. He saw it the way that seven recent college grads and their adviser wanted him to back in 2011: as an opportunity to reject the legitimacy of fossil fuels.

THIS WAS A WORST-CASE scenario for the fossil fuel industry. It was bad enough to lose a potentially lucrative export route from Canada's tar sands to the Texas Gulf Coast. But by rejecting Keystone XL, Obama had revealed a vulnerability that the industry had tried to conceal for years. I was first clued into it when I visited Washington, D.C., one chilly

February to meet and interview the oil lobbyists trying to persuade the Obama administration to approve Keystone XL. What I learned was that it's in the fossil fuel industry's best interest to debate the future in the narrowest possible national terms. To the lobbyists I interviewed, Keystone XL was merely a steel pipe—one that would create thousands of jobs, reduce America's reliance on foreign oil, and have little impact on U.S. carbon emissions. The last thing those lobbyists wanted was to debate Keystone XL on the global terms set out by 350.org. As TransCanada's CEO Russ Girling would later acknowledge, "We were ill prepared for what ensued."[40]

When I arrived in Washington that February, Canada was exporting more than 1.2 million barrels of oil per day to the United States and had plans to nearly triple that amount by 2020. Canada was by far America's largest supplier of foreign oil. But up in the tar sands province of Alberta where that oil was produced, people were unsure how long this lucrative relationship would last. During the run-up to the 2008 election, Obama's top energy adviser, Jason Grumet, had declared that carbon emissions from the tar sands were "unacceptably high." "If the only way to produce those resources would be at a significant penalty to climate change," he explained, "then we don't believe those resources are . . . going to play a growing role in the long term future."[41]

For the eight years that George W. Bush was president, tar sands oil from Canada had been an easy sell. It powered the U.S. economy. It cut reliance on the Middle East. It created jobs. By the narrow terms of national interest there was little to debate. But now Barack Obama was threatening to widen those terms. By evaluating the climate impact of the tar sands, he was proposing to make them global. That was not a debate that producers of the world's most polluting oil wanted to have. "As long as George Bush was the president, [the tar sands] had a certain umbrella, had a certain protection," one Canadian politician fretted in 2009. "It was clear [then that] the United States was not going to impose any legislative or regulatory changes that would harm our operations and our export of oil from Athabasca tar sands. But that has changed."[42]

If the tar sands industry wanted to keep selling millions of barrels of oil to the United States, it had to persuade American decision makers to think nationally instead of globally—just as they had under George W. Bush. In Washington, D.C., I arranged to meet Paul Frazer, one of the high-powered lobbyists hired by Alberta's provincial government to do the job. I thumbed through a copy of the *New Yorker* as I waited in the spartan front lobby of his downtown office. Then Frazer burst into the room with a firm handshake and a smile. "Hello! How are you?" he exclaimed. His hair was parted down the middle, and he was wearing black and white polka-dot suspenders, a yellow tie, and impossibly shiny shoes. It was the outfit of a professional charmer.

His job was to convince senators, energy officials, and other key policy makers in the U.S. capital that the climate change impact of tar sands production was none of their concern. During our half-hour chat, he provided several versions of the pitch he used. Carbon emissions in Canada were a challenge, he admitted, but companies like Exxon were doing their best to lower them. "Canada can chew gum and walk at the same time," he said. Having brushed off those concerns, Frazer quickly pivoted to the jobs, prosperity, and security the U.S. gains from having a big source of oil next door. Frazer was so confident in his approach that when fifty Democratic members of Congress wrote a letter in 2010 warning about the "climate change implications" of the Keystone XL pipeline, Frazer told his employer back in Alberta to relax. "I said, 'Take a breath, this isn't going anywhere,'" he said. "'It's not like the sky is falling.'"[43]

In retrospect, the sky was beginning to fall—at least for Keystone XL. After Frazer and I said our goodbyes, and as I stood waiting for the elevator to take me down to street level, it dawned on me that money and charm can hide the truth for only so long. For a year after the Democrats' 2010 letter, lobbyists like Frazer continued their PR offensive as if nothing happened. "The message in Washington has been that there are no problems with the oil sands industry at all," an environmentalist explained to me.[44] By the summer of 2011 that message was becoming much harder to defend. First came Hansen's prediction that Keystone XL would be "game over" for the climate, and then 350.org's two-week protest outside the White House.

Few people felt the impact more than the CEO of TransCanada.

When Russ Girling took his job in 2010, he assumed that most Americans were concerned only about their national interest—that they would easily overlook the tar sands industry's soaring emissions to gain the four thousand construction jobs and millions of barrels of oil that the Keystone XL pipeline would provide. "My job, as I expected when I came in, would be pretty much ninety-nine percent focused on running the business," Girling said. He was wildly mistaken. Within a few years he found himself trapped in a global debate about the carbon impact of tar sands. "Girling figures he spends half his time trying to assure skeptics that pipelines proposed to carry oil-sands crude, known also as bitumen, won't destroy the planet," read a *Bloomberg* profile of the CEO.[45]

Among the skeptics Girling had to assure was his own mother. One of her favorite actors was Robert Redford, who put out a video describing tar sands as "the dirtiest oil on the planet." She asked her son whether that was true. No, Mom, Girling attempted to explain, I'm not going to "blow up the planet." Another personal affront came in 2014, when Neil Young—whose music Girling described as "really, really good"—toured Canada criticizing the tar sands and Keystone XL. One colleague later explained that "I'm not sure I've ever seen Russ lose his cool." But the TransCanada CEO, who earned over $8 million in 2012, admitted that the tar sands opposition was getting to him. "These things grind on you 24/7," he said.[46]

As opposition to Keystone XL became louder and more sustained, Washington's fossil fuel lobbyists found it harder to dismiss their industry's impact on climate change. So they added another argument to their repertoire. The bluntest and most forceful version of it I heard came from Jane Moffat, executive director of the Canadian-American Business Council, a cross-border trade group with strong ties to Washington's diplomatic community. Its members include ExxonMobil, ConocoPhillips, and Shell. Moffat and I met in an office overlooking K Street, which is to lobbying what Wall Street is to finance.

Like Frazer, Jane Moffat radiated charm and energy. "So great to meet you!" she said upon my arrival. But she lacked some of his smooth-talking veneer. When I asked her about the green groups raising concerns about Keystone XL, her reply was swift and dismissive: "They just scream on the paper about a bunch of stuff that isn't even true. I don't think anybody takes them seriously." I countered that people seemed to be taking their concerns more seriously all the time. She quickly pivoted. "We're not getting off fossil fuels in the next thirty to fifty years, are we?" she asked. "We're not shutting down the pipes tomorrow." To her, the idea of shifting off oil was "naïve." And once policy makers had accepted her version of the status quo, she was certain they'd see Keystone XL as little more than a steel pipe. "The pipeline's only really about this big," she said, making a circle shape with her arms. "It's not that big."[47]

As I left Moffat's office, the gesture stayed in my mind. She wanted to shrink the terms of the Keystone XL debate to the space between her arms. But for the tens of thousands of people whom groups like 350.org had rallied against the pipeline, those terms were as large as the Planet Earth. They weren't protesting a piece of steel. "The question now is whether we continue down the path toward cataclysm or make a bold break towards a brighter future," wrote Conor Kennedy, the eighteen-year-old son of Robert F. Kennedy Jr., before being arrested outside the White House in 2014.[48] By then the fight against Keystone XL had become a referendum on the legitimacy of a status quo that threatens the planet—along with the survival of an entire generation.

The fossil fuel industry knew it represented that status quo. But its lobbyists had prepared a seemingly convincing response to people like Conor—they denied that they were the ones perpetuating it. The clearest articulation of this argument was made to me by Cindy Schild, a spokesperson for the most powerful fossil fuel lobby group in the United States, the American Petroleum Institute. I met her inside the institute's hulking Washington headquarters, which I reached by pressing an elevator button marked "API." In 2010 its members had spent $146 million lobbying Congress. They played a key role in killing the climate laws that would have pushed America away from oil and gas. But to Schild, the true blame for climate change rests with regular people—not the corporations she represented. "We certainly don't have consumers who are willing to conserve," Schild said. "That doesn't seem to happen."[49] She saw this as the main flaw in our system. Every day people across the world demanded oil and gas. And until they cut back, projects like Keystone XL would provide it.

When Obama officially rejected the pipeline in 2015, he in effect called bullshit on Schild's argument, along with the others I had heard from Washington lobbyists. In the wake of his decision, the CEO of TransCanada declared that "rhetoric won out over reason."[50] What actually won out was a new generation's worldview. It was the idea that our identities don't map neatly onto the countries where we were born. That in an era when our political and economic system literally threatens human survival, we need to think beyond national borders. Phil Aroneanu and Allyse Heartwell and 350.org didn't invent this global identity. But they provided a powerful outlet for the anxiety it created, then aimed it against a visible symbol of our status quo. Their ability to defeat Keystone XL revealed that the corporate power underpinning it was more fragile than previously thought.

It was the last victory that Phil would celebrate at 350.org. In early 2016 he announced on his blog he was leaving the group. "We've built an incredibly powerful global climate movement that is unstoppable, and for that I (and future generations) will be forever grateful," he wrote.[51] But it'd been nearly a decade since he cofounded the group. He was in his early thirties. He wanted to explore new things. One area that excited him was electoral politics. The youth-led social movement that 350.org had helped build was now wielding real power. To be truly effective, though, it had to do more than just get pipelines rejected—a fact made painfully clear when Donald Trump revived Keystone XL in early 2017. "We need to learn how to unelect people and elect people," Phil told me. "I'm hoping to spend time figuring out how to do that." In fact, a movement of young people in Canada had already taken that step. And as I'll explain in Chapter 4, what they achieved was globally significant.

4

—

Beyond Left and Right

THE YOUTH-LED POLITICAL REVOLT that toppled a petrostate leader in Canada was born in the minds of people like Andrew Frank. Andrew has always considered himself to be politically progressive. He believes we have to make profound changes to the way we live and structure our society in order to ensure a future that isn't totally screwed. But a major life decision he made several years ago affirmed his suspicion that such changes can be achieved only outside established institutions. He was working for an activist group that was trying to stop the expansion of the tar sands. He believes there is no place in a safe and stable world for the extreme oil that is produced there. Canada's prime minister responded by allegedly calling him and the group he worked for an "enemy of the state." When Andrew's superiors refused to fight back, he risked his career and reputation to do so himself. He learned that to change a system, you sometimes need to detach from it.

This particular prime minister, Stephen Harper, was a bland and emotionless technocrat. His dad had worked for the oil and gas industry. And during the nine years that Harper led the country, it seemed like he was serving the same employer. Harper hollowed out environmental laws that limited the industry's growth; pulled Canada out of the Kyoto Protocol; forbade government scientists from speaking publicly about global warming; defunded years of scientific research; attacked civil society; and obsessively tried to transform Canada into an "energy superpower." A *New York Times* op-ed described his reign as a "subtle darkening of Canadian life."[1] Harper didn't care that he was deeply unpopular with young people. He knew they tended not to vote and that his older, white, and male supporters reliably did.

Harper's number-one political goal was to a build a pipeline from the tar sands to Canada's west coast. By doing this, he would solve a vexing problem for the industry. Nearly all the oil produced in the tar sands went to only one country: the United States. But as we saw in Chapter 3, that lucrative relationship was becoming more vulnerable. Efforts to build the Keystone XL pipeline were stalled. If the tar sands industry was going to keep expanding, it needed to reach new markets. That's where a 731-mile pipeline known as Northern Gateway came in. By providing access to the west coast, tar sands companies could sell their oil directly to China. The company proposing this project, a Calgary-based pipeline builder called Enbridge, estimated it would add $300 billion over thirty years to Canada's GDP. Harper was thrilled. He deemed the pipeline a "national priority."[2]

Andrew saw it as anything but. He'd grown up in the west coast province of British Columbia, near Washington State, in the small town of Oliver. He spent lots of time outdoors in the region's arid mountains. He was the type who'd "find a rattlesnake on the road and put it on an anthill so the ants would eat everything up and then put the skeleton together and have it on my wall."[3] He became aware of climate change at a young age. He always had the sense that he wanted to contribute to "quote unquote 'saving the world.'" After going to university out east in Toronto, Andrew came back to Vancouver and earned a master's degree studying how to communicate climate change. "I immersed myself in the most up-to-date research on climate science," he said. It was pretty dire stuff. He struggled against feeling like "Oh we're just fucked anyhow, so why should I care?" Yet Andrew was convinced that regular people like him could make a difference.

To prove it, he got a job at an activist group called ForestEthics. Though based in San Francisco, it had offices in Vancouver. And around the time Andrew was hired as senior communications manager, the group had joined a coalition of civil society groups fighting against Northern Gateway. Stopping the pipeline was its number-one goal.

Andrew saw it as a direct threat to the well-being of his generation: a project that would lock us into decades of reliance on the tar sands, add enough carbon to the atmosphere each year to equal five cities the size of Los Angeles, and require 220 oil tankers each day to sail up and down a treacherous coastline that'd recorded waves ninety feet high. A spill in its pristine waters would be absolutely devastating to the ecosystem. Andrew believed that the true "national priority" should be to get Gateway rejected.

It was a daunting goal. The $57 billion Enbridge company, on which ForestEthics and its allies had declared war, was one of the largest pipeline builders in the world. All the tar sands corporations—including Exxon, Chevron, Shell, ConocoPhillips, BP, and Total—wanted to ship their oil to the West Coast. China was eager to cut its reliance on Middle East crude through Gateway, by obtaining a major new oil supply. And Harper's administration stood to gain billions of dollars of tax revenue. This was serious geopolitics. Andrew and his employer and their allies were standing up to "the full weight of Canada as a petro-state," as civil society insider Bruce Hill said at the time. "[Canada's] environmental movement has never had a fight like this before."[4]

But in order to be approved, the Gateway pipeline first had to go through extensive public hearings. And during the months leading up to those hearings, groups like ForestEthics seemed to be winning over public opinion. A survey conducted by the research group Mustel in 2010 suggested that 80 percent of people living in British Columbia opposed a pipeline project that threatened the coastline with an *Exxon Valdez*-type oil spill disaster.[5] Polling commissioned the next year by several activist groups reached a similar conclusion. "The simple fact is that despite all precaution, a major oil spill could happen on our coast," observed one environmental leader. "Do we accept the risk of catastrophe or not?"[6]

By that point, nearly 130 indigenous groups across the country had joined the pipeline opposition. "We will be the wall that Enbridge cannot break through," explained Saik'uz First Nation chief Jackie Thomas at a press conference covered by all the national media.[7] Despite being greatly outfunded by the tar sands industry, and despite lacking its access to political power, the wall built by this civil society opposition was made out of sturdy stuff. As years of delays and setbacks for the project added up, companies like the Exxon subsidiary Imperial Oil started to get worried. Gateway is a "critical factor for the projected growth" of the tar sands industry, said a company spokesperson. The Chinese were also losing patience. "They're frustrated, as we are, in the length of time it takes," said Enbridge CEO Pat Daniel. "If you don't move it along, people do lose interest. We don't have forever."[8]

Harper was listening. He knew that Canada would never become an oil and gas "superpower" unless Gateway was built. He wasn't about to let a bunch of hippie activists and indigenous groups stand in the way. And so in early 2012 he decided to attack ForestEthics where it was weakest. Harper's intention was to shut it down completely. But he hadn't counted on how someone like Andrew would react to such an attack, that he would risk his career and reputation to declare his independence from the political system, that at the same time millions of others from his generation were developing the same radical worldview, or that several years later it would cause a political revolt so contrary to popular wisdom about Millennials that the *Harvard International Review* would deem it "exciting . . . in a global context."[9] The result of it all would be to prove that when politically independent young people come together to fight for their future, their impact can be profound and immediate. It's a lesson that politicians like Harper and Donald Trump now ignore at their peril.

To TRULY APPRECIATE WHY all this was such a big deal, you first have to wrap your mind around a frustrating reality of our political era. Though years of research suggest that Millennials support profound changes to our society, we're the least likely generation to participate in the activity able to deliver them: elections. That's especially true for global warming. As we have seen in previous chapters, people my age are more likely to desire strong action on climate change than members of older generations. We're rejecting an economic system that cares only about short-term profits. Our view of the world—and how to address the existential threats facing it—transcends national borders. "The passion and energy of young people . . . is a potentially potent electoral force," explained David Roberts on *Vox*. "The problem is, too few of them vote."[10]

This problem has been building for several decades. "Between 1964 and 2012, youth voter turnout in presidential elections has fallen below 50 percent," Derek Thompson wrote in the *Atlantic*.[11] At first it seemed like Millennials would reverse the trend. In the years leading up to Barack Obama's win in 2008, youth turnout rose as more and more members of this generation became old enough to vote. But that year's 52 percent turnout among 18-to-29-year-old voters turned out to be an aberration. In 2012 Millennial turnout dropped to 45 percent.[12] And during the 2014 midterm elections, just 19.9 percent of them voted. Though turnout during midterms tends to be lower than during presidential elections, "this was the lowest rate of youth turnout recorded . . . in the past forty years," a U.S. Census analysis calculated.[13]

A similar dynamic has been observed in the UK. "According to the British Election Study, the proportion of registered 18-to-24-year-olds turning out to cast their ballot has consistently been below every other age group since the 1970s," the *Guardian* noted in 2015.[14] In the early 1990s, election turnout among young people briefly rose to 60 percent. But turnout then plummeted to an average of only 40 percent during general elections in 2001, 2005, and 2010. Early exit polls in the 2015 election that returned David Cameron to power suggested that youth voter turnout had risen to 58 percent. But "more reliable" estimates made by the research firm Ipsos months later found that youth turnout was "relatively unchanged" at 43 percent. This has "concerning implications for the future of democratic engagement," it concluded.[15]

This decline has also been observed in Canada. Less than 40 percent of young people voted in the 2011 federal election. Overall they were nearly two times less likely to cast a ballot in national elections than the broader population. Several years ago a government agency known as Elections Canada conducted a study to understand why. Many Millennials said they were too busy to vote, they didn't know how to register, or they couldn't find the polls, "but scratching below the surface, the study found that in most cases, the real issue is motivation." Young people "were generally less interested in politics, less likely to view voting as a civic duty, and more likely to feel that all political parties were the same and that no party spoke to issues relevant to youth."[16] It was a puzzle that just couldn't be solved.

And it was particularly vexing to progressive parties. Polling from the Pew Research Center has consistently found that Millennials are more likely to support progressive positions than older generations. In 2014 Pew estimated 50 percent of young people lean Democratic, compared to 35 percent Republican. The numbers for Boomers, meanwhile, were 46 percent Democratic and 42 percent Republican. A year later those figures were for the most part unchanged. "Millennials continue to be the most Democratic age cohort," Pew concluded. Young people weren't only leaning more progressive than their elders—they also seemed to be leaning harder. Among Democratic voters of all age groups, Pew found, Millennials were "more likely than older generations" to identify themselves as "liberals" rather than "moderates."[17]

This also appeared to be the case in the UK. British polling in 2015 found "young people are much more likely to back [left-leaning] Labour and the Greens than other age groups," the Guardian reported. "Offending young voters is much less of a risk for more conservative parties."[18] The same seems to go for Canada. A major survey of Millennials conducted by the Broadbent Institute suggested that about 56 percent of young people think the environment should be prioritized over jobs, compared to 46 percent of those over thirty-five. Millennials also favored greater government spending on education and health care. "More young voters support elements of a progressive political agenda than older voters," a report concluded.[19]

Yet supporting progressive policies is not the same as supporting the institutions that could actually implement them. A widely discussed 2015 survey from Harvard University's Institute of Politics found that among American Millennials, trust in those institutions was at a historic low. Only 36 percent of 18-to-29-year-old respondents trusted the White House to improve society, and less than 20 percent felt the same about

Congress.[20] This lack of faith in government wasn't confined to the United States. In 2014 Deloitte asked 7,800 Millennials in twenty-six countries to identify the big challenges facing society—climate change was in the top three—and how they could be fixed. Many respondents believed "government has the greatest potential to address society's biggest issues," the survey concluded, "but [is] overwhelmingly failing to do so."[21]

In the United States, that's not just conjecture—it's a fact. And a huge reason is record-high levels of political polarization. Not since the Civil War has Congress been so ideologically divided. A study from the Brookings Institution found that from 2011 to 2012 the most conservative Democratic member was still more progressive than the most moderate Republican. There was no cooperation on anything. Democrats and Republicans voted nearly entirely along party lines. Media like the *Atlantic* were not alone in arguing that "Congress is hopelessly gridlocked."[22] Progress on most issues became impossible. "This is particularly apparent in the steady reduction of the number of bills introduced onto the floor," explained one academic study, "suggesting that the primary negative effect of increasing partisanship is a loss of Congressional innovation."[23]

Over this same period, corporate spending on elections soared. In large part, that increase can be traced to a 2010 Supreme Court ruling known as *Citizens United*, which removed legal limits on campaign finance. In four years, outside spending on Senate elections more than doubled to $486 million. And since the ruling, spending by super PACs—outsider groups that attempt to influence elections—has surpassed $1 billion. Many of those groups are legally protected from having to reveal their donors' identities. Yet the Brennan Center for Justice found that over $600 million in super PAC spending came from just 195 rich individuals. "Does anyone believe . . . [this] does not give them disproportionate influence on the politicians they have supported?" Georgetown University law professor David Cole wrote. "This is a game played by, and for, the wealthy."[24]

On no issue is the impact of both these trends—polarization and spending—more visible than climate change. Senator John McCain

(R-AZ) was once a proponent of climate action, but by 2014 he was arguing, "I just leave the issue alone because I don't see a way through it."[25] While President Obama argued that "no challenge poses a greater threat to future generations," Senator Jim Inhofe (R-OK) called climate change "the greatest hoax ever perpetrated against the American people."[26] To David Roberts of *Vox*, this was evidence that "the issue is thoroughly, 100 percent polarized."[27] And during the same period, political spending from the fossil fuel industry reached staggering heights—nearly $700 million in the two years leading up the 2014 midterm elections, according to a Center for American Progress analysis.[28] These two trends in fact appear to be related. A 2015 study in the *Proceedings of the National Academy of Sciences* found that the political influence of companies such as Exxon and Koch Industries has helped to "polarize the climate change issue."[29]

All this has caused young people not only to distrust our political system but to reject it. A 2014 Pew survey suggested that half of people my age refuse to identify with any political party. They see themselves as "political independents." There is a prevailing sense that the choice between the Republican and Democratic parties is a false one. Only 31 percent of Millennials see any major difference between the parties, compared to 49 percent of Boomers. These are the "highest levels of political disaffiliation" that Pew has "recorded for any generation in [a] quarter-century."[30] To the coalition of young climate and racial justice activists who marched through Washington, D.C., in 2015, the explanation was obvious. "Today, we face a true crisis of democracy," they wrote. "While politicians and the media continue to talk about left versus right . . . [we are] talking about a different direction: forward."[31]

THE FIRST TIME I experienced our broken political system firsthand was in the winter of 2011, when I accidently ran into Gary Doer inside the Canadian embassy in Washington, D.C. I was in the U.S. capital to interview the oil industry lobbyists we met in Chapter 3. Doer was Canada's ambassador to the United States. His diplomatic position was among the most influential in the world. I'd sent more than a dozen interview requests to the embassy. I badly wanted to ask Doer about something I could just not wrap my mind around. Before he became ambassador in October 2009, he was among the most progressive politicians in Canada. He had stood up against the powers that be. He won accolades for fighting climate change. But something changed when he got to Washington. He became friends with all the oil companies. He began blocking the progress he'd previously fought for. What was going on?

Doer first made his name as premier of Manitoba, an often overlooked central Canadian province best known for being the place where Neil Young grew up. But under Doer's leadership, it won global recognition for its efforts to make our society less environmentally destructive. Doer was a huge supporter of the 1997 Kyoto Protocol. As the United States rejected the climate change treaty, Doer promised that Manitoba would meet its obligations two years early. He vowed to go four times beyond the Kyoto targets: "In doing so, we can help to set the stage for a new, exciting and more sustainable economy in Canada." International media soon took notice. *Business Week* picked Doer as one of the top twenty people on the planet fighting climate change. "Under Doer," it observed, "sustainable development has become an economic lynchpin."[32]

Doer had always been politically ambitious, but nobody could have predicted he would suddenly resign as premier after ten years to become Canada's ambassador to the United States. Or that instead of continuing the fight for the new economic system that he began in Manitoba, one that valued survival of the planet just as much as short-term profits, he would do the exact opposite. That he would host lobbying events with Exxon and Chevron. That he would become a tireless champion of tar sands pipelines like the Keystone XL. That he would fight climate laws that could hurt the industry's profits and describe the environmental impact of tar sands as "very small." That he would go from being an attacker of our status quo to one of its most powerful defenders. "My view is the oil is coming," he said. "It's just a question of how it gets there."[33]

None of it made any sense to me. What happened to the progressive leader who'd once declared that "we simply cannot afford to wait to take action on the very serious issue of climate change"? The one who'd promised to "leave a legacy of clean air and clean energy for our future generations"? The Canadian embassy refused to grant me an opportunity to ask. It rejected weeks and weeks of interview requests. And so on my last day in Washington, I decided to visit the embassy anyway. I had no game plan. I didn't know what to expect. I simply showed up at the hulking Arthur Erickson–designed building on Pennsylvania Avenue and puttered around the lobby. I was about to leave when I heard voices behind me. *Wouldn't it be something if one of them belonged to Doer?* I thought. I turned around, and to my astonishment, there he was.

I could think of only two plausible reasons Gary Doer had abandoned the progressive ideals he'd fought for as premier—and neither reflected very well on our political system. The first was that his ideals were simply trumped by ambition. Doer was good-looking and charming. He knew how to get people's attention. During his earliest days in politics, he drove sports cars and wore tailored suits. He must have sensed his potential to rise higher in politics than leader of an overlooked Canadian province. During a press conference to announce his resignation as premier in 2009, his excitement was noticeable to several reporters. "What am I going to do next?" he said, "Well, I'm not going to be watching soaps." The next day Prime Minister Harper announced Doer as Canada's ambassador to the United States.[34]

This was by far the most important diplomatic posting in Canada—it's among the more influential in the entire world. Doer would now have direct and regular access to the White House. His job was to represent America's largest trading partner and its biggest supplier of foreign oil. Influential U.S. environmental groups such as the Natural Resources Defense Council (NRDC) were familiar with Doer's progressive positions on the climate. They knew he'd tried to build a new type of economy far less destructive than our current one. They also knew that as U.S. ambassador, Doer would have to do the opposite. "It was very interesting to many of us to observe him accepting this [ambassador] position knowing that a big part of his portfolio would have to be promoting tar sands," the NRDC's Susan Casey-Lefkowitz explained.

But they figured that if anyone could navigate the contradiction of pushing for a new economic model while also promoting an old one, it would be him. "I thought Gary Doer would become the person that basically acknowledged we have a problem with Alberta's oil sands, but that we were doing everything possible to address that problem," said Danielle Droitsch, a senior policy analyst at the NRDC.[35] She was badly mistaken. The new ambassador used his access to the Obama administration—"visitor logs show Doer has been a frequent visitor to the White House," read a *Bloomberg* story[36]—to fight any new restrictions on the tar sands. When the EPA raised concerns about the industry's soaring carbon emissions, Doer accused it of "distortion and omission."[37]

In Canada, Doer had won the praise of environmentalists. In the United States, he now won it from oil companies. Doer worked so hard to promote the Keystone XL pipeline that the company trying to build it, TransCanada, sent him a thank-you note. "Gary," reads an e-mail from the company that I later obtained through a Freedom of Information request. "I just wanted to send a quick note to thank you and your team for all of the hard work and perseverance in helping get us this far, I know it has made a big difference." It added: "Hopefully, we can connect when I am in DC in mid September." Doer responded several days later. "Thanks," he wrote. "Look forward to seeing you soon."[38] Doer was a big deal in Washington. His phone calls always got answered. Had he simply decided to trade his ideals for power?

Perhaps. But I had a second explanation for why Gary Doer so readily abandoned his ideals: maybe he never had any to begin with. "[Doer] has contextual intelligence," the University of Manitoba professor Paul Thomas has argued. "He can read situations in a very insightful way." Historically, Manitoba has been a very progressive province. To gain and hold on to power there, Doer knew it made good political sense to fight for strong environmental policies. "He is an immensely pragmatic politician," said Keith Stewart from Greenpeace. "As premier of Manitoba, being good on climate is good politics."[39] It made less sense as U.S. ambassador. If Doer's ideals were simply a means to power, perhaps he'd dropped them when they were no longer useful.

How else could you explain the startling disparity between his actions as premier and as ambassador? In Manitoba, Doer hadn't only pushed for a new status quo—he'd actively fought the expansion of our current one. During his second term as premier, the province's utility announced a plan to build a power transmission line along the east side of Lake Winnipeg. Doer rejected it in favor of rerouting the line, which though costlier would avoid industrializing the pristine boreal forest. To Doer, the boreal forest was "the greatest undiscovered area anywhere in North America."[40] But later as ambassador, he dismissed criticisms that the tar sands were destroying that same ecosystem. "Come on up," he said. "You'll fly over a lot of Boreal Forest."[41] He didn't mention you'd also see strip mines eleven times larger than the island of Manhattan.

Here was a politician who in 2006 had signed an agreement with then-California governor Arnold Schwarzenegger, committing them "to work co-operatively to the fullest possible extent . . . to advance greenhouse gas emission reductions."[42] Three years later Schwarzenegger brought in a policy that would restrict the sale of tar sands in California, equivalent to taking half a million cars off the road—but the new ambassador told him to back off. "Doer suggested [the policy] didn't make much sense," the news agency Canadian Press reported.[43] None of it made much sense to environmentalists. "Do I think it's odd, given [Doer's] views on climate change, that he is also promoting the use of tar-sands oil in the United States?" said Richard Brooks of Greenpeace. "Certainly, on the surface, it doesn't seem to line up."[44]

Others were more direct. "What became of Gary Doer the green premier?" Environmental Defense policy director Matt Price wrote in an op-ed. "It is sad to lose Gary Doer to the tar sands." After years of fighting to change the status quo, Price lamented, "Doer is enthusiastically selling Americans on the do-nothing approach . . . on climate change." The ambassador didn't seem to care what people like Price thought. "You're green, you're not green. You're this, you're that," Doer later told a magazine in Canada. "I don't live in a world where I think you kayak to England. I do believe we can improve on efficiencies on oil consumption. But I'll still drive to the lake on the weekends. We don't live in a world of absolutes, and I don't either."[45] It made me wonder: Had Doer's professed green ideals ever been real?

That was the question going through my head as I turned around and met Doer's eye in the front lobby of Canada's embassy. Here was my chance to finally ask him. I cleared my throat and walked toward the ambassador. "Excuse me, Gary Doer?" I said. "I was wondering if I could ask you a question." Doer didn't look all that pleased and started to back toward the security checkpoint. He raised a hand defensively around hip level, and his eyes shifted from side to side. "Actually, I'm hosting something right now," he said. "But if you can give me your number I can call—or better yet, contact my press secretary." I didn't have time to answer that his press secretary had already received and rejected requests for an interview I'd been sending his office for several weeks. Before I could say anything, the ambassador was gone.

At this point, security was glaring at me. I figured I should leave. Outside, the skies opened up, and it began pouring rain. On Pennsylvania Avenue men in expensive suits held briefcases over their heads and ran for cover. I found shelter under an alcove. As I waited for the storm to pass, I tried to process the complicated emotions I was feeling. I'd been meeting with oil lobbyists all week long. But my chance run-in with Doer felt different somehow—it felt personal. I kept repeating the scene in my head—Doer's hand raised in defense, his shifting eyes—until finally I understood why. The moment he'd retreated behind the security gate was the moment when I realized our political system was broken. Left or right, it didn't seem to make a difference. So long as people like Doer ran our system, the choice was false.

ANDREW FRANK WENT TO work for ForestEthics during one of the most harrowing periods for civil society in Canadian history. It began in 2011, when the conservative political leader Stephen Harper, whose base was in the tar sands province of Alberta, won a majority of seats in Canada's parliament and was reelected prime minister. Harper had unbridled power to do whatever he wanted—much like when Donald Trump took power with a Republican Congress. "For decades, the world has thought of Canada as America's friendly northern neighbor—a responsible, earnest, if somewhat boring, land of hockey fans and single-payer healthcare," the journalist Andrew Nikiforuk wrote in *Foreign Policy*. But under Harper, "a dark secret [now] lurks in the northern forests. Over the last decade, Canada has not so quietly become a . . . rogue petrostate. It's no longer America's better half, but a dystopian vision of the continent's energy-soaked future."[46]

To fully realize that vision, though, Harper first had to push through the Northern Gateway pipeline that would let tar sands companies like Exxon sell their oil to China. And with public opposition to the project rising, he decided that civil society groups such as ForestEthics had to be neutralized. He would use the tax code as a weapon. Many activist groups are considered "charities" for tax purposes. This lets them receive funding from philanthropic organizations outside the country. The tax code prohibits charities from participating in explicitly political activities. In the past, this had never been much of an issue, but Harper realized that a strict reading of the tax code could be used to remove the charitable status of the groups fighting a pipeline he'd deemed a "national priority." It could be used to cut off their funding.

Andrew Frank's employer was particularly exposed. The entire budget for ForestEthics was funded by a San Francisco–based charity, Tides. With an annual income of almost $100 million, Tides gives out hundreds of grants supporting immigration reform, climate change activism, and many other progressive causes. ForestEthics literally couldn't exist without its charitable status. In early 2012 that vulnerability became painfully clear. Canada's natural resources minister Joe Oliver released an open letter accusing groups such as ForestEthics of using "funding from foreign special interest groups to undermine Canada's national economic interest."[47] And while on a state visit to China not long afterward, Harper vowed to "put the interests of Canadians ahead of foreign money and influence."[48] To Andrew's employer, the implication was clear: Harper's petrostate was coming after them.

Around that time Andrew and other staffers from the group's Vancouver office were called into a meeting. A senior supervisor informed them about a conversation that had recently taken place between the prime minister's office and Tides. In that conversation, Tides Canada's leader, Ross McMillan, was informed that the Harper government considered ForestEthics to be an "enemy of the state." And if McMillan didn't cut off funding and support to ForestEthics, Andrew recalled, the government threatened to "take down" the other charitable work—including activism on AIDS, homelessness, sustainable food and domestic violence—that Tides was doing in Canada. No one at the meeting believed what they were hearing. "We were just shocked," Andrew said.

One woman in the meeting, an administrative coordinator, started to cry. "She was really freaked out," Andrew said. "She had a husband who wasn't a full citizen in Canada so she was worried about the implications." Everybody was instructed to stay quiet while leaders at ForestEthics and Tides figured out what to do next. Andrew had trouble sleeping in the days that followed. He lost his appetite. There was talk about using encrypted e-mail—and even about being careful on the phone. People "began looking over their shoulder, out of fear and paranoia, because their own government might be watching them," Andrew claimed.[49]

Initially Andrew's colleagues at ForestEthics made plans to strike back. "People were talking and planning about what we should do," he said. But two weeks passed with barely a word from his superiors. Finally Andrew was informed "that we would not be going public with the story," he said. If ForestEthics had its charitable status revoked, it would lose all its funding. And Tides Canada was worried about its own existence. It too depended on charitable status to fund dozens of progressive projects.

Andrew sympathized with those fears. But did they outweigh the blatant evidence that our political system was broken? "You had the government trying to pressure and defang one of the environmental watchdogs," he said. "If it wasn't illegal, at the very least it was strongly immoral." Andrew soon came to what he described as a "huge and uncomfortable realization." The only way the story could get out was if he made it public himself: by leaking it to Canada's news media, making

the alleged threat into a matter of public record and forcing Harper
onto the defensive.

Yet in making sensitive information public, Andrew would be
disobeying a direct order from the Tides and ForestEthics leadership.
He knew that once the story appeared he was going to be fired. He
knew it'd be tough to get another job. He knew his employer would
deny everything and attack his reputation. "I also knew as soon as I
thought about it that I had to do it," he said. But there were a couple
issues he had to take care of first. Andrew had no direct proof that the
Harper government had actually called ForestEthics an "enemy of
the state"—or that it had threatened to revoke Tides's charitable status
in Canada. Andrew hadn't been in the room during any discussion
between the government and Tides. Nor had he even spoken directly
with those leaders. All his information had come at second- or
thirdhand.

Andrew assumed that the Harper government would deny everything
after he went public with his story. It wouldn't be too hard for Tides and
ForestEthics to do the same thing. Without evidence to support his allegations, such denials could easily discredit him. Andrew quietly
prepared for this scenario by speaking with several trusted colleagues at
ForestEthics and telling them about his plans to contact news outlets
about the "Enemy of the State" allegation. "They agreed to confirm off-
the-record with any media that came asking that they too had heard
about alleged threats to Tides and ForestEthics made by the government," he said.

Andrew also got in touch with a lawyer and wrote an affidavit
describing everything he'd heard from his superiors over the past weeks.
"I wanted it to look official," he explained. "Me doing due diligence
and swearing an oath." Still, none of it was any guarantee that his allegations would be taken seriously in public. "I certainly was worried
about that," Andrew explained.

He was also worried about the optics of being fired by ForestEthics.
"My biggest concern was that I'd release all this information," he
explained, "and that if I didn't time it all properly, I'd get labeled [in the
media] as a disgruntled former employee instead of a whistleblower."

So he decided to delay the inevitable as long as he could. When governments have bad news to release, they often wait until a Friday afternoon. That's when Andrew decided to tell McMillan from Tides Canada that he'd reached out to several local reporters and was going to officially go public with the story on Monday. Because the weekend was starting, "they won't be able to fire me immediately,'" he said.

Andrew and McMillan didn't really know each other. "I'd only seen him in the hallways and exchanged pleasantries like 'Hi, nice to see you'—that kind of thing," Andrew said. Their meeting was short and tense. "I went in and said, 'The story is coming out next week,'" Andrew said. McMillan was not happy. Had Andrew considered the jobs he was putting at risk? "McMillan described it as like 'setting off a bomb in your own house,'" Andrew recalled. But Andrew refused to yield. "We need to share this information with our allies and the public," Andrew said to McMillan. It was not a comfortable meeting. "You could have cut the tension with a knife," he said. About twenty minutes after it was over, Andrew's phone started ringing off the hook.

It didn't stop for two days. Andrew didn't answer any calls. "Every senior person at ForestEthics and Tides Canada was trying to stop me from going forward with the story," he said. "It was intense, it was like out of a movie." On Saturday morning his supervisor, Pierre Iachetti, left two short voice messages. "I'm sure you're probably getting [tons] of messages from various folks, but uh, you seriously need to call me," Iachetti said, according to Andrew's transcript of the phone message. "We're hearing some troubling news from Ross . . . and what I can say is if the information that we have is true there are some serious consequences as of Monday."[50] Andrew didn't respond. Soon his ForestEthics e-mail account was shut down. Andrew used his personal account to write an e-mail to the group explaining himself. "The Canadian government is attempting to silence the voice of civil society in this country," he wrote. "As a citizen, that's not something I can accept."

ForestEthics leader Todd Paglia responded on Sunday. "You have thrown this bomb whatever it is and have refused to talk to your supervisor, me, and many other staff trying to reach you so we could prepare for whatever it is you have done," Paglia wrote, according to Andrew's affidavit. "This is unprofessional and insulting to everyone on this team."[51]

By Monday morning, Andrew hadn't been fired by ForestEthics—not technically. He wanted to keep it that way until the first news reporters got in touch. At home he sat waiting for his phone to ring. Suddenly his buzzer rang instead. It was a courier sent by ForestEthics to deliver his firing papers. "I hung up on him because I didn't want to get fired just yet," Andrew explained. Yet the courier was somehow able to enter his apartment building. At Andrew's door he knocked loudly. "Then he jammed this thick envelope under the door," Andrew said. By that point the reporters Andrew had reached out to last week were starting to get in contact. When one of them called, Andrew explained, "'I've just been fired.' 'Why are you fired?' the reporter asked. 'Because I'm sharing this story with you!'" Andrew said.

On Tuesday morning Andrew posted his affidavit online, along with a letter putting it all into context. "I am taking the extraordinary step of risking my career, my reputation and my personal friendships, to act as a whistleblower and expose the undemocratic and potentially illegal pressure the Harper government has apparently applied to silence critics of the Enbridge Northern Gateway oil tanker/pipeline plan," he wrote.[52] He also put it on Facebook. "Hey everyone, I'm all in today against the Prime Minister," he said.

The first major media stories were now appearing. "Affidavit accuses PMO [prime minister's office] of threatening environmental group," read a Canadian Press story.[53] Headlines continued to mount. "PMO accused of threatening environmental group," read a headline on the CBC.[54] "Environmentalist's departure sheds light on tension felt by green groups," read a headline in the *Globe and Mail*, Canada's national newspaper. The novelist Margaret Atwood made #EnemyGate a hashtag on Twitter.

As Andrew had expected, Harper's government disavowed the entire thing. "The Prime Minister's Office denies making any of the allegations or saying any of the things that are outlined in [Frank's] statement," said government spokesperson Andrew MacDougall in a statement. He refused to comment on the matter further.[55]

McMillan was also tight-lipped. He put out a statement saying he wouldn't be doing any interviews about Andrew or his affidavit. "Tides Canada does not speak about our conversations with government, partners, the private sector or other parties," he said. "I will say that Mr. Frank did not take part in any conversations we've had with government and his account of our conversations with government is inaccurate."[56] McMillan was in a tricky position, though. If he completely discredited Andrew he would in effect be siding with the Harper government. He would be playing right into their hands. So within the week McMillan attempted to clarify his comments. "Andrew Frank had the wrong facts but the right idea," he wrote. McMillan denied that Tides or ForestEthics had ever been threatened by Harper. "But like Frank," he added, "I am profoundly disturbed by the current political atmosphere" around the tar sands.[57]

By the end of the week Andrew Frank's open letter had been viewed nearly seventy thousand times. "This is a letter, it isn't a Kardashian video," Andrew said. "People cared about it, and they shared it because it mattered to them in some way." But McMillan's comments about the letter's accuracy, even with the later clarification, left Andrew in an awkward position. "As much as I was trying to push the 'enemy of the state' story out and hit the government hard, I also had this rear-guard action where I'm trying to protect my own reputation," he said. As days went by, Andrew's frustration began to show. "The elite brand of environmentalism practiced by big foundations like Tides Canada, can, when it matters the most, be more concerned about its own political interests," Andrew wrote on his blog, than about the safe and sustainable future for his generation he had joined ForestEthics to build. "When telling the truth becomes revolutionary within a social movement, something is wrong," he argued.[58]

In doing so, Andrew Frank effectively detached himself from the partisan political process. By going public with his allegations, he'd hoped to show people that the country's Conservative government was more apt to obey the wishes of tar sands companies than those of regular people. "My cynicism comes from the fact that the government was pulling these strings behind the scenes," he said. But he'd also cut ties to many of the progressive organizations fighting Harper. "The environmental groups and foundations were under so much pressure that they acted in kind of a cynical way," he said. He was certain that the "enemy of the state" allegation he made public would've had a much larger impact if his old employer had confirmed it. "If it was up to me I wouldn't have had to worry about [them] trying to slag me and take me down because they were so worried about trying to protect themselves," Andrew said.

But that's not what happened. And in the aftermath of the scandal, Andrew often thought about where he fit within Canada's political system. Clearly there was no place for him in the aggressive expansion of the status quo envisioned by Conservatives like Harper. Yet in a moment when it mattered most, the progressive opposition had chosen—rightly or wrongly—to focus on its own self-preservation rather than on his generation's future. Andrew was not apathetic, lazy, or ignorant. He still believed that young people like him can and should make a difference. But the traditional political spectrum didn't seem to present them with very good options. "I feel like so many people [my age] want to be involved in politics," Andrew said. "But they're just not involved with the regular political parties. They're cynical about our system."

THE 2011 FEDERAL ELECTION that gave Stephen Harper virtually unbridled power to turn Canada into a petrostate (and to go after ForestEthics) was in many ways decided by young voters—or rather, their decision to abstain from participating in it. Less than 40 percent of people under the age of thirty cast a ballot in that election. If 60 percent had voted, the pollster Nik Nanos later calculated, Harper likely wouldn't have won a majority. By not voting, they increased the ballot power of Harper's older, white, and male supporters. Older Canadians "are very cynical, they have less confidence in finding solutions," Nanos observed. But younger people, his years of polling research suggested, "are actually much more hopeful, have a higher level of confidence in finding solutions." If more of them actually voted, "just the mere act of engaging them could reshape the tone of [politics]."[59]

But youth voter turnout had been getting worse and worse for decades. In the years following World War II, upward of 75 percent of Canadians voted in elections. But by the 2000s that had decreased to about 60 percent. A study by Elections Canada concluded, "This decline is disproportionately concentrated among the youngest electors,"[60] as in the United States and Britain. If the decline couldn't be reversed, "that has implications for the long-term health of our democratic system." An op-ed in the *Globe and Mail* questioned if the problem was past the point of fixing. "The decline of voting in the 21st century may become as striking a phenomenon as the decline of church attendance in the latter part of the 20th," its editorialists speculated.[61]

But many observers didn't realize that people of Andrew's age are in many ways more political than their elders. "The low voting rate among today's youth is often considered proof that they're more apathetic or lazy than any other generation before," argued the think tank Samara in 2015, but actually youth were more likely to sign a petition, run a civil society group, and share news on social media. "Across 18 forms of political activities," it found, "Canadians under 30 participate at a rate 11 percentage points higher than those 30 and above."[62] Voting was the exception. "It shows something many millennials have been saying for years. It's not that they don't care about politics, it's just that electoral politics isn't necessarily catching their imaginations," as a story in the *National Post* put it.[63]

Harper came up for reelection in October 2015. And in the months leading to the vote, no issue exemplified this challenge more than climate change. In the spring I interviewed Julie Van de Valk, a university student in her early twenties who, like many her age, considers global warming to be so urgent that "it's not something we can wait another day to address." She was so concerned about it that she spent a Saturday knocking on strangers' doors across Vancouver to raise awareness of climate solutions. But she refrained from endorsing a specific political party. None of them, neither left nor right, "are addressing climate change with the type of leadership that people who understand the issue want to see," she explained. "People of my generation, we want to see a politician commit 100 percent to a brighter future."[64]

Julie planned to vote in the October election—she wasn't going to sit this one out. But she felt deeply uninspired by her options. For a young person who believes her generation's future survival requires us to make transformative changes to our society, supporting a Conservative like Harper was completely out of the question. Yet none of the progressives seemed willing to make those changes either. Both of her left-of-center options, the Liberals and New Democratic Party (NDP), promised to take stronger action on climate change than Harper. Yet neither party could explain how it would rapidly reduce carbon emissions and shift toward clean energy. And both openly supported the tar sands. "That doesn't do it for me," she said.[65]

That left her in the same awkward political position as Andrew Frank. The three and a half years that'd passed since his decision to become a whistleblower hadn't been easy. He'd burned a lot of bridges. "People afterwards told me on the phone that 'I respect you and like working with you but I'm not allowed to talk with you,'" he said. And at first he'd a bit of trouble finding work. Several times when he applied for activist jobs, he'd made it far into the hiring process, only to be cut at the very end. "Later people would say, 'I just want to let you know I thought you had a really great application, but let's leave it at that,'" he said. "That kind of thing." He'd been able to pick up some part-time work with indigenous groups, however, and as Canada's 2015 election approached, he was teaching at a local university.

Often before a new semester even started, many of Andrew's students knew who he was. "Because they'll Google me," he explained. So he began to use the story of his departure from ForestEthics in his classes on climate change and public relations. "I tell my students, 'I'm progressive, but I'm not partisan. I'm going to share a story, but I'm not sharing it to shape your politics,'" he said. "I want to teach them to be active citizens." In his opinion, an active citizen is willing to fight for his or her ideals, even if it means detaching from the political institutions claiming to represent them. "When you say, 'I want my side to win,' there's a litmus test of ideological purity," he said. "I'm like 'No, it's not about purity, I just want to get stuff done.'"

Andrew sensed untapped power in this argument. He thought that by applying it to the upcoming election, young people like him and Julie could topple Harper's nearly decade-long petrostate. In general elections, Canadians don't vote directly for their leader, as in the United States. Instead they vote for party candidates in specific ridings. Whichever party elects the most candidates gets to make its leader prime minister. The system seemed to favor Harper. Since he was the only strong Conservative option, most right-wing votes went to his candidates. Left-wing voters had two strong options—the NDP and the Liberals—which meant that the progressive vote was often split. In 2011 this allowed Harper's party to win with under 40 percent of the popular vote. Andrew's idea was simple. Voters should figure out which progressive candidate had the best shot of winning in their riding—NDP or Liberal, it didn't matter—and then vote for that candidate. "I am not a member of a political party," he wrote. "I am a progressive . . . willing to roll up my sleeves."[66]

Across the country many young people were coming to the same conclusion. The strategy became known as ABC—Anything But Conservative. One of its leading proponents was a youth-led activist group known as Leadnow, which convinced 85,000 people to sign a pledge promoting the idea of strategic voting. Its rationale was the same as Andrew's. "Most people in Canada don't see the country through a partisan political lens or identify with a political brand," it explained. "But we want to see change."[67] Leadnow identified thirty-one ridings across the country where Conservative candidates were in close races with progressives. It pored through polling data to figure out which progressive candidate had the best chance of winning, then advised people to vote for that candidate. "I'm so curious to see what's going to happen," said Leadnow's Amara Possian. "In some ways it's a big experiment."[68]

Meanwhile more than 450,000 people, many of them in their twenties and early thirties, RSVP'd to a "Stephen Harper Going Away Party" on Facebook. For them, toppling Harper was more important than rallying behind a specific replacement. "I would vote for a centipede if it would get rid of Harper," one woman told the *Globe and Mail*. The newspaper concluded that "'Anybody But Harper' has become a kind of war whoop for disaffected voters this election"[69]—particularly young ones. One of its loudest proponents was the well-known youth activist Brigitte DePape, who traveled the country urging people her age to vote Harper out of office. "I want to do everything in my power to see a government that reflects our values," she said. DePape was confident young people would listen. "To all those who said 'the youth vote is dead,'" she argued, "I believe that our generation will prove you wrong."[70] And on Election Day, it did.

MY PARTNER, KARA, and I got up early on October 17 to vote. We'd done our research and concluded that the NDP candidate had the best chance of defeating a Conservative in our riding, so that's who we voted for. Like most people we know, we see ourselves as political independents. We believe our society needs profound structural changes, but we weren't picky about who implemented them. For now the most important thing was to get Harper out of office. You couldn't build a new status quo until you rejected the old one. That message was everywhere. As Election Day approached, my social media feeds were flooded with anti-Harper news stories. People who'd never seemed political to me were posting them. You could feel the revolt building. Even the HBO comedian John Oliver urged Canadians: "Don't vote for Stephen Harper!"

That evening we packed into a friend's living room to watch the results. It was a party atmosphere. People were slamming beers and rolling joints. But everyone was a bit on edge. Could we really endure four more years living in a petrostate? And then suddenly the election was over. We watched in silence as Harper conceded his loss to the charismatic young Liberal leader Justin Trudeau. "We gave everything we have to give, and we have no regrets whatsoever," Harper said. "God bless all of you. God bless Canada." With that his reign was over. Harper walked off the stage and announced he was leaving politics. All the TV stations cut to Trudeau. "It's time for a change," he said. "A positive, optimistic, hopeful vision of public life isn't a naive dream. It can be a powerful force."[71] For ten years the status quo had looked impenetrable. And in one night it was swept away.

My generation was a big reason for it. Elections Canada found that voting among 18-to-24-year-olds was 18 percent higher than in the 2011 election that gave Harper his majority. "[This] is believed to be a major factor behind the resounding Liberal Party victory," Jessica Dorfman wrote in the *Harvard International Review*, calling the outcome "exciting . . . in a global context." Youth voter turnout had been in steady decline for decades in the United States, Britain, and Canada. "[This is] a problem faced across the board in developed democracies," Dorfman explained. But Canada's election proved that it can be fixed: "This decline is not inevitable, and it does not have to be permanent. After years of bemoaning voter apathy . . . there is finally reason to feel optimistic."[72]

In the weeks and months after the election, a consensus seemed to emerge that the reason so many young people voted was because of Trudeau's charm, his relative youth—he was forty-three—and his hopeful message of change. He took countless selfies with young supporters. His Liberal platform mentioned young people more than sixty times. The *Washington Post* called him a "rock star." The *Guardian* remarked on his "charisma and popularity." Many others compared him to Obama. "Mr. Trudeau is a political leader young Canadians feel understands them and that they can relate to," read a report from Abacus Data and the Canadian Alliance of Student Associations.[73] But I wasn't sure. To me, Trudeau's victory seemed to be the byproduct of something larger. He hadn't won because young people embraced his party. He won because of people like Andrew Frank. He won because they rejected the political system. That was the story the data told.

For it to make sense, you first to have understand why so many young people wanted Harper out of office. During his nearly ten years in power—but especially during the four years he had a majority—his Conservatives governed with a set of values that was hostile to those of many Millennials. Harper was not at all keen about gay marriage— he once called it "vile and disgusting." He was distrustful of diversity—he'd referred to Muslim culture as "barbaric." He argued marijuana is "infinitely worse than tobacco." He passed intrusive anti-terrorism laws that the journalist Glenn Greenwald referred to as a "fear-mongering" power grab.[74] He said that the unsolved deaths of indigenous women aren't "high on our radar." Such positions didn't endear Harper to many 18-to-34-year-olds. The polling firm Abacus Data concluded that "this is the weakest age group for the Conservative Party."[75]

But it was Harper's obsession with the tar sands that arguably turned off young people the most. As we have seen, Millennials are more likely than members of older generations to support far-ranging climate solutions. They want an economic system that values those solutions as much as profits. And they desire leaders with the global mindset necessary to implement them. Polling suggests young Canadians are no exception. A national survey commissioned in 2014 by the publication *Alberta Oil* found that only 9.3 percent of 18-to-34-year-olds consider the tar sands to be "essential" to the country's future, as opposed to 18 percent of the broader population.[76] Separate polling in the same year suggested that 42 percent of young people believe the government can address climate change and create jobs at the same time, compared to 32 percent of people older than 55.[77]

Harper called that idea "crazy." He declared tar sands pipelines to be a "national priority." He deemed anyone who disagreed a "radical." So it wasn't surprising that in 2015 one of the top issues for young voters was the environment. An online survey of 164,704 Canadians conducted by the CBC suggested it was the second most important issue for voters after the economy. "I don't think that the environment would have been pegged second several years ago," said University of Ottawa law professor Penny Collenette.[78] Millennials were more likely to select it—15 percent of them said it was the most important issue, compared to nine percent of people over 55. "Today's young people are about to inherit decades of climate woes," explained the *Toronto Star*, "and they want a government that is willing to address these problems now."[79]

It was consistent with years of opinion research. "If you're a younger Canadian," the pollster Nik Nanos found, "you're twice as likely to say that the environment is a top national issue of concern" than older voters.[80] Harper's most reliable voters were in their sixties or older. They won't live to see the true impacts of climate change. But the Millennials who voted against him will. "We are hungry for change," DePape the activist wrote. "We want a good life . . . where the water, air, and earth isn't eaten up by unsustainable energy projects, with future generations and youth left to deal with the consequences." She added, "We're going to fight for it."[81] Many young voters yearn for a future where they won't have to worry about civilization collapsing. But as the election approached, they didn't seem all that particular about which party created it.

In April 2015, no political party held a commanding lead among young voters. Polling from Ekos Research Associates showed Millennial support was evenly split among Harper's Conservatives and the two progressive parties—NDP and Liberals—trying to replace him. "Very little appears settled," the firm concluded. One statistic, though, had remained consistent. Support for the Conservatives among people 65 and older hadn't dipped below 39 percent for months. Harper had "a huge lead with seniors," Ekos found.[82] Only days before the October election, the polling data was mostly unchanged. Millennial support was divided almost evenly among the three main parties, while senior support for Harper was at 39 percent. If Trudeau's charisma was truly invigorating young voters, the polling data wasn't showing it.

What it did show was most young people had no firm attachment to any political party. Polling in July 2015 from Abacus Data found that Millennial voters leaned toward progressive options. Nearly two-thirds of young respondents were open to supporting the NDP or Trudeau's Liberals, compared to less than half for Harper's Conservatives. Yet the data suggested that most Millennials were ambivalent about their options. About 84 percent of young people said they weren't "firmly decided" on which party they wanted to vote for. This was 12 percentage points higher than the Canadian average. "Millenials are the most 'up for grabs' voters today," Abacus concluded. "All major parties can win sizeable proportions of [their] vote."[83] It also implied something else: Millennials were detached from the political system.

On October 17 many of them seemed to vote in a way that expressed that. In British Columbia, where Harper wanted to build the Northern Gateway tar sands pipeline, voter turnout surged by over 10 percent, much of it due to new young voters. They were more likely than any other age group to engage in strategic voting—that is, to choose the candidate that had the best chance of defeating Harper, instead of embracing a particular party. A poll from Insights West suggested that 42 percent of Millennials in BC voted strategically, compared to 27 percent of people over 55.[84] These trends seemed consistent across the country. After NDP polling numbers dropped in the final weeks of the race, a surge of progressive voters, many of them young, decided to vote Liberal. "It was strategic voting on a grand scale by voters who wanted Harper gone and who did not particularly care whether the NDP or Liberals finished the job," wrote former Harper adviser and University of Calgary political science professor Tom Flanagan.[85]

In the end, it was Trudeau who became Canada's new prime minister. But the data suggest his youth and charisma weren't the main reason. His victory was rather the byproduct of a generational values shift that had been building for years in the minds of people like Andrew Frank. Many older people weren't even aware it was occurring: to them, young people's reluctance to turn out for elections was evidence of apathy and cynicism and ignorance. Andrew's departure from ForestEthics hinted at the true cause. The reason he risked his career and reputation as a whistleblower was that he yearned for a better future for his generation, and he believed that our political system is more interested in self-preservation than in building it. It was a dramatic expression of a view widely held by people Andrew's age: that partisan politics, at least in their current form, are a barrier to social progress.

Canada's election showed what can happen when young voters coalesce around that worldview. Across the country, record numbers of Millennials came out to vote. By doing so, they played a crucial role in toppling Harper's petrostate. They decisively rejected its legitimacy. The *Harvard International Review* believed the election was globally significant, proving that "Millennials aren't inherently lazy, or unin-formed, or even nonpolitical. They just need the right motivation and conditions to exercise their democratic rights."[86] The election also proved that our political and economic system is more fragile than it appears. When politically independent young people decide to vote together for their future, the impact is profound and immediate.

Less than a month after becoming prime minister, Justin Trudeau announced that he would be moving forward with a moratorium on all oil tankers off the northwest coast of B.C. "Crude oil supertankers just have no place [there]," he later explained.[87] It was a major setback for the Gateway tar sands pipeline that Andrew had been called an "enemy of the state" for fighting. One indigenous leader referred to the project as "dead in the water."[88] In some ways it was a vindication. "Needless to say, I was pretty happy with the election results," Andrew said.

It added to what had already been a big year for the Millennial generation. In 2015, we'd amplified a labor crisis in the oil and gas industry; convinced President Barack Obama to reject the Keystone XL pipeline; and now kicked Harper out of office. We'd proven what can be achieved by rejecting the status quo. And in Part II of this book, I'll describe the new one that we're building to replace it.

Building a New One

5

Why Wall Street Is Changing

THE HARVARD STUDENT WHO helped launch a $3.4 trillion challenge to the global economic system has spent much of her life trying to protect her home from its expansion. The first threat to the forested wilderness surrounding Chloe Maxmin's home in rural Maine came from a real estate developer. The second came from an oil and gas transporter. The third came from the $5 trillion industry that the corporation belonged to—a threat so big that it could potentially cause human civilization to collapse. Chloe came to believe that her personal struggle to protect her home was symbolic of the challenge her generation faced from climate change. She decided that the only hope we have for a long-term future on this planet is to reject the financial logic that threatens it. She knew that a better alternative was already growing in the hearts and minds of millions of people her age.

Chloe grew up on a farm midway up the coast of Maine. Both of her parents were overachieving intellectuals, holding doctorates in social studies. Chloe's mom was a professor at Harvard, and her dad was a former CEO at Volvo. They had more than ten thousand books in the house, and when she was ten, they published their own: *The Support Economy: Why Corporations Are Failing Individuals and the Next Episode of Capitalism*. Chloe's rich intellectual surroundings were mirrored by her rich natural ones. She spent countless hours in her youth trekking up mountains, exploring dense forest, scrambling along Atlantic coastline, swimming in lakes, and snowmobiling across them. "Ever since I can remember I've felt like that land was a part of my soul," she said. "I've always felt like it was my best friend."[1]

When Chloe was twelve, she became convinced that it was in danger. The threat came from the Seattle company Plum Creek Real Estate, which in April 2005 submitted the largest development plan in Maine history. Plum Creek wanted to transform the pristine shoreline of Moosehead Lake into 975 houses, two resorts, a golf course, a marina, three RV parks, and more than one hundred rental cabins. Chloe used to snowmobile there every winter with her dad and her brother. "It is the largest tract of undeveloped woodland east of the Mississippi, so it's this really rare jewel," she said. "I didn't ever want to see it destroyed." She joined a growing public opposition to the project. She wrote letters to the governor, to the land use commission, and to local newspapers. She testified at public hearings. She also graduated from junior high.

Even at that young age, Chloe understood that Plum Creek was only one player in a larger global struggle. All across the world fragile ecosystems were under siege by "these huge external corporate forces," she said. She knew she would spend her whole life fighting against them. "When I was thirteen, we held my bat mitzvah in our back garden," she wrote. "I stood up that morning and pledged my spirit to the cause of saving the beauty and integrity of the natural world."[2] She can't recall exactly when she first learned about climate change. "Like for so many of us," she explained, "it's always just been part of my life and my awareness." But by the time she entered high school, she saw it as the defining challenge of her generation.

Most people seemed to talk about climate change—that is, if they talked about it at all—as if it were this far-off thing, a scientific curiosity, troubling but distant. Chloe saw it much differently. To her—as to many others her age—climate change was the pervading sense of dread that came anytime she thought about the future. It felt intensely personal. "There's a really interesting psychological phenomenon among our generation," she explained. "What is it like to grow up with this huge looming disaster in your life? How do you find your hope and your love?" In high school she created a student group, the Climate Action Club. She saw its mission in global terms: "If we can make a difference and be recognized for it, it will be obvious that every single person on earth can make a difference."[3]

Chloe decided to prove this theory by going after plastic bags. She believed the reason we humans are screwing up the atmosphere is that we make wasteful decisions. We constantly choose short-term payoffs with little regard for the long-term consequences. We drive too much. We don't recycle. We don't use the right lightbulbs. Maxmin thought she could change that with the right incentives. She and the others in the Climate Action Club raised money for nineteen hundred canvas bags and gave them to local businesses. "This is not a one-time thing, but an ingrained change in behavior," she said.[4] Her program kept seven hundred thousand plastic bags from going to landfills. She graduated from high school in the top of her class. That fall she got into Harvard.

Most people spend their first year in college trying to figure out where they fit in. Chloe was no exception. In addition to embarking on a degree in social studies, she joined every major environmental club at Harvard. Her goal was to "learn about their projects, goals, and strategies," she said. "It is a time commitment, but the best way to find 'your' group is to understand all the groups and their distinct perspectives and priorities." One focused on the green economy. Another pushed for energy efficiency on campus. The third rallied for renewable energy. They ran the gamut from "vanilla actions like holding a banner" to "slightly more radical." None of them were quite the right fit. "I still haven't committed myself to one group exclusively," she said midway through her first year.[5]

But later that summer she read something that gave her the clarity and purpose she'd been seeking. It was an essay published in *Rolling Stone* by the climate change activist and author Bill McKibben. "Global Warming's Terrifying New Math" was based on a simple premise: if we are to limit the rise in global temperature to relatively safe levels, then 80 percent of oil, coal, and gas reserves must stay in the ground. But instead of letting that happen, companies like Exxon and Koch Industries were doing the exact opposite. In 2012 the industry as a whole spent $674 billion finding and developing new fossil fuel reserves. "Given this hard math, we need to view the fossil-fuel industry in a new light," McKibben explained. "It has become a rogue industry, reckless like no other force on Earth."[6] For Chloe, the essay came as a revelation. "We are being coerced into a broken system without even knowing it," she said.

Having that knowledge was one thing. But how could a Harvard student ever expect to do something about it? How could she break the power of the $5 trillion fossil fuel industry? In the final paragraphs of his essay, McKibben offered a suggestion. In the 1980s students at Harvard and a few other campuses had discovered a novel way to take action against apartheid. They had gone after their schools' financial endowments—big investment portfolios, essentially, whose returns fund the school's activities. The 1980s campaign to have those investments pulled from companies tied to South Africa's racist leadership eventually spread to hundreds of colleges and universities across the world. Archbishop Desmond Tutu later credited it with helping to end apartheid. McKibben urged college students to do the same for fossil fuels. "If their college's endowment portfolio has fossil-fuel stock," he wrote, students should pressure their college to dump that stock.[7]

Chloe didn't know it then, but the ideas contained in McKibben's essay would define the rest of her time at Harvard. They would inspire a college movement that within several years had spread across the world, ignited a passionate debate within the financial sector, and influenced trillions of dollars worth of economic activity. The movement ultimately demonstrated that our current means of generating wealth is not inevitable, that our system is not based on inviolable economic laws, that it's actually based on a series of human decisions. And when enough young people come together to demand a system that makes better decisions, it listens. "There are these critical moments in the story when something pivots and something changes," Chloe said. They are the moments when people realize a better future is more attainable than it appears.

WHEN CHLOE MAXMIN READ Bill McKibben's essay in the summer of 2013, the tactic of divestment had been around for more than three decades. To understand why her generation's iteration of it spread so rapidly, you have to go to 2001, however, when Swarthmore College undergraduate Morgan Simon made an exciting discovery. Simon found that with $2,000 you could invest in a corporation—pretty much any publicly traded one you wanted—and file a resolution requesting changes to its corporate policy. She thought it could be a powerful tool in the hands of college students like herself. To test out her theory, Simon and a few others decided to see whether they could get Lockheed Martin, the biggest weapons maker in the United States, to adopt new policies protecting LGBT rights. "The nice thing about young people is we think we can do anything, regardless of whether or not it is realistic," she said.[8]

With Swarthmore's support, they filed a resolution asking Lockheed to add sexual orientation to its antidiscrimination policy. They wrote letters to more than five hundred large institutional investors asking for their support, and soon reporters started to call. Morgan Simon found herself running out between classes to do interviews with Fox News. That April she flew to Lockheed's annual shareholder meeting in San Diego. "You get exactly two minutes to state your case in front of the board of directors and executive staff before, literally, two buff men in black suits lead you away," she said. Lockheed execs mocked Simon's resolution. What was next, they laughed—a policy on eye color discrimination? But her resolution received enough shareholder votes to survive until the next year. And several months later she read in the *Wall Street Journal* that Lockheed had decided to adopt it. "We were overjoyed," she wrote. "I had never felt like my actions could have such an immediate, powerful effect."[9]

That success led Simon and four other student activists, in 2004, to launch the Responsible Endowments Coalition (REC). Its goal was to get students across the United States to look at the social and environmental impacts of their schools' investments—and how those investments might be leveraged to advance a whole suite of progressive goals. "Most universities directly and indirectly fund injustice through their investments, making money off of the dirty work of coal companies, private prisons, tobacco companies, and more," explained a 2011 REC handbook. "As a student, you have both the power and the responsibility to transform the way your school invests."[10] The wide focus of the

REC's call to action allowed it to spread to more than one hundred college campuses. But it also limited the organization's reach. What REC offered to student activists was in effect a powerful toolset. It lacked the purpose of a tightly structured campaign.

The ideas that induced people like Chloe to take REC's ideas global can in many ways be traced back to James Leaton, the head of research for a think tank called the Carbon Tracker Initiative (CTI). In 2012 he set out to answer a simple but underexplored question: how much of the world's known oil, coal, and gas reserves had to stay in the ground if we were to have any hope of limiting global warming to safe levels? A lot, as he would later find out, up to 80 percent. The reserves of ExxonMobil, BP, Gazprom, Chevron, ConocoPhillips, and Shell alone contained enough carbon to use up over 25 percent of our warming budget. "This research provides the evidence base which confirms what we have long suspected," explained a CTI report. "There are more fossil fuels listed on the world's capital markets than we can afford to burn." The report, called *Unburnable Carbon*, stated, "The missing element in creating a low carbon future is a financial system which will enable that to happen."[11]

Carbon Tracker quantified what McKibben and many others had always known: that the number-one obstacle to an economic system that values human survival as much as profits is the fossil fuel industry. "What all these climate numbers make painfully, usefully clear is that the planet does indeed have an enemy," he explained in "Global Warming's Terrifying New Math." "We need to view the fossil-fuel industry in a new light . . . it is Public Enemy Number One to the survival of our planetary civilization." Since the industry was driven by our relentless search for short-term profits, McKibben figured the best way to fight it was to demand a new system. An obvious place to start would be on college campuses. In the 1980s a divestment movement had helped end South African apartheid. If that tactic were directed at fossil fuels, "it could," he concluded, "give rise to a real movement."[12]

McKibben's essay immediately went viral. Within two weeks it had been shared over 100,000 times on social media. "It is getting monster social media numbers of the kind usually reserved for pieces on *HuffPost* about Kim Kardashian in a bikini," wrote the climate blogger Joe Romm.[13] McKibben seemed to have tapped into a latent feeling of frustration that had been growing for years. To a majority of Millennials, it made no sense to sacrifice the future for short-term financial returns. They believed that businesses should be improving the world instead of destroying it. And their rejection of industries like oil and gas was already challenging our status quo. McKibben's essay pointed the way toward a new one.

"Global Warming's Terrifying New Math" had a profound impact on the worldview of people like Chloe. It made their broad anxieties about our society clear and definable. It gave them a sense of power and control over their destiny. It turned climate change in their minds from an impossibly big global challenge into something that regular people like themselves could influence. Chloe would later say that the essay "changed my life and the course of my career as a climate activist." It caused her to view the fossil fuel industry, and the wider economic system it represented, as a "moral outrage."[14]

What made the industry even less acceptable was that alternatives were becoming more viable all the time. For years, renewable energy had been perceived as an expensive and unreliable luxury that could never take the place of fossil fuels. But China and Germany were determined to prove that false. In the 1990s Germany began subsidizing the development of renewable energy and set targets to phase out the use of fossil fuels. The result was that in 2011 about 20 percent of the country's electricity was generated by low carbon sources. China's 2006 Renewable Energy Law would create a similar outcome. From 2005 to 2009 the country's wind power industry doubled in size every year—and then doubled again by 2012. Within two years of passing the law, China was leading the planet in solar cell production.

The global impact is hard to understate. From 2009 to 2015 the price of solar energy fell 75 percent. Wind power dropped 30 percent. Major investment players such as Deutsche Bank were soon calculating that within a decade clean energy would be less expensive than fossil fuels in much of the world. By 2013, in fact, countries were adding more renewables to the electricity mix (143 gigawatts) than all fossil fuels combined (141 gigawatts). And the following year more than $242 billion was put into renewable energy, as a report from the Frankfurt School of Finance and Management explained—"far above the figure for net investment in additional fossil fuel capacity, at $132 billion."[15] When college students like Chloe set up their first divestment meetings in the fall of 2012, these shifts were just starting to be felt. They might not have realized it then, but the ground was rumbling beneath them.

The work of REC and others had given them an effective strategy for taking on corporations. Carbon Tracker and McKibben had provided a clearly defined enemy. And China and Germany were proving that alternatives to our current model were viable. Chloe and her fellow students were now in control of a powerful narrative. "It's that a better world is possible—clean, high-tech, prosperous, and just—and that fossil fuel companies are using their enormous legacy wealth and power to prevent the transition to that better world," wrote Vox columnist David Roberts.[16] And when they began acting on that narrative, when they used it to demand a safer future for their generation, it wasn't very long before the rest of the world took notice.

BY THAT POINT WALL Street was already paying attention. For several years now its leading financial institutions had been noticing something peculiar about members of Chloe's generation. Investors born after 1982 or so seemed to have a completely different worldview than their financial elders. They seemed to think that Wall Street—and our global economy at large—should aspire to more than just making the highest profits possible with little to no concern for the consequences. "I was taught in [business] school that the purpose of a corporation is to maximize shareholder value," said Peter Roselle, vice president at Morgan Stanley, a global financial services firm overseeing nearly $2 trillion in assets. "Millennials, though, have identified the improvement of society as the primary purpose of business."[17]

I was sitting across a boardroom table from Roselle in midtown Manhattan when he explained why. I and about twenty-five others had gathered on the invitation of a national sustainability group to learn how people my age were potentially reshaping Wall Street's priorities. It's fair to say that I felt a bit out of my element. Most of the meeting's participants were in their forties or fifties or older. All of them seemed to know each other. And their job titles—strategic officer, co-inventor, chairman, managing director, general partner, senior analyst, operations coordinator, vice-president—sounded much more legitimate than the introduction I kept giving: "Yeah, um, I'm a journalist from up in Canada." Also I should mention that I had a killer hangover.

The night before this meeting I'd watched my friend's band play in a sweaty and smoke-filled East Williamsburg warehouse. My goal, of course, had been to drink only one or two of the Miller High Lifes that the bartender with a neck tattoo and beard was selling for five bucks a bottle. "I have to go meet some serious finance people tomorrow," I'd explained to my friends. But the opening band's unholy mash-up of psychedelic jazz and Lynyrd Skynyrd–style roots rock was so unexpectedly weird and awesome that I threw back one High Life after another. And now here I was, less than twelve hours later, in a boardroom high above Rockefeller Plaza, listening to financial professionals many years older than me discuss "the millennial challenge" facing Wall Street.

The problem, as Peter Roselle described it, was that our financial system simply wasn't set up to accommodate the demand that so many young investors were now making—namely, that their investments be used to improve the world rather than destroy it. "Consumers, especially the 'Millennials,' have widened the scope of their investment lens," a short description of today's meeting had noted. Morgan Stanley was in the business of making a lot of money really fast. But improve society? The weird thing was that Roselle seemed intent on convincing the room that he was trying. In his opinion, Morgan Stanley was now at "the early stage . . . of a movement" toward a more socially conscious economy. Let me remind you that I was the only journalist attending this meeting. Nobody there seemed exactly sure how I'd been invited.

So this wasn't a large press conference or anything. This was a vice president at one of the "top five" Wall Street investment banks telling a small group of colleagues that the financial system as we know it was changing, and that the pressure for that change was coming from people of my generation. It was at this point in the meeting, and after my third cup of coffee, that my mind snapped into focus. What was I supposed to make of Roselle's remarks? Morgan Stanley, after all, had been one of the leading underwriters of risky subprime mortgages in the run-up to the 2008 recession. Its industry's heedless pursuit of profits had melted the global economy. Now it wanted to throw $10 billion into meeting challenges like climate change? What was going on here?

I leafed through the Morgan Stanley pamphlet that I'd been handed at the beginning of the meeting. Hopefully it would contain some answers. Immediately the pamphlet's corporate title made me cringe: "Sustainable Investing: Imperative and Opportunity." But as I read on, the language started to sound a lot more Greenpeace than Wall Street. "The global challenges we face in the decades ahead pose critically important questions not only for society at large, but also for each of us as individuals, citizens, parents, business leaders, and also policy-makers," it read. "How do we ensure that the demand curves of the future do not spell a world of intensifying resource scarcity, economic inequality, and ecological damage?"[18]

Morgan Stanley hoped to proactively avoid that world by investing in companies that were committed to building a better one. Or that was the sales pitch, anyway, of its "investing with impact" program. "Whether it is low-carbon air travel, vertical farming in high-rise struc-tures, or zero-waste buildings and cities," the pamphlet continued, "businesses and entrepreneurs have the potential to create products and services that enable a more populous planet to thrive within its carrying capacity." In November 2013 the investment bank announced a plan to invest $10 billion in such companies over five years. Its competitor Goldman Sachs launched a $250 million "social impact fund" only a few days afterward. By Wall Street standards, this was not normal behavior. Capitalism wasn't supposed to care about society.

In truth it wasn't as if these banks had suddenly gained a social conscience. The head of Morgan Stanley's global sustainable finance group was pretty up front about the fact that the pressure for these changes was coming from outside her company. "You are definitely seeing a next [generation] effect of younger investors who want to change the ways that their families or institutions invest," Audrey Choi explained.[19] This now seemed to be common wisdom among major financial players. Across the boardroom table from me, a vice-president at Deutsche Bank weighed in. "One thing that really appeals to the millennial generation is not thinking just about finance," Sam Marks offered to the room. By which he meant that people my age seemed to view our financial system as the means to a greater end and not necessarily an end unto itself. All around the room, people were nodding in agreement.

I wondered what my friends at last night's warehouse show would think. Like me, I imagined they'd be a little bit incredulous. Sure, the $10 billion that Morgan Stanley had committed toward society-improving investments sounded impressive. But the numbers needed to be put into context. At the time of this meeting, Morgan Stanley oversaw assets worth $1.94 trillion, or more wealth than that generated by the entire Canadian economy. The company's $10 billion in "sustainable" assets would be worth less than one percent of its wider business—zilch, basically. And more to the point, why would I trust the altruism of a Wall Street bank whose own self-interest had helped crash the global economy in 2008? Yet dismissing it all as public relations seemed overly simplistic. The more pertinent question, I decided, was what Morgan Stanley stood to gain by making the world a better place.

The first thing would be to gain a less toxic public persona. In the aftermath of the financial meltdown, Wall Street became one of America's most hated institutions, especially among people my age. One study from Harvard's Institute of Politics found that 86 percent of 18-to-34-year-olds distrust companies like Morgan Stanley.[20] "If you went to a cocktail party in 2009 in New York and somebody asked you what you do, [you'd] kind of cringe a little to say you work for an investment bank," Roselle said. "So there's an intentional shift to try to change the image."[21] At this point, I'll admit, my bullshit sensors went on standby. Yet as the meeting continued, I learned a few things about Morgan Stanley's plan that kept them from being fully triggered.

They had to do with demographics. At the moment, much of the world's wealth is controlled by Baby Boomers. That's quickly changing, however. As more and more members of this generation retire or pass away, their wealth—over $40 trillion globally—is being transferred to Millennials. With that transfer comes a completely different perspective on capitalism. "This new socially conscious generation of 80 million strong," a 2014 report from Brady Capital Research noted, "will be looking to invest in innovative companies that are disrupting the status quo and doing social good." Many of its members desire an economic system that heals the planet rather than profiting from its demise. As Millennials ascend to positions of power in society over the next few decades, the Brady Capital report went on, their worldview will be "an influential force on corporate America and Wall Street."[22]

In a sense, you could see Morgan Stanley's $10 billion commitment to a less broken economic system as an early hedge against the more socially conscious future that people my age are demanding. Once again, by Wall Street standards it's a minuscule investment. But it's not totally insubstantial either. It's one-tenth of what developed countries like the United States have promised to poorer nations for fighting climate change. Morgan Stanley was entering a rapidly growing market too. In the United States, investments in companies that pursue social and environmental progress alongside profits grew from $3.74 trillion in 2012 to $6.57 trillion in 2014. "There seems to be a powerful but latent demand" for a less destructive economic system, financial executive Elizabeth Littlefield observed. "My guess is if you build it, [investors] will come."[23]

Once those investors come, moreover, they are likely to stay. Or so it would seem, according to Morgan Stanley's own research. Conventional economic logic holds that companies aspiring to make a positive difference in the world will be less profitable than ones driven only by their bottom line. As it turns out, that assumption is deeply flawed. After reviewing seven years of data for more than ten thousand mutual funds, Morgan Stanley "observed that sustainable funds tend to exhibit slightly higher returns and lower volatility than their traditional counterparts, barring a few exceptions."[24] The reason has to do with efficiency and risk. Companies with lower ecological footprints often use fewer resources, for instance, and are less exposed to the price volatility that comes with them. A 2014 study from Ceres found that clean energy is already saving America's largest corporations more than $1.1 billion per year.[25]

At the same time, the financial risks of destroying the planet are growing. Carbon Tracker has estimated that if and when governments take serious steps to limit global warming to relatively safe levels, more than $300 billion worth of oil, coal, and gas reserves could become effectively worthless. In the meantime, such investments are becoming less and less socially acceptable—a trend that Morgan Stanley, for one, has attributed directly to student activists like Chloe Maxmin. "Though divestment has a mixed track record as an investment strategy, it often leads to increasing public pressure to take regulatory action," the bank concluded. "It has sparked a robust debate among investors about how to address fossil fuel risk in their portfolios."[26]

Suddenly this strange meeting I was attending in Manhattan started to make more sense. Of course banks like Morgan Stanley were aware of how much people my age distrusted them. And of course it was in their best interest to present a less greedy image to the world. But when Roselle closed the meeting by stating, "We have to start measuring things [differently]," I was inclined to agree with him. The steps that Morgan Stanley was taking toward a new economic system were for now far too small to make any tangible difference. As I waited for the elevator, I nevertheless reflected on how remarkable today's meeting had been. Here was one of the "top five" investment banks in the world acknowledging that the economic system demanded by people my age was more profitable and less risky than the system we currently have. And with a ding, the elevator doors opened.

ONE OF THE REASONS Bill McKibben's *Rolling Stone* essay affected Chloe Maxmin so deeply is that it struck a personal note. It coincided with an experience that showed her how our economic system really works. The path that would lead her there began when she joined a campaign to keep Canada's tar sands out of Maine, which centered on a 236-mile pipeline from Portland to Montreal. Since 1941 the pipeline had pumped conventional oil from the East Coast up into Canada. But with Canada's tar sands booming, demand for use of the pipeline had shrunk. In 2009 its operator, the Portland Pipe Line Corp., which Maxmin would later discover was mostly owned by ExxonMobil, began exploring the option of reversing the pipeline's flow. Doing so would enable it to move tar sands oil from Canada to the east coast and provide a badly needed export hub for the landlocked industry. By 2012 a coalition of environmental groups had sprung up to oppose the idea.

To Maxmin, it was like a repeat of the Plum Creek standoff. Once again her home was being threatened by a company that cared only about profits. The Portland-to-Montreal pipeline crossed hundreds of waterways. It ran next to Sebago Lake, the drinking water supply for over 15 percent of Maine's inhabitants. Leaks had not been an issue for decades, but tar sands can be more corrosive than regular oil—especially on a pipeline more than seventy years old. One day Maxmin decided to go actually see what she was fighting. "I drove through dense woods and followed yellow poles that marked an underground pipeline," she wrote. "Most people didn't know that toxic sludge could soon be running under their feet."[27]

As protests against the pipeline reversal became louder, the Portland Pipe Line Corp. did something strange. It denied that such a reversal was even under consideration. "Its website says there are no active plans to move [tar sands] from western Canada through Maine," read a local news story.[28] A major tar sands transporter up in Canada also denied it: "We have been absolutely clear on the fact that the company is not pursuing" oil transport through Maine, said the pipeline builder Enbridge (the same one Andrew Frank was fighting in Chapter 4).[29] Yet behind the scenes both of these companies were quietly pursuing the permits and approvals needed to get tar sands to Maine's east coast. "Now that they are being watched, Big Oil wants to hide the ball," read a blogpost that summer from the National Wildlife Federation. "But their plans to bring tar sands to New England are becoming increasingly clear."[30]

Chloe Maxmin couldn't believe it. In public, fossil fuel companies assured people they had no interest in Maine. But in reality they were trying to set up a transport route that would endanger her homeland and increase tar sands consumption at a time when our world badly needed to reduce it. "It just blew my mind," she said. "The more I got to understand the fossil fuel industry and how it acts, I realized we were dealing with a systemic problem." It was a system that put profits before the survival of her home and generation. Until then Chloe had assumed climate change was caused by people's daily choices—each time, for instance, they chose plastic bags over canvas ones. But after reading McKibben's essay, she realized this was only part of the bigger picture. "We are being coerced into this system," she said.

Chloe returned to Harvard that fall determined to do something about it. What, though, was unclear. To achieve any kind of meaningful change, she would have to take on the $5 trillion fossil fuel industry—one that in 2012 alone had spent $153 million opposing Obama's clean energy policies.[31] How could one college sophomore ever hope to challenge that kind of power? In early September the youth-led climate group 350.org, which we met in Chapter 3, reached out to one of the environmental clubs Chloe belonged to with a potential solution. It was looking for students interested in taking up McKibben's call for a divestment campaign. Instead of fighting the fossil fuel industry head-on, students would pressure their schools to remove oil, coal, or gas stocks from their financial endowments. If enough colleges decided to divest like this, it would send the message that fossil fuels are morally unacceptable investments.

After some initial discussions, Chloe, along with student activists at twenty-nine other U.S. colleges, agreed to give it a shot. She knew it wouldn't be easy. Harvard's endowment of $31 billion was the largest in the world. An estimated $79 million of it was invested in oil, coal, and gas companies.[32] At the first meeting she scheduled in the fall, only nine students showed up, "and none of us knew what we were doing," she recalled. But she was undeterred. "My goal was to get Harvard to stop investing in the companies that were fucking up my home [back in Maine]. That is what I devoted myself to."

Her first goal for the new campaign was to get a referendum on whether Harvard should divest from fossil fuels into that fall's student government election. She and other activists spent hours gathering signatures in heavily trafficked areas like the Harvard Yard. They had a simple but compelling argument. "Our schools invest in our future," Chloe would tell the students who stopped to listen. "Yet at the same time, they are supporting corporations that are actively threatening the future of all life on earth." Within a week and half of their first meeting, her team had gathered 550 signatures. "The Harvard campaign is picking up steam," she declared. By the end of the month, she had all the signatures needed to get divestment into the student election. On voting day in mid-November, she was astounded by the results: 72 percent of voters supported it. "This is an incredible milestone," Chloe wrote in response. "We launched this campaign a little over two months ago, and it has become one of the major issues on campus."[33]

Not only at Harvard, it seemed, but across the country. Over that same period, divestment campaigns had spread to one hundred colleges—a more than 300 percent growth rate. Partly it was due to the tireless activism of Bill McKibben. Beginning in November, he set out to leverage his viral *Rolling Stone* article "Global Warming's Terrifying New Math" by going on a months-long Do the Math speaking tour across the United States. "Everyone who came was asked to join a growing [divestment] movement," read the tour's website. By December, divestment had made it into the *New York Times*. "In recent weeks," read the front-page business section story, "college students on dozens of campuses have demanded that university endowment funds rid themselves of coal, oil and gas stocks." Student organizers such as Chloe were described as "the vanguard of a national movement."[34]

DIVESTMENT PROVIDED A POWERFUL outlet for young people's frustration with the world's political and corporate leadership. In an era of gridlock and polarization, it let students take direct action on their campuses against a very clear target: their school's fossil fuel investments. The campaign immediately forced school administrations into a debate about the morality of the fossil fuel industry. "It's simplistic but it's true: Are you going to keep investing in an industry that is literally destroying our planet, and everything we love and care about, or are you going to take a stand and chart a new course?" Chloe later explained. "The choice defines the person or institution." All those local choices, and the student-led actions that caused them, were then amplified by the larger divestment movement. They became plot points in a developing story. "It's an inherently empowering framework," she said.

Which helps explain why divestment grew so fast. As the year progressed it would take root on more than three hundred university campuses around the world. It "has spread extraordinarily rapidly," Harvard professor David Keith remarked. "The divestment movement marks the first time in my quarter century involvement with climate change that I have encountered such a strong and disciplined commitment to activism."[35] Even as its reach grew, however, divestment's arguably most critical battleground remained under Chloe's command. "Not only is Harvard the richest university in the world," read a story in the Canadian oil and gas publication *Alberta Oil*, "but its divestiture would be a symbolic victory for leaders of a much wider movement."[36]

The first major step Chloe took toward achieving it came in early February 2013, when school trustees agreed to meet with the Divest Harvard leaders. Students filled the administration building's halls in anticipation. "Overall, the tone of the meeting was very positive," Chloe later recalled. "The trustees recognized the urgency of climate change and the moral authority of younger generations who will be feeling the impacts of [it]."[37] Yet they were hesitant about divesting Harvard from fossil fuels. They argued that society is built on fossil fuels, and that billions of people across the developing world can't escape from poverty without them. It wasn't at all convincing to Chloe, but the meeting achieved its aim. It had initiated a moral debate about our status quo with the Harvard administration—one that she was convinced she would win.

For the next seven months, Divest Harvard did all it could to keep that debate alive. It rallied hundreds of students in the Harvard Yard, got 67 percent of law students to vote for divestment, delivered thousands of student and faculty signatures to the school's administration, and kicked off the fall 2013 semester with a teach-in and more demonstrations. The wider global movement continued its rapid growth, but it had yet to convince a major university to drop fossil fuel stocks from its financial endowment. The objection from schools like Vassar, Middlebury, and Swarthmore was consistent and predictable: that divesting could hurt the school's financial returns and was unlikely to have any impact on fossil fuel companies.

Harvard president Drew Faust had barely said a word about divestment this entire time. The $31 billion endowment she presided over was the largest of any school in the world. So the entire movement paid attention in October 2013, when she released her decision on divestment: an eloquently worded *no*. Divestment would gamble the school's income, turn it into a "political actor," cut its ability to influence fossil fuel firms as a shareholder, and do little to lessen reliance on oil, coal, and gas. "The endowment is a resource, not an instrument to impel social or political change," she wrote.[38] Chloe was disappointed, of course. But Divest Harvard had forced Faust to make a decision about the morality of our economic system. And as Chloe and several others wrote in the *Nation*, "she has chosen the wrong side of history."[39]

Later that spring Stanford University became the first major U.S. college to choose the other side. In May 2014 it decided to divest its $18.7 billion endowment of all investments in coal-mining companies. Stanford remained invested in oil and gas, as well as power and steelmaking companies that burn coal. It was nonetheless a gigantic victory. "Stanford, on the edge of Silicon Valley, is at the forefront of the 21st century economy; it's very fitting, then, that they've chosen to cut their ties to the 18th century technology of digging up black rocks and burning them," said McKibben.[40] To Chloe, it was proof that a new economic paradigm was emerging, that "we can align our values without sacrificing anything financially."

That continued to be a tough sell to Harvard president Faust. Since deciding against divestment in October, she'd refused to meet with Divest Harvard. Its members had to find creative ways to confront her. Earlier that spring divestment activist Alli Welton followed Faust into Harvard Yard and got her to state on camera that it "is not the case" that fossil fuel companies are blocking the transition to clean energy.

("Does Faust seriously believe that?" the climate blogger Joe Romm wrote in response.⁴¹) That May campus police arrested another student, Brett A. Roche, after activists blockaded all the entrances to Faust's offices in Massachusetts Hall.

By the time Chloe began her last year at Harvard, divestment had spread to four hundred campuses. With that growth came a backlash, particularly from older observers. They argued that the tactic was polarizing. That it would have no impact on fossil fuel companies. That it was diverting attention from more meaningful causes. That it would hurt financial returns for colleges. That it was fundamentally naïve. Harvard professor Robert Stavins patronizingly urged divestment leaders "to focus on actions that can make a real difference, as opposed to actions that may feel good or look good."⁴² The world-renowned climate scientist Mike Hulme dismissed it as "gesture politics." A former premier of the Canadian province of Quebec deemed it "inappropriate."⁴³ An ExxonMobil vice-president said it was "out of step with reality." To some student activists, all this attention was good. "It's proving that we're being effective," one explained.⁴⁴

To CHLOE MAXMIN, IT proved that many older people just didn't understand what she was trying to accomplish. Divestment's primary goal was never to have a direct financial impact. It was to force a debate about our economic status quo—and to rebrand it as immoral. But as the movement grew bigger, something unexpected happened. Mainstream investors began to take it seriously. They debated whether a financial system without fossil fuels could still be profitable. One executive described it as "one of the fastest-moving debates I think I've seen in my 30 years in markets." Two months after Stanford divested from coal, the global clean energy research group Bloomberg New Energy Finance released a paper examining if it would be feasible to redirect the nearly $5 trillion invested in fossil fuels into less destructive alternatives. Its conclusion: "not yet." But the paper's author, Nathaniel Bullard, argued that "perception can change this paradigm." He went on: "for all of the tools available for financial analysis, institutional investment remains fundamentally human. People choose portfolios, and people assess risk."[45]

The Swiss financial services giant UBS, which holds over $2 trillion in assets, was coming to a similar realization. Throughout 2014 it held a series of meetings with its clients to determine their views on divestment. In the meetings a consistent pattern emerged. "Interns and young professionals feel very strongly about the need to move away from fossil fuels," UBS explained in a research note. This, coupled with the fact that divestment is primarily a student-led movement, struck the bank as extremely significant. "It is the consumers, voters, and leaders of the next several decades who feel so strongly about fossil fuels," UBS noted. "In our view, this single fact carries more weight than any other data point on the planet for this issue." The bank predicted it could have a profound impact on our global economic system: "We would not necessarily expect a sweeping step change in the immediate future. But we do think the fossil fuel divestment campaign indicates a long-run change."[46]

Meanwhile student activists were doing all they could to change Harvard's position on divestment. By that November they still hadn't succeeded. So seven law students decided to take matters into their own hands. They sued. The $79 million Harvard was estimated to have invested in oil, coal, and gas companies would jeopardize "the ability of students to study and thrive free from the threat of catastrophic climate change," the students argued.[47] Major news outlets covered the lawsuit, including the *New York Times,* ABC News, the *Guardian*, and the *Daily Mail*. And though a judge dismissed the lawsuit that March, law student Joseph Hamilton was undeterred. "We are viewing this as a longer process," he said, "and this is just a first step."[48]

By then, Divest Harvard wasn't only making a moral argument; it was making an increasingly strong economic one. In the final months of 2014, a global oversupply of oil caused the price to plummet from $100 a barrel to less than $50. In 2015 it would fall a further 30 percent. With it went the earnings of the planet's largest oil companies. ExxonMobil, for one, saw its revenues drop by $26 billion. Its rival Chevron lost $14 billion over the same time period. *Fortune* magazine warned of "major disruptions in the oil industry in the near future."[49]

At the same time, clean energy investment soared. A study called Tracking the Energy Revolution found that a record $367 billion was invested in clean energy in 2015, almost 50 percent more than in fossil fuels. "It's clear that clean energy is going mainstream," its authors concluded.[50]

For Chloe and other student activists, the irony was hard to miss. The Harvard administration had argued for years that divesting from fossil fuels would threaten financial returns. But in the spring of 2015 an investment firm called Trillium Asset Management determined that the reverse was true. Plunging oil prices had wiped an estimated $21 million from the school's endowment. "Harvard's continued investment in fossil fuels . . . has diminished the financial strength of the endowment," said Trillium's Matt Patsky. "This staggering potential loss is only half of the story. Opportunity cost is the other half. If Harvard had sold off its fossil fuel holdings, it would have reinvested the proceeds, presumably with broad market exposure."[51]

Instead of distancing itself from fossil fuels, however, Harvard decided to get even closer to them. In April the school appointed Thomas Hollister, a former oil industry and banking executive, to oversee its financial endowment. A spokesperson for the school defended the decision by stating that "Harvard remains deeply committed to confronting climate change." But to the members of Divest Harvard, administration leaders seemed more committed to doing the opposite. "This university continues to uphold the status quo that enables climate change and condones the fossil fuel industry," Chloe told a *Bloomberg* reporter. "This action is inconsistent with the morals that we are taught in the classrooms of this university every day."[52]

Several weeks later she graduated from Harvard. As the frenzy of schoolwork and activism that had defined her last four years there gave way to the long hot days of summer, she reflected on what she had achieved. Despite everything she'd done, Harvard's administration still refused to divest from oil, coal, and gas. Yet at home on her family farm in Maine, that didn't trouble her as much as it could have. When she looked back at a movement that began on twenty-nine campuses in the fall of 2012, then spread around the world to more than four hundred, she was inclined to think that in one important way the Divest Harvard activists had already won. By forcing one of the most prestigious schools in the world into a moral debate on fossil fuels, they'd created "a cultural stigma around business-as-usual," she wrote. "We have won in symbolic ways, and we will soon win when Harvard commits to divestment."[53]

In the meantime, divestment continued to gain global momentum. In late May the University of Oxford announced it would "avoid any future direct investments in coal and oil sands" companies.[54] That was followed in June by the largest divestment action in the movement's history: Norway's parliament approved a plan to sell off over $8 billion of investments in 122 coal companies from its $900 billion sovereign wealth fund. A panel tasked with exploring the feasibility of divestment concluded that "good long-term returns are dependent on sustainable development."[55] Dropping coal simply made financial sense. "The significance of the Norway decision is that, because of their size and reach, this will act as a major signal for other investors to follow," said Carbon Tracker Initiative founder Mark Campanale. "This will certainly create a wave."[56]

It surged even higher in the lead-up to the international climate talks in Paris that December (which we'll be looking at in depth in the next chapter). In early fall the state of California passed legislation requiring its two largest pension funds to sell off investments in coal mining firms. A month later the London School of Economics divested its $140 million endowment from coal and oil sands. Halfway through the climate talks, 350.org calculated the value of these commitments. Since divestment began, institutions worth $3.4 trillion had joined the movement (a number that's now surpassed $5 trillion). Though it represented only a fraction of global economic activity (about 3 percent), 350.org believed "investors are reading the writing on the wall and dramatically shifting capital away from fossil fuels."[57] A new status quo was quickly emerging. The Swiss bank UBS agreed. This was "a social movement with legs," it argued. "Time, youthful energy and stamina are on the side of the fossil fuel divestment campaign."[58]

Chloe was at the Paris climate talks when the $3.4 trillion figure was released. As a key leader of the divestment movement, she should have been overjoyed. But when the climate negotiations ended a week and half later, she found herself alone on a Paris side street at one A.M. with tears in her eyes. All she could think of was how the system that she wanted, one where the survival of her home in Maine was worth as much on a balance sheet as the latest profits, felt so far away. "My heart broke at the thought of all that I love most falling prey to the chaos of . . . climate change," she wrote in the *Nation*.[59] But in that moment she vowed to keep fighting. She wouldn't stop until she lived in a world that cared about more than just financial returns. Only then would her home be safe. "We have to break free from the systems that created this crisis," she explained. "We need something different."

AT THAT MOMENT A new status quo was rapidly emerging. In the three years since people like Chloe Maxmin launched the divestment movement, it had become impossible to ignore. In many ways it was being driven by simple economics. It was the realization that the old way of generating wealth, whereby we extract as many resources from the Earth as possible and ignore the long-term consequences, was inefficient. That lessening humankind's impact on the natural world can also create massive returns. And that the technologies that are enabling this shift, particularly new forms of energy like wind and solar, are becoming less expensive all the time. Not long ago I was invited to a three-day gathering of global elites in New York who are trying to build this new economic system. They believe it can be done with the right combination of market forces and government incentives. By the end of summit, though, I realized it would never succeed without people like Chloe.

The summit was hosted by Bloomberg New Energy Finance, one of the world's top trackers of our transition to a less destructive economy. Over its three days more than 1,033 world leaders, CEOs, investors, academics, activists, journalists, and other delegates from over forty countries gathered in the dimly lit ballrooms of New York's Grand Hyatt hotel. Its A-list included Secretary of Energy Ernest Moniz, General Electric chairman Jeff Immelt, former New York mayor Michael Bloomberg, and European climate commissioner Connie

Hedegaard. The men and women who I saw streaming into the Hyatt were for the most part wealthy and privileged. Some had even made fortunes in fossil fuels. But these weren't your typical one-percenters. For one reason or another, they'd come to the conclusion that our current means of generating wealth was hurtling us toward destruction. While fossil fuel CEOs and Republicans denied that there was a crisis, they wanted to profit from solving it.

If this movement had a guru, it was Bloomberg New Energy Finance chairman Michael Liebreich, who'd made a career out of translating the moral imperative of climate change into language that could make investors salivate. He bounded onto stage to the musical accompaniment of Bruno Mars. "The structure of the future will be different from the past," he said. Wind and solar energy is getting "unthinkably" cheap, he explained. So cheap, in fact, that it may soon provide more economic value to society than fossil fuels. If this persists, Liebreich and many of the delegates were convinced, it will allow us to dismantle the fossil fuel industry's monopoly control over the global economy. In doing so we can create a safer and more prosperous future. Though the specifics of that future are "very difficult to predict," Liebreich said, "what we do know is that it's going to be built by the people in this room."[60]

Everyone in the room seemed to share in common a belief that market forces would be the main driver of this transition. They were aware of the immense political and economic power invested in the fossil fuel industry. They knew that it was worth $5 trillion. They knew that 90 percent of the planet's electricity came from it, as well as the fuel for almost every vehicle, boat, and plane. Yet they believed the fossil fuel industry would ultimately wither and die, because the new economic system they were building was more profitable in the long run. "[It] will require an enormous amount of investment" to shift off oil, coal, and gas, said Maria van der Hoeven, executive director of the International Energy Agency. "But it is precisely that . . . an investment, and one that will pay out."[61]

The financial data seemed to back her up. Ever since Germany and China started pumping out wind turbines and solar panels on a massive commercial scale in the mid-2000s, the price of renewable energy has plummeted. It's now over one hundred times cheaper to produce a solar panel than it was in the 1970s—and it continues to get cheaper all the time. In the United States solar prices have dropped more than 70 percent since 2009. Those market forces, along with generous federal tax credits, have caused new U.S. solar installations to expand tenfold from 2011 to 2015. The solar industry expects that growth to double in 2016. If these trends continue, it's plausible that clean energy by 2050 will provide over 80 percent of America's electricity, a Department of Energy–funded study recently predicted.[62]

But what Liebreich didn't mention was that the fossil fuel industry has fought this new economic system every step of the way. As solar power exploded across America, it ate into the profits of coal- and gas-burning utilities and posed a threat to the entire fossil fuel business model And so some utilities, along with groups funded by the billionaire Koch brothers and Exxon, decided to lead "a fierce, rear-guard resistance at the state level," according to *Rolling Stone*. "Their efforts have darkened green-energy prospects in could-be solar superpowers like Arizona and Nevada."[63] A similar resistance was growing in Europe. After regulators there decided to phase out subsidies for clean energy by 2017, the *Guardian* revealed that "the policy decisions were . . . requested by BP, Shell, Statoil and Total, and by trade associations representing a plethora of oil and gas majors."[64]

The fossil fuel industry is fighting for its survival. Though it may not look like it—especially with Donald Trump in power—it is starting to lose. In Europe that process is further advanced than North America. As wind and solar accelerated over the past decade, Europe's top twenty coal- and gas-burning utilities lost over half a trillion dollars in value. According to the *Economist*, those utilities are now faced with "an existential threat."[65] At the Bloomberg summit, clean energy mogul Jigar Shah told me it was only a matter of time before the same thing happened in the United States. He predicted that within a decade or so "90 percent of all [fossil fuel] utility companies will go out of business." If that happens, it will be because of people like him. "I'm working to destroy [their] business model," Shah told a packed breakout session.

These trends are playing out across the globe. The first fossil fuel to fall victim to them will likely be coal. After surging over the past decade, global coal demand is now in a precipitous free fall, thanks in part to cleaner and cheaper alternatives like wind and solar. Worldwide consumption declined by up to 180 million tons in the first nine months of 2015 alone. Greenpeace deemed it "the largest drop on record."[66] It wasn't long before Wall Street took notice. In September, Goldman Sachs advised its clients that "peak coal is coming sooner than expected." And Moody's Investors Service later estimated that in North America the coal industry's earnings fell 25 percent in 2015.[67] So when Peabody, the largest and oldest U.S. coal company, filed for bankruptcy in 2016, many took it as a sign that the end of coal was near.

But the same market forces that are killing coal may also lead to a dangerous resurgence of it. This is due to the "green paradox": that as coal's demise gets nearer, producers could decide to sell off their reserves as quickly as possible at rock-bottom prices. "It's the difference between having no profits and having some profitability," explained Fergus Green, an energy and climate change researcher at the London School of Economics.[68] Australia, for instance, currently plans to double its coal exports to places like India, which is right now deciding whether to overtake China as the world's largest coal consumer or to develop its economy with renewable energy instead. "Coal or the sun," read a recent *Wired* story. "The power source India chooses may decide the fate of the planet."[69]

Even retired fossil fuel executives now believe the sun makes more financial sense. At the Bloomberg summit, James Rogers, the former CEO and chairman of the coal-burning utility Duke Energy, explained that small-scale clean energy is rapidly becoming more efficient, reliable, and affordable than fossil fuels. In a ballroom full of investors, journalists, world leaders, and CEOs, Rogers mused that if he could reenter the power industry as an idealistic twenty-five-year-old, he'd do it as an "attacker" of the fossil fuel model he used to run. Today's large incumbents "tend to be resistant to anything that attacks their core business," he said. "There's always an instinct to hoping all these new technologies go away. But the reality is, that won't happen."

Rogers and everyone else at the summit had good reason to think so. Beginning in 2013, the world began adding more renewable energy each year than every other coal-, gas-, or oil-based power source combined. "Fossil fuels just lost the race against renewables," read a story in *Bloomberg* at the time. "And there's no going back."[70] Deutsche Bank, for one, predicts that solar energy will soon become cost-competitive with coal and gas power across the entire world. In 2015 investment in clean energy reached a record high of $328.9 billion. All this is starting to finally have an impact on our climate. The International Energy Agency (IEA) has calculated that global emissions have stayed flat for the past two years while the economy has grown. "This is yet another boost to the global fight against climate change," said IEA executive director Fatih Birol.[71]

But the simple fact remains that unless 80 percent of the planet's oil, coal, and gas reserves stay in the ground, none of it will make any difference. That was the warning that McKibben delivered midway through the Bloomberg New Energy Finance summit. "There's no way to finesse the future," he said. The Arctic is melting, sea levels are rising, and oceans are acidifying. "We're producing the beginning of real chaos," he said. Either the Exxons of the world stop extracting fossil fuels immediately, "or the planet burns up." Beside me several delegates shifted uncomfortably in their seats. This was the brutal reality of our economic system: that even as a safe, stable, and prosperous future is taking shape, the status quo still threatens to destroy it.

At that moment I realized that market forces alone can't ensure the survival of my generation. The elites gathered in this Hyatt ballroom lent deep financial credibility to an economic system where protecting the planet was just as important as earning profits. But they couldn't offer the moral urgency needed to defend it. The same market forces that are making this new system economically viable are also making it vulnerable to fossil fuel industry attacks. That is why this new system will never succeed without the shift in generational values expressed by people like Chloe Maxmin. We need them to remind us that a status quo where the profits of a wealthy few put the rest of us in mortal danger isn't just broken—it's immoral.

What the divestment movement proved is when enough young people come together to demand that their survival be taken seriously, our economic leaders are forced to listen. The reason banks like UBS and Morgan Stanley are paying such careful attention to people like Chloe is that they know that the frustration and anger that divestment channels isn't going away. That it's the reason a small youth-led revolt grew into a $5 trillion movement in only a few short years. And that when her generation takes control of society, it will bring this desire for radical change with it. Our system isn't run by market forces, after all. It's run by people. Their values decide its shape and form. It was clear to me as I left the Bloomberg summit that a better world can be attained by changing those values. Indeed, it's the only option we have. And in the next chapter I'll show how that same lesson helped end a thirty-year diplomatic stalemate on climate change.

6

Staying Alive in Paris

THE YOUNG PEOPLE WHO helped end three decades of international stalemate on climate change tend to have the same ambivalence toward national borders as Erlend Knudsen. They were also scared shitless about the future that world leaders were negotiating on their behalf. Erlend saw dystopian versions of the future play out over and over again in the research he did for his Ph.D. in climate science. The twenty-nine-year-old Norwegian knows that unless we make profound changes to our status quo, Greenland's 650,000 square miles of ice sheets—an area nearly the size of Texas—could melt into the ocean and flood every major coastal city on the planet. For a while he assumed that "our politicians or whoever is in charge will understand the importance of the data and act upon it," he said. "But it doesn't really work like that."[1] So in late 2015 he set out on a harrowing journey in the hopes of creating a world where it would.

Erlend grew up around snow and ice. He was born and raised in Sandefjord, a midsize town in the south of Norway known for its proximity to ancient Viking settlements. As a child, he spent pretty much every Sunday on skiing or hiking trips with his family. As he got older, he began to take trips without them. "Those trips got longer and more adventurous," he said. Many of them were spent exploring Arctic regions in Norway's far north—remote places where, as he described it, "there're more polar bears than humans." He loved the Arctic's austere beauty. "The calm and cold white surfaces of the snow and ice attracted me," he once said. Erlend's attraction to the Arctic was metaphysical as well. "It is very hard for humans to survive there," he said. "You really learn how vulnerable as a human being you are in nature."

Erlend was also learning how vulnerable nature is to humans. At the University of Bergen he came to appreciate a troubling fact about climate change's impact on the Arctic. Normally ice and snow reflect the sun, but when that ice and snow melt, the water or land beneath them starts rapidly absorbing heat, which is why the Arctic is warming at rates double the global average. During nine years of academic research, Erlend dealt with so much scary climate change data that he "stopped getting shocked about it," he said. But there was one "jaw-dropping" fact that the young scientist found impossible to accept: after decades of scientific research into the causes and impacts of climate change, world leaders still failed to take the threat seriously: "I was like 'If we already know all this, then why don't we do anything?'"

Climate scientists had been asking that question for nearly as long as Erlend had been alive. Starting in 1988, when the UN General Assembly decided that climate change was a "common concern of mankind," the world's nations met every year to debate what should be done about it. But in those meetings leaders fought to ensure the weakest possible target for their countries rather than humankind's survival. Emissions soared as a result, growing from six billion tons a year in the early 1990s to ten billion tons by the time Erlend completed his Ph.D. in 2015. It was difficult for the young scientist to write research papers that few people ever read about a global threat that grew larger each year. "I knew that I had to reach out in a new way," he realized. "I couldn't just sit behind my desk anymore producing more data."

Around that time a friend and fellow climate scientist, Daniel Price, got in touch. Daniel had felt the same sense of frustration while studying the impact of climate change on Antarctica. "He called me up and said, 'Hey man, I have a crazy idea,'" Erlend recalled. In November 2015, leaders from almost every country in the world would be meeting in Paris to negotiate a treaty capable of limiting global temperature rise to two degrees. Groups such as the International Energy Agency had called it "our last hope" to avoid the worst damages of climate change. Daniel said, "I'm going to bike from New Zealand to Paris. Do you think you want to run from the Arctic?" Erlend told me. "'Right away I was like 'Yeah sure, I'll do it.'"

Both scientists would blog and tweet and Instagram and Facebook each day of their trips in order to bring attention to an obvious but underappreciated fact: that climate change isn't some far-off threat—it's happening right now. And that unless we rapidly change the way we structure our society, it literally threatens human existence. To reach the Paris talks, Daniel planned to cycle 7,500 miles through Australia and then across much of southeastern and central Asia, where changing weather patterns are wreaking havoc on food production. But in some ways Erlend's 1,500-mile run from Norway's rapidly melting Arctic would be harder.

There was no way his knees and joints could survive a four-month pummeling on hard asphalt roads, so he decided to take softer paths through the mountains instead. In doing so, he had to prepare for altitude gains nearly equivalent to climbing Mount Everest seven times, and the bitter cold of Norway's alpine regions. Erlend was pretty sure that his body could handle it. "I've been running long-distance races since I was a teenager," he said. And he had years of experience in extreme Arctic environments. What worried him more was his mind. "The mental part is the hardest," he said. "Every morning I would ask myself, 'Why am I doing this?'"

It wasn't easy to answer. In November leaders from every country in the world would be in Paris for the UN climate talks known as COP21, which, as I would later learn firsthand, were seemingly designed to exclude young people like Erlend. Hunkered deep inside a converted airport hangar guarded by the French military in the Parisian suburbs, those leaders would spend two weeks trying to negotiate an international climate treaty for the year 2020 and beyond. By some measures, the talks were a failure before they even began. Emissions-cutting plans submitted in the lead-up by 187 countries would at best get us to 2.7 degrees of warming by the end of the century, an outcome University of Oxford scientist Ray Pierrehumbert predicted would likely cause "massive disruptions" to the Earth's natural systems.[2]

Not even the official UN target of two degrees could avoid those disruptions. At that level of warming, for instance, Greenland's ice sheets would still melt into the ocean. "Most people are like 'Two degrees, that doesn't sound too bad,'" Erlend says. "But it's an enormous number— it's beyond repair." Pretty much any level of atmospheric warming will disrupt food production, bring more weather disasters, and acidify the oceans. Yet the science produced by researchers like Daniel and Erlend suggests that such impacts can still be managed at 1.5 degrees. Achieving the target would require a "massive acceleration" of emissions cuts from every world nation, Daniel says. We'd have to fully ditch oil, gas, and coal by the year 2050. We'd need to start seeing ourselves as a global whole rather than as members of competing countries.

As Daniel and Erlend began their journeys to the Paris talks that summer, such an outcome appeared very unlikely. Within the negotiations, a target of 1.5 degrees was perceived as a political deal-breaker. No major world power would support it. Their leaders—most of whom were in their forties, fifties, or sixties—saw it as something that would make their countries less competitive with others. But people like twenty-year-old A. J. Alik from the Marshall Islands, a low-lying country in the Pacific Ocean, saw the target in terms of global survival. Without a commitment of 1.5 degrees, rising waters would swallow his home. He knew that some version of this threat awaited his entire generation. "I am here to add my voice to other young people from other parts of the world to tell world leaders not to spoil our future," Alik explained.[3]

If the Paris talks were anything like previous climate negotiations, though, there was little reason to expect that the voices of people like Alik and Erlend and Daniel would actually be heard. But during the talks something unexpected happened—something that flew in the face of conventional wisdom about international politics or even human nature. One by one all the major world powers decided to endorse the only target that could ensure the survival of young people across the planet. Their leaders did so without an immediate short-term payoff. In fact, the benefits might not even be realized in their lifetimes. But the result was that after three decades of diplomatic stalemate, world leaders agreed—at least on paper—to set aside their national differences and fight a shared threat together. And to a large extent this agreement could be traced back to unique global worldview of Erlend's generation.

ERLEND KNUDSEN AND DANIEL Price weren't the only Millennials to make epically long trips to the Paris climate talks. An American, Morgan Curtis, could also lay claim to the title. The inspiration for her 6,200-mile bike trip from Vermont to Paris came to her one night while she was knitting. She had recently graduated with a degree in engineering from Dartmouth College. She was living in a small cabin on the coast of Maine. During the day she taught environmental issues to high school students. At night beside her woodstove, the twenty-three-year-old often reflected on the future—and on climate change's role in shaping it. While at Dartmouth, she had led a campaign like the one we saw in Chapter 5 to divest the school from fossil fuel stocks. She saw climate change as the defining challenge of her Millennial generation. "The two words for me elicit a physical reaction," she would later write. "My heart aches, the pain of the injustice of continued fossil fuel extraction [is] almost overwhelming at times. Yet my soul soars, buoyed by the inspiration, optimism and joy [of] imagining a better future."[4]

Morgan believes that a safer and more stable future requires a radical shift in worldview—one that is already firmly entrenched within her generation. We have to construct "a different story of humanity," she explained, in which people stopped seeing themselves as "separate individuals floating through the earth competing for these scarce resources."[5] Instead we have to conceive of ourselves as small parts of a global whole. Doing so requires us to see past the national borders constraining our identities. Only by expanding our sense of self can we achieve the collective global action necessary to keep Earth from burning up.

At home one night in her cabin, Morgan mulled over all this as she knitted beside her woodstove. Her thoughts turned toward the COP21 talks happening later that year. "I knew that the world's eyes would be turning towards Paris," she said. "This presented a huge opportunity."[6]

By attending the climate talks, Morgan could join people her age from all over the globe to demand that their survival be taken seriously. Together they'd show world leaders that the last century's paradigm of national self-interest had no place in the current one. But if Morgan was going to argue in front of the world that humankind wasn't merely a collection of selfish and competing nations, she wanted to have some evidence. So she decided to get to Paris by biking. She asked a friend her age, Garrett Blad, to join her. They'd follow a six-month route through Canada, Iceland, the U.K., Ireland, Norway, Sweden, and Germany—and meet people fighting for a better future along the way. "I hope to come away from this trip with a better sense of my own place in this world," she said.[7]

Morgan and Garrett also hoped "to bring the stories and lessons from the trip into the [COP21] conference space." She knew it wouldn't be easy. Once she got to Paris, she'd have accreditation to enter the conference as a member of the youth activist group SustainUS. But if past COP meetings were any indication, it was no guarantee that her voice—or any of the stories that she gathered along her journey—would actually be heard. Each year's climate summit was premised on the long-standing theory of selfish human nature that she so badly wanted to change. World leaders arrived with great fanfare, promising to save the planet, and instead they fought each other behind closed doors for national advantage. The talks were conducted in a legalistic UN jargon inaccessible to the public. And for as long as she had lived, their outcome was always the same: a continuation of our destructive status quo.

But every once in a while, a young voice shook things up. At the 2013 climate talks in Durban, South Africa, U.S. negotiator Todd Stern was addressing delegates from 190 nations when twenty-one-year-old Middlebury student Abigail Borah stood up and interrupted him. "I am scared for my future," she said. "We need an urgent path to a fair, ambitious, and legally binding treaty. You must take responsibility to act now, or you will threaten the lives of the youth and the world's most vulnerable. You must set aside partisan politics and let science dictate decisions." Borah received a loud ovation from the room, and as she was led away by security, a reporter chased after her. The reporter asked what group she belonged to. "The United States youth," Borah said, then added, "The United States government does not speak on my behalf."[8]

Todd Stern is a career diplomat who speaks with the slow and precise cadence of a professor. He is not prone to emotional outbursts. And as Borah was led out of the room, he looked slightly uncomfortable. Until that point he had argued that it was not possible for the United States to negotiate a climate treaty until the year 2020. But Borah's global world-view made Stern reconsider his national one. "The vastly experienced bureaucrat later [told] a colleague in an EU delegation he was shaken by the intervention," reported *Climate Home*, a respected tracker of the process. "The anger from someone so young was not something he could forget." The next day Stern made a surprising announcement. Instead of delaying a global climate deal until 2020, the United States was open to negotiating one at the 2015 talks in Paris. *Climate Home* claimed Stern had been "stung into action by a student protester."[9]

The chances of a deal being reached in Paris grew stronger over the next two years. In the fall of 2014 the United States and China, two of the most bitter opponents at previous talks, jointly promised to reduce their emissions. Coal consumption in both countries, and hence world-wide, began to slow. And as we saw in Chapter 5, the business case for renewable energy was getting better all the time. A record $329 billion had been invested in it over the previous year. To all those factors, Morgan Curtis wanted to add one more: the emerging global conscious-ness of her Millennial generation. "Our story is one of interconnected people power," she wrote. "[We are] a generation that has a collective identity beyond borders."[10] Their future depended on an ambitious climate deal in Paris. And they were less attached than their elders to the national divisions that were preventing it.

It isn't hard to understand why. In Chapter 1 we saw how young people like Morgan are more vulnerable to the impacts of climate change than their parents or grandparents. If climate scientists like James Hansen are correct, a Millennial living today could potentially be in his or her late seventies when every coastal city on the planet is flooded. Global warming threatens young people's future more tangibly than that of older generations. "[We] are the first generation to have had very little choice but to accept the many harsh realities of our world," argues David Burstein, the CEO and founder of a youth-led political group called Run for America. "With climate change, we are the generation that will have to live with its impact more than previous generations."[11]

And as we saw in Chapter 3, that acceptance is one reason young people are more global in their worldview than any other age cohort in history. From a formative age, people of Morgan's generation have known that the impacts of climate change will be experienced around the entire planet. They've been forced to accept that the national borders they were born in are no protection against them. That their future is inextricably tied to the future of strangers all over the entire world. And that the decisions made today will determine whether that future is a safe, stable, and prosperous one, or one more like the dystopian scenarios described by scientists like Hansen. For young people, it doesn't make sense to privilege the national interest over the global one, because in the end they're the ones who will suffer the most from doing so.

Which is why, as COP21 began in late November of 2015, there was a noticeable generation gap between the conference's younger delegates and the older world leaders and diplomats tasked with negotiating their future. The months that Morgan Curtis spent biking to Paris had made her especially attuned to it. "This is what the negotiators and UN officials don't understand," she wrote midway through the summit. "Unlike those who have staled in a lifetime of bureaucracy, young people still have the capacity to imagine a just and stable future."[12] They can imagine a political system premised on more than just the national interest. Indeed, it is the only option they have. "When I hear words like 'unreasonable' or 'impractical' or 'impossible,' that's how I feel about a two-degree world," she later said. "That's how my generation feels about the continuation of the status quo."

I CAME TO THE Paris climate talks hoping to take part in history. But by the end of the first day, I came to the same conclusion as many other delegates my age: that the leaders and diplomats gathered in the heavily guarded airport hanger in the suburb of Le Bourget had every intention of deciding the future without me. Day one started as I waited for the laminated ID badge that would grant me entry to the conference. It was hard to wrap my mind around all that was taking place here. Over the next two weeks, negotiators from 196 countries would be meeting to figure out how to keep the atmosphere from frying us. They would be joined by tens of thousands of activists, journalists, celebrities, and CEOs. And on this opening day of the negotiations, world leaders such as Barack Obama, David Cameron, Angela Merkel, Vladimir Putin, and Narendra Modi—150 in total—would also be in attendance. Somehow they'd all fit into a venue no larger than several football fields. I was about to squeeze in.

It was difficult to know how to feel about being in Paris. For months leading up to the summit, there had been a sense of giddy and unrestrained hope. "Those who have consigned the world to its doom should reconsider," *New York* magazine's Jonathan Chait argued in a widely discussed story in September, which pointed to the global trends in clean energy that we discussed in Chapter 5. "The game is not over. And the good guys are starting to win."[13] For my generation, it had been a banner year. In October, we'd toppled Stephen Harper's petrostate in Canada. In November we'd gotten the Keystone XL pipeline rejected by Obama. And in December, as I'd soon learn, we'd convinced institutions worth over $3.4 trillion to divest from fossil fuels.

But all that was overshadowed by the horrific terrorist attacks in Paris that took place just seventeen days before the talks began. My mom phoned me immediately. "Did you see the news? There are 130 people dead," she said. "Is it still safe to go?" At first nobody was sure. Former French president Nicolas Sarkozy said the climate talks should be postponed. The current one, François Hollande, countered that going forward with them would be the "best response" France could offer to the attacks. Yet a dark mood had fallen over Paris. "The streets are less busy," a friend explained after my partner, Kara, and I arrived. "I go out, but I look over my shoulder. I'm afraid of another attack." "It feels like we are at war," another explained. "The whole city is on edge." There were soldiers all over. And one night an uneasy silence fell over us as we walked by the Cosa Nostra Pizzeria and saw bullet holes across its facade.

With ISIS vowing further attacks in retaliation for the French bombing in Syria, the government canceled a massive climate protest that was supposed to draw 200,000 people. "They cannot guarantee safety at the march, and so it will not happen," said the head of Greenpeace France in a statement. "This is a source of huge regret, but we must respect the decision."[14] Yet many activists chose to ignore it. The year 2015 had been the warmest in recorded history—and there was every reason to expect 2016 to be even warmer. On an overcast afternoon the day before the climate talks began, thousands of people marched through central Paris to remind world leaders of their continuing failure to transform the status quo. Police in full riot gear showed up to confront them and fired tear gas into the crowd. More than 280 people were arrested.

All this was on my mind as a cheerful green-vested UN volunteer scanned my ID badge and ushered me into the Le Bourget conference area. As I made my way down a wide open-air corridor that organizers had named the "Champs-Élysées," it was easy to forget there even was an outside world. On my left I passed French bakers pulling steaming loaves of bread out of a wood-fired oven, while to my right several African delegates took photos with selfie sticks. Off in the distance I saw a thirty-foot-tall Eiffel Tower replica lit up in red. All around me, men and women in expensive suits rushed by in various states of stress and fatigue. I decided to go looking for a croissant.

My search took me into the media zone, where thousands of journalists from every major news organization in the world would at some point end up during the talks. A set of stairs led me into an elevated area that peered out over row upon endless row of workstations. It looked like an assembly line for the production of meaning. Back on the ground, and still croissant-less, I bumped into a friend from Canada. This was his fifth COP summit. "It's sort of like Burning Man," he said. "All these people coming out to the middle of nowhere and setting up a temporary city that just goes away in two weeks, except there's a little more clothing and less drugs."

The analogy proved apt in more ways than one. Anyone who's been to a summer festival has at some point experienced the unique form of psychic stress known as FOMO, or the Fear of Missing Out. You know there's too much to take in all at once, but in committing to one activity, you invariably hear later about all the better stuff you could have been doing. After finally finding a croissant, I sat down to check my e-mails. In the hour I'd spent aimlessly walking around the venue, I'd received nearly fifty of them—press releases, mostly, alerting me to events that were now over. Bill Gates had announced an alliance of billionaires to fund financially risky low-carbon technology. Obama and nineteen other world leaders had pledged $20 billion for the same. The Paris talks were just getting started, and already I felt like I was missing out.

It didn't help that my media badge gave me only the most basic level of access to what was going on. I could walk up and down the halls and poke my head into, say, a forum being hosted by International Energy Agency leader Fatih Birol, but the truly A-list stuff was inaccessible. "Are you on the list of preapproved media?" a handler for John Kerry asked when I tried to get into his event. Likewise, I was restricted from entering the zone where any of the actual negotiations took place—and where on this opening day one leader after another, from Putin to Obama to Merkel, made speeches to the world. I watched them on my laptop instead. It was like getting backstage at a concert only to realize that the dressing rooms were off-limits.

So you can imagine my excitement when in the late afternoon I heard that Prime Minister Trudeau would be holding an event open to people like me. By definition no Canadian leader could ever be on the A-list of global elites, but the forty-four-year-old Trudeau was getting close. The UK *Mirror* had recently pondered whether he was "the sexiest politician in the world."[15] And at the APEC summit in November, he and Obama had acted like the best of friends, referring to each other by first names and prompting media to speculate about their budding "bromance." "You should try to get a selfie with him," my mom said before I left for Paris. The problem was I only had ten minutes to find Trudeau's event, and nobody could tell me where it was.

I ran up and down the media zone until finally I stumbled upon a cluster of Canadian premiers and staffers who looked just as lost as I was. Pausing to catch my breath, I struck up a chat with Torrance Coste, a young climate change activist from Vancouver who was part of the Canadian Youth Delegation. Trudeau had pledged $2.65 billion earlier that morning to help developing nations fight and prepare for climate change. Obama had called him "extraordinarily helpful" on the issue.[16] But Torrance wasn't sure. If Canada was to actually do its part in preventing the world from overheating, it would have to go fossil-fuel-free by 2050. That meant no more tar sands. Was this a future Trudeau was prepared to accept? "We've asked him to meet with us youth several times," Torrance said. "We'll see if he follows through."

Inside the press conference, Torrance sat in the front row with other members of the Youth Delegation. They wore large stickers demanding JUSTICE AND CLEAN ENERGY NOW. "It's great to see so many engaged young people at #COP21!" Trudeau later tweeted. But during the event he refused to give details about how Canada would meet any climate target coming out of Paris, other than to say that "we have started putting elements in place for a plan." And when it was over, he was whisked out of the room by security without saying a word to the young people up front. Outside the event Torrance was fuming. "Trudeau spoke for almost half an hour without really saying anything," he said. "What we're getting is a shiny veneer on the same old inaction and foot-dragging that we youth are used to from the government."[17]

Torrance wasn't the only young delegate to feel shut out of the summit. "Negotiations here at the conference happen behind closed doors," Morgan Curtis wrote. "No press, no civil society observers. We cannot see any progress in the averting of suffering."[18] I was finding it difficult to see anything either. After Trudeau's press conference, I took off in a jog across the "Champs-Élysées" to a media room where India's prime minister was about to announce a twenty-nation solar energy alliance. As I arrived, a security guard was closing the door. "Sorry, sir, it's all full," he said. I thought about getting some food. But the line at the nearest cafeteria was insane. And the food—"13 famous French chefs cook for you," it bragged—felt a bit too fancy for me.

So I made my way to the exhibition hall, where a youth-led

discussion on intergenerational equity was about to begin. In contrast to the carefully tailored power suits I'd seen all day among the summit's older delegates, the style here seemed much more relaxed. Half of the fifty or so young people in attendance were wearing jeans. Over in the corner I saw my first man-bun of the climate talks. "We are the first generation to really feel the impacts of climate change," said Irene Garcia, a project manager at the World Future Council, "and possibly the last to avert it." Beside me several people my age nodded in agreement.

But to what avail? I wondered. The talks were just getting started, yet it seemed like all the real decisions were being made in places off-limits to the young people who would be most affected by them. The young Dutch activist and Yale University Ph.D. candidate Ralien Bekkers made the point most strongly. "Are there any negotiators in the room?" she asked during her presentation. I looked from left to right. Not a single young person raised their hand. Bekkers seemed to take it as a confirmation for the point that she raised next. "The future of my children and my children's children is in the hands of old men, and that doesn't feel right to me," she lamented. "Young people are still not taken seriously when it comes to our future."

It was early evening when the panel discussion was over. I decided to call it a day. But before I could reenter the real world, I first had to wait in line with hundreds of other delegates to get through the conference area's single exit. No one was doing much talking. Most people seemed just as tired as me. Day one of the climate talks had been more surreal than I expected. But as I lifted up my ID badge for the green-vested UN volunteer to scan, I kept repeating Ralien Bekkers's words in my head: that here in this airport hanger, the fate of my entire generation was *in the hands of old men*. The future we ultimately had to live in was being negotiated without us.

FEW PLACES IN THE world are more remote than Svalbard. The Norwegian archipelago is separated from Europe by 450 miles of Arctic Ocean. Its vast icefields, mountains, and glaciers are only 640 miles from the North Pole. When Erlend Knudsen was twenty-three, he and five other friends set off on a ten-day ski trip across a wilderness where polar bears outnumber people. It was more of an adventure than they had expected. Right away one of his friends got sick. "There's no roads up there, and so the way you transport yourself is by snowmobiles," Erlend said. "But because there was a big storm he had to be evacuated by helicopter." The group pressed on without him. A few days later they got walloped by another storm. "It was a bit of a tough trip," he said.

Yet by his standards, it was a success: "The Arctic is so harsh. When you are in those surroundings your main concern is just to survive—that's something I really enjoy." At the time of his expedition Erlend was living in Longyearbyen, a town of two thousand people on Svalbard's western coastline. He was there for a semester of research on the high Arctic while he completed a degree in science from the University of Bergen. "You can relate the numbers to something when you live there," he said. In that type of environment, climate change wasn't just an abstract issue. The thick ice that used to cover Svalbard's bays was now often too thin to safely support a snowmobile, and glaciers receded by hundreds of feet a year.

"Seeing those changes really caught my attention," Erlend said. "I decided that I wanted to pursue this further by going into climate research." During the five years it took him to earn a Ph.D., he was exposed to so much alarming data about climate change that he became numb to it. "The new numbers are so shocking all the time that I stopped getting shocked," he said. While researching his master's thesis, for instance, he learned that thousands of glaciers in the Mount Everest region could disappear by the end of the century—and that with them would go a crucial water supply for millions of Asian farmers. "To me what's surprising is how hard it is for people to realize how extremely important it is that we do something about climate change," he explained. "Because it's affecting people around the world right now."

To residents of island nations like Kiribati, in the Pacific Ocean, it was already an existential threat. For years they've watched waves wash farther and farther onto their shores. In 2008 the Association of Small Island States commissioned a scientific study to learn how much temperature rise its members could survive. At two degrees, low-lying nations such as Tuvalu and the Maldives would be swallowed by the ocean. They decided to push for a target of "well below" 1.5 degrees at the 2009 climate change talks in Copenhagen, arguing that anything less would drive them "extinct." But world powers like China saw the target as unrealistic and tried to remove it from the text. The issue became so divisive that at one point it "brought negotiations to a standstill," as the *Telegraph* reported.[19]

The island nations were undeterred. In the aftermath of Copenhagen, they kept pushing for global recognition of their right to survive. They gained an unexpected ally in 2011. "Two degrees is not enough," UN climate chief Christiana Figueres warned. "If we are not headed to 1.5 degrees, we are in big, big trouble."[20] It was a huge symbolic victory—not only for small island nations like Kiribati and the Marshall Islands but for much of the developing world. The havoc wreaked by rising temperatures could "push more than 100 million people back into poverty over the next fifteen years," estimated a 2014 report from the World Bank. "And the poorest regions of the world—Sub-Saharan Africa and South Asia—will be hit the hardest."[21]

That is why forty-three developing countries now belong to a global alliance known as the Climate Vulnerable Forum. Its founders include nations as diverse as Tanzania, the Maldives, and Bangladesh, which are dangerously exposed to the impacts of climate change despite playing relatively little role in causing it. That injustice is amplified by the fact that they have some of the youngest populations in the world. More than half the people living in Tanzania are under seventeen. The median age in the Maldives is twenty-three, and in Bangladesh it's just over twenty-five. For nations like these, climate change could stunt an entire emerging generation. "My eyes go moist . . . because I understand how it feels to see my future and be forced to let it go," the young Maldives climate activist Mohamed Axam Maumoon has said.[22] Now compare that age data to the rich nations with the most historical responsibility for climate change. The U.S. median age is nearly thirty-eight, the UK's is forty, and in Germany and Japan it's over forty-six.

Those global divides are reflected at each year's round of climate
talks. Richer and older nations make most of the decisions, while poorer
and younger ones live with the consequences. "It is the future of the
young people who are alive now—not to mention the generations not
yet born—that is up for negotiation," wrote two young climate activists
from the United States and Brazil.[23] For years the Climate Vulnerable
Forum has tried to change how those negotiations happen. It urges
nations to see themselves not as separate entities fighting for national
gain but as members of a collective global whole doing all it can to keep
civilization alive. "At the moment, every country arrives at climate negotiations seeking to keep their own emissions as high as possible,"
Mohamed Nasheed, the former president of the Maldives, has observed.
"This is the logic of the madhouse, a recipe for collective suicide . . . We
want a global survival pact."[24]

In Norway, Erlend Knudsen was trying to bridge a different sort of
generation gap. The older scientists he worked with while earning his
Ph.D. in climate research produced reams of alarming data about rising
global temperatures. But many of them believed it wasn't their role to
tell members of the general public why they should care. That was for
politicians and activists and journalists. "They think the only work you
have to do is publish papers," Erlend said. Scientists like himself see
things otherwise. "The younger generation of climate researchers thinks
we have to spend more time on outreach," he says. "We have to make
clear the consequences of our research and all the data we produce
because the moral implications of it are just enormous."

Erlend is joined in that opinion by climate scientist Daniel Price,
whom he met while they were both students in Svalbard. They shared a
deep interest in science—"and also adventures," Erlend said. Though
Daniel now lived in New Zealand, where he was completing his Ph.D.
on sea ice in Antarctica, they'd kept in touch periodically throughout
the years. "We both felt like there was a general mismatch of understanding about climate change in public and academia," Erlend said.
Most regular people think of global warming as a vague and distant
threat. But the data produced by scientists like him and Daniel show
that it is already affecting "our biodiversity, our migration patterns, our

economy, the way we live," Erlend says. "It's not just a climate change problem, it's a society problem."

So when Daniel called him up and suggested they travel half the globe by foot and bicycle to reach the Paris climate talks, Erlend quickly agreed. "I was like 'Yeah, sure,'" he said. On their solo journeys they'd be able to meet people already affected by climate change. They made a website called Pole to Paris where they could share those stories with the world. Erlend's motivation was also personal. It's hard to sit at a desk all day worrying about a threat you feel unable on your own to fix. By running more than fifteen hundred miles from Norway's remote Arctic regions to Paris, he hoped to feel part of something bigger than himself or the country he was born in. He wanted to join people his age from all over the world to fight for a better future. Plus it was a good excuse for adventure.

ERLEND BEGAN HIS RUN 286 miles north of the Arctic Circle in the Norwegian town of Tromsø. It was early August when he departed. He hoped to make it to Bergen, in the country's south, by mid-October, a distance of over eleven hundred miles. He'd effectively have to run nearly a marathon every day. Not only that, but for much of the trip he'd be on steep footpaths in the mountains. The amount of altitude he gained would be almost equivalent to climbing Mount Everest seven times. As he left Tromsø, Erlend was carrying about thirty-three pounds of supplies on his back: enough food to last him ten days, a compass, a smartphone, a covered sleeping bag—"so I could survive outdoors," he explained—and a flag of the North Pole. To assuage his parents' concerns, Erlend had a GPS tracker that could be followed online. "They were really worried," he said. "With this tracker they know exactly where I am, and I can signal out if there's something wrong."

Erlend's days followed a steady routine. He started each one by asking himself "Why am I doing this?" It was meant to be motivational. Paris felt so far away, he needed to focus on the present. Maybe he'd be crossing a spectacular mountain pass that day, or giving one of the thirty or so school presentations that he'd scheduled along his route.

Satisfied with his answer, he would begin his run. Typically he'd cover twenty to thirty miles, stopping to eat every hour. "Up in the mountains I'd drink energy powder," he said. He refilled his supplies every few days. "I'd had parcels shipped to different places along the way," he said. Many of his nights were spent in public cabins in Norway's alpine regions. "The wind outside sounds like it's going to lift the whole cabin," he later recalled.[25] Before he fell asleep, he'd ask himself one more question: "What are you thankful for today?"

Some days the answer was obvious. Not long after leaving Tromsø, he met a Sámi woman named Laila Inga. For thousands of years her indigenous ancestors had herded reindeer across northern Europe. Now climate change is making that way of life much harder. Warmer temperatures meant more precipitation, often falling as rain instead of snow in the winter, which caused a hard layer of ice over the lichens and plants that reindeer need to survive. Sámi people like Inga were spending more and more of their income on extra food for the reindeer—without it, many would die of starvation. Inga wondered if the day would come when the Sámi would have to abandon herding altogether. "Everything is changing for her," Erlend said. "She doesn't know what the future will be like for her kids. Her story had a strong impact on me."

It gave him the resolve to keep going. There were days when he definitely needed it. In one particularly remote region of Norway, the snowmelt came later than usual and caused several rivers to swell to the size of lakes. "There were no bridges, so yeah, I had to cross them by walking through them," he said. "It was very tough. You're up to your knees or thighs in water, and it's cold, like crazy cold." He later told the *Guardian* he "was very much on the edge physically and mentally."[26] Yet he faced an even more "extreme situation" only days before finishing the Norway section of his run. "Before I reached Bergen, I had to cross a mountain area," he said. "It was very cold, and a blizzard started. There was no one else around at this time of year, and I was tripping on all the rocks because they were so slippery from all the snow and ice."

Finally, he arrived in Bergen. Erlend needed some rest before he could fly to the U.K. to begin the second part of his run. He was covered in blisters. His legs felt like they were going to fall off. "It takes its toll," he told the *Guardian*. "It was so painful I could almost not walk anymore. It has been a very hard stress on my muscles and ligaments."[27] He did physiotherapy, acupuncture, and electroshock therapy. But with his pain came the elation of completing phase one of his trip. "I was very thankful and happy afterwards," he said. "Those kinds of experiences make you tougher."

As Erlend nursed his legs back to life, a team of people his age continued the run to Paris without him. Starting in Edinburgh, they headed to London. The plan was for Erlend to join them in Cambridge. Meanwhile, Daniel Price was cycling across the Gobi Desert in central China. He was covering about sixty-two miles a day with over eighty pounds of gear. By that point he'd already cycled through Australia, Indonesia, Malaysia, Thailand, and Bangladesh. "It's been absolutely, massively eye opening for me just to appreciate just how many people are at risk [from climate change]," he later said. In Bangladesh, for example, more than 30 million people live less than three feet above sea level, "and a lot of them are already living on the fringe so it is pretty worrying how these communities are going to adapt and how far they can adapt."[28]

In the months leading up to the Paris negotiations, Climate Vulnerable Forum members like Bangladesh were adamant the world commit to a 1.5-degree target. The "two degree goal would not be sufficient," Bangladesh's environment secretary Nurul Quadir said in June. "We need to take forward a 1.5 degree goal."[29] Floods and cyclones were hitting the country more frequently. Changing weather patterns were making it harder to grow food. "We have inherited a world where unchecked levels of carbon emissions have led to unprecedented global warming," wrote the young Bangladeshi activist Sohara Mehroze Shachi. "Youths are not responsible for the climate crisis but will be bearing most of this burden now and in the future."[30]

Each year the world fails to decrease its greenhouse gas emissions, that burden grows larger. Thus far we've warmed the planet by one degree. There's so much pollution in the atmosphere that many climate scientists think it will be impossible to avoid hitting 1.5 degrees. Climate commitments announced by over 180 nations in the lead-up to Paris would at best get us only to 2.7 degrees of warming. Yet some scientists are hopeful that the much safer target of 1.5 degrees can still be met. Humankind would need to fully transition off fossil fuels by 2050 and reduce global emissions to effectively zero. It would be a profound shift—and a radical transformation of our political and economic system. But not an impossible one, explained a 2015 paper in the prestigious scientific journal *Nature Climate Change*. "Early reductions are key," it argued. And those carbon reductions must happen quickly because "the window for achieving [1.5 degrees] is small and rapidly closing."[31]

Erlend Knudsen arrived in Cambridge determined to help keep it open. He was now joined by several other runners from the wider Pole to Paris team. He figured the rest of the trip to Paris would be a breeze compared to Norway. But the day before he reached London, terrorists killed 130 people in the French capital. When Erlend arrived in Brussels a week later, the entire city was in lockdown. "The subway, shops, and schools— everything was closed," he said. He had to cancel a big climate event where he had planned to speak. "At the last minute the police turned it off," he said. As he entered the final stretch of his journey, one event after another was canceled or downscaled.

In the French town of Maubeuge, for instance, only six people came to hear him speak at a venue big enough for fifty. "The question of 'Why am I doing this?' became much harder," he said. "My goals weren't that strong anymore, and I started to get injured more." By the time he reached Paris, he was so exhausted it didn't even really register—"I didn't have any reaction at first." But as he sprinted to reach the Eiffel Tower, the enormity of his fifteen-hundred-mile journey from the Arctic began to sink in. "I saw Daniel coming towards me, and I allowed myself to think that, yes, I'm finally here," he said. Erlend and Daniel embraced, and "it was a wonderful feeling."

For Morgan Curtis, her elation of finally making it to COP21 was short-lived. On day one of the climate talks, she and Garrett Blad cycled from central Paris out to the northern suburb of Le Bourget, where more than 150 world leaders would be meeting. They'd spent the last five months biking through eleven different countries to get there. But when the two of them arrived at the venue, they couldn't find a bike rack. "We were handed off from a security officer to a policeman to UN officials asking where we can park our bikes," Morgan said. "And they were like 'Oh, we don't know, we didn't think about that.'" She saw it as symbolic of a much wider disconnect: "I was shocked by how detached the [COP21 venue] felt from the realities of climate change."

All along her 6,200-mile bike journey from Vermont, she'd been confronted by those realities. But she and Garrett had found plenty of reasons to hope they could be overcome. They met cancer survivors fighting against a tar sands pipeline in New Brunswick. Norwegians pushing their leaders to transition away from oil. A human geographer studying racial injustice and climate change in Sweden. "These are people who've devoted their whole self to building a better world," Morgan said. At a Conference of Youth in Paris before the climate talks began, she met many more like them. "Young people came from all over the world to share their stories," she recalled. "You could really feel like we were all one community and moving in one direction together."

But that feeling was harder to sustain behind the security perimeter of Le Bourget. During the opening day of the talks, leaders from thirty climate-vulnerable nations gave a press conference to demand that global temperature rise be limited to 1.5 degrees. To do so would require a complete phase-out of fossil fuels before 2050. It was the "strongest call to date for full decarbonization of the world economy," the Climate Vulnerable Forum claimed.[32] It was also a pledge for the survival of young and future generations. "My daughter is seven days, twenty hours old," the Philippine youth commissioner Dingdong Dantes told the room. "I really should not have left her, or her mother, but I am here, speaking for her."[33] Few reporters were there to listen. The press event was drowned out by coverage of more powerful leaders like Obama, Modi, and Putin.

Youth leaders tried again the next day. They held a press conference demanding the world eliminate all its emissions by 2050. This time only four journalists came. "Not everyone's voice is heard at the UN,"

Morgan Curtis observed.[34] In frustration, she and dozens of other young delegates planned a protest through the hallways of Le Bourget. They stayed up late the night before painting banners and drafting press releases. On the day of the event, one hundred youth from around the world gathered outside the media zone. Each of them had painted a zero around their right eye to symbolize a future without oil, coal and gas. "I was ten years old when I realized the urgency of climate action," twenty-year-old Nepalese delegate Sagar Aryal told a growing crowd of reporters. "I began to see the mountains melt, glacial lakes flood, and the human impacts of the climate crisis."[35]

After the event, Morgan and some others left the COP21 venue to join a group of unaccredited young people outside. As bystanders stopped to watch, they chanted the unofficial slogan for climate vulnerable nations: "One point five to stay alive." The group got larger and louder as it marched toward the publicly accessible Green Zone of the climate talks. A line of police officers blocked them from getting in. "We were soon surrounded," Morgan wrote. "The police closed up the banners and summoned representatives from the UN secretariat." And with that, the protest was officially over. "Our voices as youth are structurally silenced," she lamented. "When nothing we can do will ever be enough, what can we do?"[36]

But as the climate talks reached their midway point, some young voices seemed to be heard. "I see your tweets, youth," said Canada's environment minister Catherine McKenna at a stakeholder meeting. "I wish I had more time to meet with all of you." Shortly afterward UN secretary general Ban Ki-moon urged a gathering of ministers and negotiators to remember just whose future they were deciding. "Today I speak for . . . all the young people of the world," he said. Ki-moon told the story of a Kiribati islander whose home was threatened by rising seas, and of young Norwegians like Erlend Knudsen watching their Arctic rapidly melt. "I say to you," he told the gathering, "that your decisions can lay the foundation for a sustainable future."[37]

Tony de Brum didn't need reminding. As foreign minister for the Marshall Islands, he was at COP21 fighting for the survival of his country. "Anything over two degrees is a death warrant for us," he told

NPR. "It means the islands go under." The seventy-year-old de Brum, a grandfather of ten, was accompanied throughout the climate talks by eighteen-year-old Marshall Islander Selina Leem, who had seen sea levels rise since she was a child. "Last year there was an inundation, and for the first time the water actually washed into our house," she said.[38] De Brum was in Paris for people like her. "We should never forget that the future we are fighting for belongs to our youth," he tweeted at one point. "I'm fighting for them."

Few could have guessed that de Brum would be one of the most influential voices at COP21. But for months he'd been readying a plan to ensure that whatever deal was reached in Paris protected his grandchildren's future. During an earlier Paris climate meeting in July, he invited fourteen ministers for informal drinks. The group included representatives from Tuvalu, Norway, Angola, Mexico, the EU, and Colombia. He proposed they form an unofficial coalition that could pressure other world leaders to set a long-term target of 1.5 degrees and establish a five-year review cycle for achieving it. The ministers met in secret at least twice more before COP21. De Brum became the coalition's de facto leader. A Colombian minister later called him the "brilliant mind behind it."[39]

Yet in the first week of Paris negotiations, the coalition struggled to get its demands heard. Both China and India were wary of a 1.5-degree target, and neither was keen on reviewing global climate progress every five years. As the talks entered their final week, de Brum and several other ministers met with Todd Stern, the lead U.S. negotiator, at a Michelin-starred restaurant called Droaunt—"famous for its fine wines, foie gras and oysters," as *Climate Home* reported—in central Paris. "Over dinner there was general agreement that the Paris climate talks were not going as many had hoped," the site wrote. "There were growing fears they were heading toward a weak deal." But by the end of the meal, Stern agreed to join the push for a much stronger one.[40]

This is "exactly what we need right now," he later explained.[41] By joining de Brum and the other ministers in their effort to get 1.5 degrees accepted by all the world's nations, Stern was effectively embracing the global worldview that Abigail Borah, the young student protester, had confronted him with back in Durban. He was formally agreeing with de Brum's conviction that the "future belongs to our youth." And he was looking beyond America's immediate self-interest to make sure that future was safe, stable, and prosperous. Out at the conference hall, young people like Morgan Curtis were struggling to have their voices heard. But inside the restaurant that night, a major world power finally recognized their uniquely global worldview. Stern suggested they rename de Brum's group the "high ambition coalition." And with U.S. support, it started burning "rocket fuel," Stern said. Within days of their meeting, more than one hundred countries had joined.

There was resistance at first within the negotiations. With the dead-line for an agreement fast approaching, China dismissed the whole thing as a "performance." But that stance was harder to hold after Brazil, an ally of China and India at the climate talks, joined the coali-tion. Its decision to break ranks was a game changer that deprived China and India of the political cover to fight the 1.5-degree target, the EU climate commissioner Miguel Arias Cañete later said.[42] And as COP21 came to a close, China and India joined 196 nations in prom-ising to keep global temperature rise "well below" two degrees and "to pursue efforts" to hit 1.5 degrees. De Brum was first to address the assembly hall after the treaty became official. "We have grabbed this once-in-a-generation opportunity to lay the foundation for a peaceful, prosperous, and safe planet for our children," he said. Then he gave the mic to Selina Leem. "This agreement should be the turning point in our story," the eighteen-year-old Marshall Islander said; "a turning point for all of us."[43]

PRETTY MUCH THE LAST thing you want when you're struggling to get over a nasty flu is a face full of tear gas. Which is why I was more than a bit apprehensive to attend an illegal public protest on the final day of the Paris climate talks. What had started as a nagging sore throat several days earlier soon became one of the most brutal viruses I'd ever caught. In retrospect, it wasn't all that surprising. I'd been in a constant state of stress at Le Bourget, working twelve-hour days, drinking wine late into the night with friends, and subsisting on little more than cheese and bread. In fact, the sickness that such a routine will produce was so common at each year's COP it even had a snappy nickname: "the COP cold." For a feverish couple of days, I'd been deep in its clutches.

But the journalist in me demanded I get out of bed to see what would happen when thousands of people blocked one of the avenues leading to the Arc de Triomphe—and in doing so flouted a ban on protests imposed by the French government after the previous month's terrorist attacks. "Bring wipes for eyes and water in case of tear gas," a friend who'd been in contact with protest organizers advised. "And maybe a scarf or something for over your mouth." Out on the street, I bought a small pomegranate juice and walked somewhat groggily toward the Métro station at République. On the train I was joined by ten or so people my age who were clearly headed to the protest. They were carrying a large red banner that read SYSTEM CHANGE, NOT CLIMATE CHANGE.

At each Métro stop, more and more young protesters squeezed on. No climate treaty had yet been announced, but it seemed almost certain that by the end of the day 196 nations would sign off on a historic promise to eliminate all the world's emissions by midcentury or later. If they acted on that promise, it would provide humankind a chance— albeit a slim one—of meeting the 1.5-degree target. The treaty could send "a powerful signal to global markets, hastening the transition away from fossil fuels and to a clean energy economy," as the *Guardian* described it. It had potential to be a crucial step toward a less scary future for my generation. So how come thousands of people were risking a face full of tear gas to protest it?

Many of them didn't trust the promises of political leaders. There was an obvious gap, after all, between the goals of the treaty and what had been proposed to achieve them. Climate plans submitted in the lead-up to Paris by 186 nations would at best keep the temperature rise to 2.7 degrees. At worst they'd cause 3.5 degrees of warming, "which is more or less the same as hell," argued Bill McKibben. Then there was the fact the deal made no specific mention of ending fossil fuels, was vague on how much financial assistance richer countries should give to poorer ones, and contained targets that for the most part weren't legally binding. "So if you want to be cynical about the Paris agreement, there's plenty of reason," McKibben said.[44]

But as I got off the train and walked with dozens of people my age toward the Arc de Triomphe, I didn't get the sense that cynicism was what brought them here. For all its shortcomings, the deal that was about to be signed in Paris had already provided something crucially important to the world—even to the deal's harshest critics. Once signed, it would create a whole new framework for understanding the future. Around the world, people my age now had something very tangible to fight for. "Here's the thing," McKibben continued. "The world's governments have now announced their intentions." They'd promised 1.5 degrees. "Even if we harbor suspicions that they didn't quite mean those words, we will use them again and again. We'll assume they really want action. And we'll demand they provide it. Game on."[45]

I'll admit that my game day face looked a little apprehensive as I turned onto Avenue d'Iéna and saw a line of police in full riot gear— shoulder armor, shields, batons, and masks—blocking my path. Above us a helicopter did figure eights in the sky. When one of the young protesters I was with tried to walk past the police as if it were the most casual thing in the world, he was quickly redirected. "*Non, monsieur*," said an officer who looked like an NFL linebacker. But clearly there was a demonstration going on behind the police line. It was impossible not to hear it: a cacophonous mixture of bongo drumming, air horns, sing-along chanting, and megaphones.

So I ducked down a side street, walked parallel to the protest, and came out right into the center of it. After spending the last two weeks at Le Bourget, it was like entering a parallel universe. Up in the sterile conference halls of COP21, all the signage had been crisp, flawless, and corporate. Down here on the streets it was messy and handmade and idiosyncratic—like the large banner urging people to UNFUCK THE SYSTEM. Instead of blue and yellow ID badges, everyone here was wearing red to symbolize the "red line" of 1.5 degrees that our world can't safely cross. I couldn't see a single suit and tie. The fashion was freaky-casual, a mixed bag of jeans, face paint, polar bear costumes, hoodies, sneakers, tattoos, and yes, some hemp sweaters. And the food was a lot simpler than at Le Bourget. No French pastry chefs, just a guy with dreads stirring a cauldron of vegan curry.

This definitely wasn't the type of scene I was used to frequenting. I'm not moved to dance by anarchist brass bands. I don't join singalongs. I'll probably never wear a pink wig and suspenders out in public. But after all the countless hours I'd spent listening to UN delegates drone on about "ratcheting mechanisms" and "intended nationally determined contributions," the energy and the passion and the humor all around me were a catharsis. It felt important to be here. "I don't consider myself a climate activist," a Londoner my age, Jon Wiltshire, explained at one point. "But look at the science. If we don't make major changes, we could be locked into three degrees. If civil society doesn't keep the pressure on, then who will?"

Part of that pressure came from reminding the world again and again what is being destroyed right now by our addiction to oil, coal, and gas. "Our people are suffering," a Lakota woman from North Dakota, Eaglewoman, told a crowd of people at the far end of Avenue d'Iéna. "They're killing our people on the front lines of fossil fuel extraction." It was equally important to remind ourselves that we are all in this thing together. That our identities should transcend the national borders we were born in. I looked around. There was a dude playing the tuba. A South Pacific woman urging people to defend "Mother Earth." Students taking selfies on their iPhones. A French intellectual silently smoking his pipe. If we truly wanted a less destructive status quo, there could be no more us versus them. We had to discard the notion that we're all isolated members of competing countries.

To Chloe Maxmin, the young divestment leader we met in Chapter 5, the climate talks had proven there could be no more "human as usual" for her generation. "The agreement represents the best of what humans have learned to do over centuries: to use the political arts of compromise and negotiation to overcome conflict and unite disparate groups," she wrote. "But here's the thing: COP21 demonstrates that even the best of what humans have learned to do is not enough. The climate emergency demands something else, something that lies beyond the known threshold of human political arts." She went on: "We need to find new ways of being in which we are all on the same side, supporting one another as we confront the limits of physics."[46]

Today's demonstration seemed to provide a tiny glimpse of what such a world could look like. "Climate change is a global issue, and we need to fight together," Ekaterine Mghebrishvili explained when I asked why she had traveled more than a thousand miles from the Republic of Georgia to be here. We looked out across the crowd in front of us: people from every part of the world singing and dancing and laughing. "It's important to feel this energy," the young woman went on, taking a drag on her cigarette. "When it's all over, we need to take all this energy back to our countries, because the climate is not just a problem for Paris, it's everyone's problem." She put out her smoke and disappeared into the crowd.

I figured it was time to go. Though it seemed unlikely anyone was going to be teargassed today, I didn't want to push my luck. As I got onto the Métro that would take me back to the echinacea pills and herbal tea and other flu supplies I'd stockpiled at my Airbnb in central Paris, I reflected on the events of the last two weeks with equal parts hope and cynicism. You could make a compelling case for both. The year 2015, after all, had been the warmest in history. "It was much, much warmer than 2014, and 2014 itself was a record," the NASA climate scientist Gavin Schmidt later explained.[47] Yet the year also contained some surprisingly positive news. Global greenhouse gas emissions were set to decline 0.6 percent in 2015 after growing an average of 2.4 percent a year over the last decade. This was achieved "despite strong growth in gross domestic product worldwide," noted the Stanford scientist Rob Jackson.[48]

There is no guarantee this trend will persist. Much of it depends on declining coal consumption in China. If India's appetite for coal simply takes place, and Donald Trump makes good on his promise to revive America's ailing coal industry, it's difficult to imagine how we can limit temperature rise to the 1.5 degrees necessary to ensure a stable future on this planet. "We are a long way from where we need to be," Erlend and Daniel wrote in a Facebook post on the final day of COP21. "But today for the first time the world has said we will try and get there together." The agreement that 186 leaders had signed was an historic renunciation of a status quo that for three decades of climate talks had put national interests over the global one. "From here it is up to all of us to ensure that the pledge the global community has made on this day is met," they wrote.

On that final point, Morgan Curtis wholeheartedly agreed. To her, the deal signed on the final day of COP21 was "woefully inadequate." It lacked any binding protections for the world's youngest and poorest citizens. "The text has no mention of fossil fuels," she observed. "And we know who is to blame: the corporate interests that have ensured it doesn't."[49] But she didn't the consider COP21 to have been a waste of time at all. The two weeks she'd spent with young people from more than 196 different nations had given her a clearer sense of her place in the world. She now saw her own actions as part of a global struggle: "Taking that step to be a part of something bigger than yourself only gives you a sense of meaning."

And that, perhaps, was the most important realization to be had in Paris. People my age had grown up in a world that encouraged them to distrust others. We were told that life is a competition, and that whoever doesn't put self-interest first will lose out to someone who does. Our attempts to imagine a better future were deemed unfeasible and naïve. But in Paris thousands of young people found a collective voice in their demand for 1.5 degrees. And thanks to allies like de Brum, the moral urgency of the demand, and the global worldview it represented, it became impossible to ignore. The Métro was pulling into République. As I left the station, I no longer felt as powerless as I had on day one. Paris held out the possibility of a new status quo, a better way of structuring our world, a new way of being. And in the next chapter, I'll investigate the young Silicon Valley movement claiming to put that promise into action.

7

The True Meaning of Sharing

ELLE-MÁIJÁ TAILFEATHERS HAS A radically different perspective on our society than the Silicon Valley leaders who claim to take inspiration from her culture. It comes from the fact that she's spent much of her adult life making films about the injustices inflicted upon indigenous people. Her work is rooted in her experience as a young indigenous woman with deep ancestral ties to two continents. She thinks that those ties—and all planetary life—are threatened by the prevailing political and economic structures of our modern world. Elle-Máijá's films are a radical challenge to them. "I feel like I have a responsibility to do something that effects positive change," she says.[1] In that regard she has an unlikely potential ally. A leader of the new youth-driven economic model arising from Silicon Valley claims to be directly influenced by indigenous cultures. He says he desires the same future as Elle-Máijá: one that's fairer, safer, and less destructive to the planet. Yet the $335 billion industry he's helping to create has been accused of building the opposite.

To understand how Elle-Máijá sees the world, you have go to back in time to before she was even born. "My parents have this sort of mythical love story," Elle-Máijá once told CBC Radio.[2] They first met in 1981 at a global conference for indigenous peoples in Australia. Elle-Máijá's mom is a Blackfoot woman from the Blood Reserve in southern Alberta, who at the time was involved in a national social movement to get indigenous rights recognized in the Canadian constitution. Her dad, meanwhile, is Sámi, the Indigenous peoples of northern Europe. For years he'd been fighting a hydroelectric dam that was going to flood territory that Sámi people had lived on for thousands of years. At the conference they noticed each other immediately. In Elle-Máijá's telling, it was love at first sight. The very first thing her dad said to her mom was "You're going to be my wife." "And yeah," she said. "The rest is kind of history."

Elle-Máijá Tailfeathers was born in Canada about four years later. She spent her childhood bouncing from one country to the next. Her first move was to Norway, where she lived until she was about five or six. Then her mother decided to enroll in medical school, so the family moved to North Dakota. By then her parents' mythical love story had begun to unravel. The family eventually moved back to Canada. But when Elle-Máijá was sixteen, her parents divorced. Her dad left for Norway. "From around my early teens to the point they split up, I'd say things were really difficult between them," she told CBC. "And it was largely because of my father's battle with mental health issues."[3]

Elle-Máijá moved on her own to Vancouver in her early twenties. She ended up taking a degree in First Nations and gender studies at the University of British Columbia. She often reflected on the many layers of her identity. She was young and culturally aware. She lived in a global city on the Pacific Ocean and listened to experimental music and saw herself as an artist and a feminist and an intellectual. Unlike many of her peers, though, she also felt deep ancestral ties to indigenous territory in Alberta and Norway. "I often feel torn between the two places, because that's where my ancestors are from," she said. "But then there's also the other side of the coin where if it wasn't for globalization I wouldn't exist."

Elle-Máijá's sense of history extends far beyond the time horizon of most North Americans. She sees the arrival of European settlers in the late 1400s—and the centuries of disease, warfare, displacement, and discriminatory policies that they inflicted upon indigenous peoples—as the beginning of a colonial conquest that North America's first peoples are still struggling to overcome. As Elle-Máijá got older, she felt the impacts firsthand. She learned why most fossil fuel extraction takes place on or near indigenous lands, why aboriginal women are up to three to five times more likely to experience violence than their white peers, and why indigenous communities remain among the most politically and economically marginalized in North America. Those experiences led her to conclude that "our people are subject to colonial violence every day." She added, "There's this trauma my generation of indigenous people inherently carry . . . The question is how do you move forward?"

Rarely do white North Americans acknowledge that trauma or the existence of a vibrant culture that persists despite it. But by some accounts, the worldview of indigenous people is at the heart of a new economic model emerging rapidly from Silicon Valley: the sharing economy. Unlikely as it might seem, one of the leading architects of that economy, which could be worth $335 billion by 2025, has directly credited the indigenous people he met during a summer exchange on the Pine Ridge Indian Reservation in South Dakota for inspiring his business model. "Their sense of community, of connection to each other and to their land, made me feel more happy and alive than I've ever felt before," John Zimmer told *Wired* in 2014. "We now have the opportunity to use technology to help us get there."[4]

Zimmer is the Millennial co-founder and president of Lyft, a rideshare company that at the time of this writing was valued at $5.5 billion. Along with others such as Uber and Airbnb, Lyft is at the forefront of an economic shift where people pay for access to things—cars, power tools, vacation homes—instead of owning them. Zimmer argues he is helping to "build community, save people money, and reduce our impact on the environment."[5] The politics of this shift are often difficult to figure out. "Is it Republican, Democrat, Libertarian, or Green?" asked one observer.[6] But people like Zimmer have captured the imagination of influential thinkers. The author, futurist, and European Union adviser Jeremy Rifkin, for one, thinks the sharing economy is leading us to "a new understanding of ecological sustainability"—one that potentially "provides the means to lift hundreds of millions of human beings out of abject poverty."[7]

Yet the sharing economy has inspired an equally fervent backlash. Companies such as Lyft have been accused of trampling unions, underpaying workers, undermining competitors, and making bold environmental claims that amount to little more than greenwashing. All of which has led *Salon*'s Andrew Leonard to dismiss the sharing economy as "the living, breathing essence of unrestrained capitalism."[8] He is not alone in thinking people like Zimmer are more interested in profits than in the values of indigenous culture. "For-profit 'sharing' represents by far the fastest-growing source of un- and under-regulated commercial activity in the country," the *New Republic*'s Noam Scheiber wrote in 2014. "Calling it the modern equivalent of an ancient tribal custom is a rather ingenious rationale for keeping it that way."[9]

Tech companies are well known for making grandiose claims about their social impact. But in this case the rhetoric and reality are difficult to sort out. For the past six years Harvard sociology professor Juliet Schor has studied the sharing economy. Funded by the MacArthur Foundation, her team has conducted more than 150 interviews on it. She concluded that "the reality is more complex" than its boosters and detractors often acknowledge. "Will the sector evolve in line with its stated progressive, green, and utopian goals, or will it devolve into business as usual?" Schor wrote midway through the project. "It is too early for definitive answers to these questions, but important to ask them."[10]

If it's true the sharing economy somehow reflects the worldview of indigenous peoples, or is even aspiring to, then Elle-Máijá Tailfeathers has questions of her own. She agrees that indigenous peoples have a vital role to play in building a safer and more equitable future on this planet. "Our people have been in our communities since time immemorial and have never lost our connection to the land," she said. "I do think there's a lot to be learned from indigenous people." Yet they're dealing with the worst impacts of climate change—and of the political and economic system causing it. (The battle to protect Standing Rock Indian Reservation's water from an oil pipeline is one example.) A new business model that purports to draw inspiration from indigenous cultures can't ignore that. For its claims to be credible, it "can't just take bits and pieces of Indigenous knowledge systems," she said. "It has to acknowledge the fact that so many of our people are in basic survival mode." And more importantly, it has to do something about it. The new generation of tech leaders to which Zimmer belongs actually has to challenge the status quo instead of perpetuating it.

JOHN ZIMMER WAS NOT the first young Silicon Valley leader to cite the influence of North America's native peoples. That title likely belongs to Mark Zuckerberg. Over dinner one night, the technology journalist David Kirkpatrick asked Zuckerberg to explain Facebook's impact on society. Their exchange was described in Kirkpatrick's 2010 book *The Facebook Effect*. "Are you familiar with the concept of a gift economy?" Zuckerberg said. "I'll contribute something and give it to someone, and then out of obligation or generosity that person will give something back to me. The whole culture works on this framework of mutual giving."[11] Zuckerberg was referring to an ancient gift-giving ceremony called the potlatch, which has been practiced for thousands of years by the Kwakwaka'wakw peoples of British Columbia's southwestern coast.

In those ceremonies, which were accompanied by feasts and dancing, tribal leaders would give away blankets and flour and other supplies to the community. Important guests sometimes received silver bracelets or boats. The potlatch provided a way for indigenous communities to create alliances, redistribute riches, undermine rivals, and of course, flaunt their wealth. "The potlatch has always been the structure that enables people in our society to work together," Kwakwaka'wakw hereditary chief Bill Cranmer explained to the *New York Times*.[12] To Zuckerberg, Facebook is the foundation of a digital potlatch. "When there's more openness, with everyone being able to express their opinion very quickly, more of the economy starts to operate like a gift economy," he told Kirkpatrick.[13] Such a shift presents a chance to restructure our society, since "a more transparent world creates a better-governed world and a fairer world."

Zimmer is the same age as Zuckerberg. And the sharing economy he's creating is in some ways an extension of the Facebook founder's thesis. It rests on the conviction that the more people become connected through digital technology, the more open and trusting they'll be. This enables behavior that previous generations would have considered unthinkable: inviting strangers into your car, giving them the keys to your house, letting them borrow your power tools. Zimmer's contribution to this so-called sharing economy is the ride-share company Lyft, which lets anyone with a smartphone access a large fleet of ad hoc taxis driven by regular people. In a 2013 interview with *Fast Company*, Zimmer explained that Lyft's business model was inspired by his visit many years earlier to the poorest native reservation in the United States.

Zimmer grew up in the small New York suburb of Greenwich, Connecticut, a place where "people were focused on the corporate ladder, or success being defined by material objects." In high school he spent a summer volunteering at Pine Ridge in South Dakota, where the average household income of its eighteen thousand Lakota inhabitants is $3,500. Only 40 percent have electricity and running water. Unemployment is 90 percent. Yet Zimmer was struck by a worldview that felt more meaningful to him than the one he grew up with. "By going to see this other culture, where they valued connection to the people and the nature around them, it really impacted me," he said. "I felt more alive and more happy than I'd ever felt."

It changed how he saw his hometown in Connecticut. "I came back, and I was like 'What's wrong with everyone here? Why is everyone so focused on these material things? How come they don't know about all these other people who are living in poverty?'" he said. "I think everyone, myself included prior to that trip, just didn't have that perspective." He claims that spending time at Pine Ridge changed the direction of his life. "I decided that whatever I did long term, I wanted to help build real community, genuine people-to-people connection, because I felt like we were all starved for it," he says. "If there was a way to use entreprencurship to help [get there] . . . that would be my dream."[14]

Zimmer moved to Silicon Valley in 2008 with a friend, Logan Green. Four years later they launched Lyft. At first it offered little more than a niche service in San Francisco. But by the end of 2012 the company had done forty thousand rides. Two years later the number was 2.2 million, and by early 2016 the company was valued at $5.5 billion. Its main competitor, Uber, has grown even faster, from a $49 million valuation in

2012 to more than $50 billion in 2015. Meanwhile, Airbnb's valuation rose by over $23 billion over the same period. "Over the past few years, the sharing economy has matured from a fringe movement into a legitimate economic force," wrote *Wired* in a 2014 cover story.[15] PricewaterhouseCoopers has predicted that by 2025 the sector's annual revenue could total more than $335 billion.[16]

Much of that explosive growth is being driven by people between the ages of 18 and 34. A 2015 survey by Zogby Analytics suggests that more than half of Americans in this age group have patronized Uber, Lyft, Airbnb, or some other sharing economy company. And about 54 percent of those young respondents "say they expect ride and home sharing services to become even more popular in the coming years."[17] Further research, from Vision Critical, has suggested that 18-to-34-year-old Internet users are "more interested" in the sharing economy than older generations. Across North America, members of this demographic are 12 percent more likely to book a hotel room through Airbnb, 11 percent more likely to hail a ride from Lyft, and 13 percent more likely to buy homemade gifts through Etsy.[18]

They're also more likely to work in the sharing economy. A 2015 report on the sector conducted by several Silicon Valley investors and Stanford graduates found that 68 percent of its workforce was composed of people between the ages of 18 and 34, a significant statistic considering that Millennials represent just one-third of all U.S. workers. "It makes sense that workers in the sharing economy . . . would be different from the population at large," read an analysis of the report by *Bloomberg Business*. "They're probably younger, for instance, since people who have grown up with mobile phones attached to their arms are going to be more comfortable with apps and the cloud."[19] And, apparently, with letting strangers into their cars and homes.

"There is now an established comfort level that has opened the door for sharing personal property via the Internet that may have seemed unfathomable even a few short years ago," said John Burbank, a vice-president at the global research company Nielsen. In 2014 Nielsen helped lead what is likely the largest survey ever done on the sharing economy: an online poll of over thirty thousand people in sixty countries. What it found was consistent with research in North America. Around the world, 35 percent of 21-to-34-year-old respondents were likely to participate in some form of sharing, as opposed to 7 percent of Baby Boomers.[20] "Millennials are the foot soldiers driving this change," argues sharing economy researcher and author Rachel Botsman.[21]

The sharing economy seems to share this generation's political independence. As we saw in Chapter 4, years of polling suggest that many young people lean progressive but are detached from partisan allegiances. They're more interested in improving society than in supporting a particular party. The politics of the sharing economy, and of Silicon Valley at large, reflect this ambivalence. Though Democrats like Hillary Clinton have promised to "crack down" on labor violations at companies like Lyft,[22] the sector's progressive positions on issues such as climate change don't fit the worldview of Republicans—Jeb Bush, for instance—who've vocally not supported it. If the sharing economy has a political perspective, it may be "that active communities can solve problems better than either the market or the government alone," explained Gregory Ferenstein on *Vox*. "In essence, it is a civil society completely oriented toward innovation."[23]

For some indigenous people, the irony of all this is hard to miss. "The 'new' sharing economy isn't actually all that new," Anthony Caole, a former tribal administrator from the Alaskan village of Kwinhagak, wrote in 2013. "The Native community has already been practicing this economy for centuries," as in the Kwakwaka'wakw potlatch ceremony, where "the status of any given family was raised not by who had the most resources, but by who distributed the most." But the European missionaries of the nineteenth century saw the potlatch as wasteful and blasphemous, an obstacle to the assimilation of Native peoples. It was outlawed in Canada in 1874. After more than a century, however, says Caole, "the Western business world is finally catching on and seeing the wisdom and value of sharing."[24]

That business world also sees "sharing" as the source of massive revenues. Which has made it hard to assess whether companies like Lyft or Facebook are actually embracing indigenous values. Canadian aboriginal leader Wab Kinew believes that people like Zuckerberg are sincere in their appreciation of a culture and history that isn't theirs. "New ways of thinking about [global] problems should come from indigenous people," the musician, journalist, and university administrator observed in 2015. Facebook "has generated a huge amount of wealth, and some part of their innovation was created by learning about aboriginal culture." Yet that on its own doesn't undo centuries of systemic oppression and violence. "Our traditions are rich and complex and have a tremendous depth that I don't think is really appreciated," Kinew says.[25]

MY INTEREST IN THE sharing economy was initially piqued by a prescient Canadian businessperson, Nicholas Parker. Back in 2002, he came to the conclusion that clean energy and other environmental innovations would someday be worth a ton of money. At first few businesspeople took his concept of "cleantech" (short for clean technology) seriously as an investment. But by 2014 the industry was worth $170 billion. So I paid close attention when Parker spoke at a climate change forum I was attending one rainy morning in Vancouver. A desire by people my age for a less destructive economic system, and a faith in technology to achieve it, he said, is blowing open our options on global warming: "We're seeing a very exciting shift."[26]

Parker was specifically referring to the sharing economy. For more than four decades we've been urged over and over again to consume less of the planet's resources. The problem is that our society isn't set up to offer very good alternatives. If you live in Los Angeles, for instance, you'll likely find it difficult to get to work, buy groceries, or meet friends without a vehicle. Ride-share companies like Lyft and Uber promised to address the problem by giving you access to a large network of vehicles, meaning that you had less need to actually own one yourself. And the vehicles that are on the road are potentially more efficient: they're moving people all the time rather than sitting idle in a garage. The same can apply to many consumer goods: appliances, clothing, electronics—whatever you can think of. It has the potential to transform how we relate to each other and the natural world. Parker, for one, thinks it is rewriting the rules of mass consumption. And unlike most progress on climate change, the sharing economy doesn't require much in the way of new legislation. It can be scaled up rapidly outside our political system.

That is the theory anyway. Not long after seeing Parker speak, I traveled to San Francisco to find out more about the reality. My arrival in California coincided with a drought so bad that Governor Jerry Brown had recently called it "epochal." Almost two-thirds of the state was facing crisis-level dryness. And across the interior, dust clouds caused a tenfold rise in infections from the toxic *Coccidioides immitis* fungus. Yet in the cozy Airbnb room I'd rented in San Francisco's Excelsior, a working-class district that had yet to feel the rapid gentrification of more northern areas like the Mission, only a small bathroom Post-it Note hinted at crisis: "Every drop counts."

On my first morning in town, I went to meet Joey Marquart in a French café on the edge of Chinatown. He blamed Lyft for his arrival ten minutes late. "The driver was new," he apologized with a laugh. "So we got a little lost." Marquart works for the global public relations firm Edelman. He is vice-president of cleantech, meaning that his job is to keep track of emerging technology trends that have the potential to create a more sustainable economy. These days he is watching the sharing economy closely. "This concept of sharing and not necessarily owning something is powerful," he said. "It has incredible ramifications." I asked for an example. By using Airbnb instead of a hotel, he said, you require far less power and water during your stay. "It's using technology to consume things differently." I recalled that Post-it Note: "Every drop counts."[27]

A 2014 study conducted by the Cleantech Group appears to back Marquart up. It found that Airbnb users in North America consumed 63 less energy than typical hotel guests. "That's enough energy to power 19,000 homes for one year," the company said. The reduction in water usage was equal to conserving 270 Olympic swimming pools. Yet an analysis of the study in Corporate Knights noted, "It's tough to know for sure if there's substance to these claims. The study was not scientifically rigorous and was based on many assumptions."[28] After saying goodbye to Marquart, I couldn't help feeling underwhelmed. Even if the

Airbnb study's figures were accurate, the implications of saving a little bit of water and energy were hardly revolutionary.

But as I walked down California Street toward downtown, I mulled over another sharing economy claim. "You could actually start seeing the majority of millennials in the next five years or so saying there's no reason I should get a car," predicts Zimmer from Lyft. "The car used to be the symbol of American freedom. [Now having] a car is like owning a $9,000 ball and chain, because you have $9,000 in expenses on your car every year."[29] In the short time I'd been in San Francisco, I'd already seen several cars with his company's pink mustache on their grills (a design feature that Lyft has since scrapped). Yet the impact of the sharing economy on car ownership—especially among people my age— is hotly debated.

An *Atlantic* story from 2012, "The Cheapest Generation," reported that young adults were buying fewer cars than older age groups, driving fewer miles, and often not even getting a license. "The fact is, today's young people simply don't drive like their predecessors did," it reported. A key factor, the article suggested, are the smartphones that "allow us all to have access, just when we need it, to the things we used to have to buy and hold."[30] In other words: the sharing economy. But three or so years later one of the article's authors, Derek Thompson, retracted some of his predictions. Research from J.D. Power & Associates had found that Millennials were overtaking Gen Xers as buyers of new cars. "Now that I have seen the data, I can report: Millennial demand for cars is growing quickly," Thompson wrote. "New vehicle sales among young people are rising as if drawn on a ruler."[31]

Millennials appeared to be no different than earlier generations in their love of vehicles. Indeed, that same year MTV released a poll suggesting 75 percent of 18-to-34-year-olds think cars are more impor- tant to their way of life than social media. "It seems like the death of the automobile has been prematurely reported," wrote *Autoblog*'s Greg Migliore.[32] But a deeper analysis of the data showed a more complex view. Though it is true young people bought more cars than Gen Xers in 2014—27 percent of sales compared to about 23 percent—that was simply because there are more Millennials in the world than Gen Xers.

If you adjust the data to reflect this reality, as *City Observatory*'s Joe Cortwright did in 2015, it would seem "the typical [Millennial] is actually 29 percent less likely to buy a car than the previous generation."[33] The real question to be asking is why.

There's no single explanation. Many people my age are still struggling to recover from the recession. They have massive student debts and are waiting longer to start families. At the same time, many 18-to-34-year-olds are choosing to live in densely populated urban areas, so they have less need to own a car. The smartphone in their pockets provides them with access to ride-share services like Uber and Lyft that simply didn't exist a generation earlier. "It is too soon to assess the impact of these new services on driving among young people," read a study from the U.S. Public Interest Research Group, "but the potential exists for these new services to provide an affordable alternative model of mobility to private car ownership."[34]

Just how viable that model is was studied in 2015 by researchers with Deloitte University Press. They looked at a range of sharing economy programs across the United States before estimating that "carsharing could reduce nationwide vehicle ownership by nearly 2.1 million."[35] That's an impressive number but not earth-shattering. Yet automakers are following the trend closely. "Surveys we do tell us young buyers are less interested in owning cars," a Toyota marketer told Reuters. "They either don't have the financial leeway or they're substituting car ownership with ride-sharing or car-hailing services like Uber."[36] After General Motors invested $500 million in Lyft, its president predicted that the auto industry will likely "change more in the next five years than it has in the last 50."[37]

By now I was amid the glass and steel towers of San Francisco's financial district. I was still struggling to see the "exciting shift" that Parker had breathlessly described back in Vancouver. The sharing economy definitely had potential to reduce cars on the road and save some energy in hotels, but as far as posing a serious challenge to our status quo, I wasn't so sure. Which is why when I arrived at the art deco Hearst Building on the eastern edge of downtown, I was hoping that Ted Howard could help me see the bigger picture. Howard is the climate change program manager at the San Francisco branch of Agrion, a global network of business leaders and thinkers convinced that our economic system should value the planet's long-term survival as much as short-term profits.

Up on the fifth floor, he greeted me with a firm handshake. "The income gap is the biggest it's been in decades," he said. "There's lots of alienation. People feel a mental and physical need to connect with others." To him, companies like Lyft and Airbnb were tapping into that desire. But he saw them as the first stages of a much larger societal shift.

I asked if he could describe where it was all heading.

He started with vehicles. Let's assume, he said, that they all go electric in the next few decades. The energy to charge them will need to come from somewhere. In an ideal world, rooftop solar panels would provide it. If all the panels on a city block were hooked up to something called a microgrid, people could generate clean energy, share it, charge up their electric cars, and share those as well. In such a future, he said, "you really can help yourself as well as helping others."[38]

The biggest impacts of that system, assuming you could replicate it globally, might be felt in the developing world. In nations such as India, argues Jeremy Rifkin, the futurist and EU adviser, some version of the sharing economy could "provide the means to lift hundreds of millions of human beings out of abject poverty and into a sustainable quality of life."[39] His argument starts from the fact that smartphones and Internet connectivity are becoming more common across the planet—even in its poorest villages. Add to it the plunging costs of clean energy we saw in Chapter 5. If you put a microgrid in every village, and solar panels on all its rooftops, you could give clean and cheap power to most of the planet. "This process represents the democratization of energy in the world's poorest communities," Rifkin says.

Solar energy that's shared house to house would make villages independent of huge centralized coal power plants. And smartphones that are charged by that energy could give village farmers the digital tools to deliver small-scale crop yields directly to consumers in larger urban areas. "Energy and environmental costs are further reduced," Rifkin argues, "by eliminating plastic packaging and the long-haul transport of produce." I have to admit this all sounds a bit too good to be true. But Ted Howard assured me that if such a future is possible, the path toward it will be laid by people like me, since "this whole sharing economy is definitely a mentality that's coming up with the current generation more than older generations."

I left the Hearst Building with my mind spinning. It was obvious that our society needed a dramatic overhaul if we had any hope of achieving the 1.5-degree target that world leaders agreed to at the Paris climate talks. But the real question to me was whether the political and economic revolution described by people like Rifkin had anything to do with the pink-mustached Lyft cars that kept driving past me as I waited for a bus back to my Airbnb in the Excelsior. What was the sharing economy exactly? Could a vision of the future built around local farming and decentralized clean energy also include the "sharing" strategies now being adopted by Walmart, BMW, and Home Depot? And when really you got down to it, who was truly benefitting from all this "sharing"?

LIKE MANY PEOPLE HER age, Elle-Máijá Tailfeathers finds it difficult to think about the future. Not the future as conceived as coming days or months or even years, but that hazy point off on life's horizon where climate change turns human survival into a question mark. "I get really stressed out," she explained during an interview on the podcast Silent X. "I have these climate-change-related anxiety attacks where I just think about everything that's happening, and it's just so overwhelming." Her perspective as an indigenous woman makes it even more so. To Elle-Máijá, it isn't enough to simply conserve energy, drive less, and shift to solar power. No solution to climate change will be adequate unless it also addresses centuries of systemic violence inflicted upon indigenous peoples. And as she got older, she learned firsthand how destructive and pervasive that violence still is.

Amid all the turbulence of her adolescence and early adulthood—the constant moves, her dad's depression, her parents' divorce, the complexities that came from exploring her indigenous identity—Elle-Máijá's

love for the Blood Reserve has stayed constant. Its 545 square miles on
Alberta's southern plains are home to forests of spruce and aspen and
balsam fir. Out on the open prairie, the sky feels infinite. "It's one of the
most beautiful places on Earth," she says. Her Kanai First Nation
ancestors lived there for more than six thousand years. Her mom and
grandparents and lots of other relatives still do. When she goes back to
visit, she feels a sense of belonging lacking in Vancouver. "When you
live in the city sometimes you have these moments of trying to find a
deeper meaning to your existence," she says. "But when I'm home I
never question that." The land to her is much more than dirt and grass
and air. "It has a spirit to it, it has life."

More than half that land was signed away to an oil and gas company
from Arkansas in the fall of 2010. The $50 million deal was negotiated
by the Blood Tribe chief and council. It gave Murphy Oil, along with a
small company known as Bowood Energy, the legal authority to drill
hundreds of oil and gas wells on Blood Reserve territory over five years.
The companies would inject millions of gallons of water and toxic
chemicals into the Earth at high pressure. This process of "fracking"
shatters rock formations and lets oil and gas be sucked to the surface.
It releases up to 80 percent more carbon emissions than regular drilling.
In places like Dimock, Pennsylvania, fracking has made tap water
undrinkable.[40] Yet the Blood Tribe leaders saw those damages as a
necessary economic trade-off for a community with nearly 80 percent
unemployment and a median income $50,000 lower than the rest of
Alberta.[41]

These types of deals have become more common as a fracking boom
has taken off across North America. Its epicenter is in North Dakota,
which by 2012 had turned from a sleepy farming state into America's
second largest producer of oil. The boom came so fast that many North
Dakota tribes suddenly found themselves sitting on land worth billions
of dollars. Yet the lowball deals hastily offered by oil companies
allegedly cheated several of those tribes out of $1 billion and left them
with a huge ecological cleanup. "The rush to get access to oil on tribal
lands is part of the oil industry's larger push to secure drilling rights
across the United States," read a *ProPublica* analysis.[42] A similar story

was playing out downstream from Canada's tar sands, where the Athabasca Chipewyan First Nation earned modest profits from oil contracts but struggled with a rare form of bile duct cancer and river water that they could no longer safely consume.

Many Blood Reserve members weren't even aware their chief and council had been negotiating with Murphy Oil. "I found out about it when somebody shared this little article from a Calgary business magazine on Facebook," Elle-Máijá recalled. At the time she didn't know what fracking was. But once she learned about its heavy impact, "the idea of it happening next to my grandparents' home or mother's home just really hit me quite hard," she said. "I was like 'how is this even legal?'" It got even worse once an eight-hundred-dollar check arrived in the mailbox of Elle-Máijá's mom. Blood leaders mailed them out to the reserve's ten thousand members in late December. "I don't know too many people who would turn down eight hundred dollars ten days before Christmas," she said. "Especially if you're broke, if you're a single mom living on social assistance."

Elle-Máijá didn't know what to do with her check. "At first I was like 'No, I don't want to take this money—it's blood money,'" she said. "But obviously I was a broke student at the time." For weeks she struggled with the dilemma. "I was going to bed and staying awake for hours thinking about it," she said. "I felt so morally conflicted." But one night as she was tossing she came to a realization. She was taking a film course as part of her undergraduate degree at the University of British Columbia. "I had access to all this amazing film gear," she said. And many of her indigenous friends worked in the film industry. So she decided to use her eight-hundred dollar check to finance a short experimental film protesting the fracking deal on her ancestral homeland. She called it *Bloodland*.

It's not an easy film to watch. *Bloodland* begins with a wide shot of a forest clearing in British Columbia's Fraser Valley. It's winter, and the trees are barren. A ghostly Earth woman played by Elle-Máijá rises from the clearing. The film cuts to a close-up of dark feet walking toward her. Suddenly two men grab the Earth woman. After another quick cut, she's being tied down to a table by two oil workers. As she writhes and screams, they aim a hand drill into her stomach. A series of quick edits switch between shots of her belly being ripped open and an oil drill entering the grassy Earth. A close-up of the Earth woman's last heartbeats fills the screen. Dark blood pours off the table. Then the credits roll: "This film made generously possible by Murphy Oil, Bowood Energy, Kainai Resources Inc, Blood Tribe Chief and Council." The irony was impossible to miss. "I credited the oil companies and our chief and council for funding the film," Elle-Máijá explained. "It was a way to subvert what they were doing."

AMONG THE HIGHEST HONORS an indigenous warrior on North America's Great Plains could earn during wartime was counting coup. It was bestowed on those brave enough to charge up to an enemy and strike them with a long, and sometimes elaborately decorated, shaft known as a coup stick. But *counting coup* also has a less literal meaning. "In Blackfoot culture we have these counting coup moments where you have an opportunity to kind of stick it to your enemy but do so in a very clever way, sometimes a really funny way," Elle-Máijá Tailfeathers explains. In some ways *Bloodland* fits the criteria. "I guess I would equate it to that," she says. "It was kind of a moment of counting coup against the oil and gas companies and our chief and council."

For Elle-Máijá, making *Bloodland* was an awakening. Its imagery is both symbolic and literal. She'd wanted to express a feeling that was difficult to put into words—that Murphy Oil was threatening not only her homeland but her identity. "There's this idea of looking at the land as our mother—it's the thing that birthed us all," she explained. "When I'm on it, I have the same sort of comfort and familiarity that I have with my mother." For the next nine months she did all she could to keep Murphy Oil far away. She joined a small but vocal resistance comprised of Blood Reserve members unhappy with the fracking deal and social justice groups like the Council of Canadians. They mailed letters to every level of government. They sent out press releases. They tried to schedule meetings with the Blood Tribe chief and council. They reached out directly to Murphy Oil.

But none of it seemed to make a difference. Murphy Oil and Bowood Energy arrived in the summer of 2011 with big industrial machinery. Semi-trucks blasted down the Blood Reserve's back roads. Exploration teams surveyed its windswept fields for oil and gas deposits. Elle-Máijá visited her mom in September. She felt defeated. "We'd basically reached our wit's end because we'd done everything we could to stop this fracking from starting, and it felt like it was all done in vain," she said. But one morning her mom woke her up with some news. Two well-known older activists in the community—Cathy Brewer and Lois Frank—were planning to block a road that Murphy Oil needed to access fracking sites. She decided to join them. "I was like 'Oh shit, I'd better go,'" Elle-Máijá said. "It was motivated by love for the land and our people."

She and her brother and a couple friends arrived to find the two women standing in the middle of the only road leading to the site. Lois Frank was holding a handmade sign that read, "Notice, we only have one homeland—protecting what is sacred to Kanai." Elle-Máijá decided to stay. The protest, which throughout the day grew to about 15 people, demanded that Blood Tribe leaders put a halt to the fracking until all of the reserve's members had been properly consulted about its implications. Until then they'd prevent any workers from getting onto the well site. "That also meant not letting the people on the site off," Elle-Máijá said. But the atmosphere was calm and respectful and peaceful. "We even fed the security guard dinner," she said.

Elle-Máijá filmed a few videos of the blockade on a friend's iPhone and posted them on YouTube. Some reporters started calling. Then the tribal police showed up. By that point it was nighttime. "We were given an ultimatum," she claimed. Either the protesters moved into the ditch and stopped blocking the road or they would all be arrested. Lois said, "Well, I'm not going anywhere." Any hesitation that Elle-Máijá felt about being arrested disappeared: "I wasn't about to let this older woman with diabetes go to jail by herself, so I decided that I wasn't going anywhere either." Another woman, Jill Crop Eared Wolf, also stayed put. The scene was eerily reminiscent of *Bloodland*: three indigenous women being hauled away by males in uniform.

They were thrown into a tribal holding cell, "this concrete room with a steel door and a steel toilet with a camera pointed at it," Elle-Máijá later recalled. There was no toilet paper. After ten hours Elle-Máijá and Lois Frank and Jill Crop Eared Wolf were released. It was now morning. "I was nowhere prepared for the media onslaught that happened after that," Elle-Máijá said. For two weeks she did one media interview after another. The actual court process took six months. All three women were charged with intimidation, assigned community service, and given probation officers. In Elle-Máijá's recollection her officer was slightly confused. "I don't really know why you're here," the officer said, "because what you did was an act of community service." The officer wrote a letter on Elle-Máijá's behalf, and the charges were cleared.

By then Elle-Máijá had entered a deep depression. Her arrest and imprisonment were "one of the most dehumanizing moments of my life." But the bigger injustice was the one inflicted on her ancestral homeland. In the months that followed her arrest, two small fracking-related earthquakes were recorded on the Blood Reserve. "The distinct fume of sour gas is seemingly always present near the well sites," she later wrote. On a windy day that December, several schoolchildren became physically ill after breathing in fumes.[43] Elle-Máijá had trouble sleeping. "I had anxiety attacks thinking about what was happening to the land and water." She was quick to anger. She felt alienated from herself and her community. "I mean, how is it that three unarmed women from our tribe were arrested by tribal police for protecting the land, the one thing that is most sacred to us?" she wondered.

It took her a long time to answer that question. What she eventually came to realize was that her arrest was a microcosm of centuries of violence toward indigenous peoples—and particularly women. From the first days of European contact onward, governments passed policies to control and disenfranchise Native communities. In Canada, for instance, the 1876 Indian Act was created with the express aim of eradicating First Nations culture. When an indigenous woman married a nonindigenous man, the woman lost her right to live on her reserve or have any say over her lands. "There is this long and ongoing history of indigenous women being dispossessed of their land and resources and rights to practice their culture," Elle-Máijá said.

Centuries of policies like that helped turn indigenous women into one of the most marginalized groups in North America. They're especially vulnerable to violence. At least eighteen hundred aboriginal women have been murdered or gone missing in Canada since 1980—a "human rights crisis," according to Amnesty International. Overall they're 2.5 to 3 times more likely to experience violence than the general North America population.[44] It gets even worse near oil and gas extraction sites. The male workers flooding into North Dakota have caused a surge of violence. Visitors to one women's shelter, for instance, grew 300 percent from 2009 to 2011. "In North Dakota's oil boomtowns," *Pacific Standard* reported in 2015, "rape, sex trafficking, and domestic violence rates are spiking, with American Indian women suffering the most."[45]

Elle-Máijá came to see her arrest as part of this wider legacy of violence. "I finally understand why that experience left me feeling so dark," she said. Out at the Blood Reserve well site, she and Lois Frank and Jill Crop Eared Wolf had stood up against an economic and political system that in many ways is rigged against indigenous peoples. In her arrest she'd felt the full weight of its power. "All of this fits under this whole system of colonialism," she said during a forum on indigenous people and climate change at New York's New School. "Industry doesn't give a damn about indigenous people because it's always been about taking our land and taking our resources and erasing us as a people." Her eyes were flashing. "But we're still here."[46]

THE SAME YEAR ELLE-MÁIJÁ was arrested, her dad shared some troubling news about his past. Her relationship with him had been strained for years, starting around the time her mom began medical school. Elle-Máijá was eight years old. She remembers that her mom was really busy and that her dad started to act strange and depressed. By the time Elle-Máijá was sixteen, their marriage had fallen apart. Her dad left the family to move to Norway. "Growing up, there was definitely resentment toward my father," Elle-Máijá says, but she's done her best to move on—"[I] just closed that door to the past." She didn't know at the time that her dad had been "going through one of the darkest moments of his life."

It was the result of trauma that he'd buried for decades. From the late nineteenth century until the 1960s, governments in Canada, Norway, Finland, and Sweden attempted to assimilate generations of indigenous children by forcibly enrolling them in a system of boarding schools. Ripped from homes and families, these children were taught to renounce their indigenous culture. Living conditions were terrible. Beatings were common. More than four thousand Native children died within Canada's system, and untold numbers were sexually abused. Elle-Máijá was twenty-five years old when her dad first told her about the years he'd spent in a Sámi boarding school. "He was taken away from home and forced to speak Norwegian," she explained. "He was subject to a lot of awful things." Suddenly the events of her childhood became far less confusing.

"It was like I had this awakening," Elle-Máijá said. "Once I learned about this part of his past, everything made sense." It wasn't enough for her to make the leap from understanding to forgiveness—"that's one of the hardest things," she told CBC.[47] But in the fall of 2013 she got a new opportunity to try. By then Elle-Máijá had devoted herself to film-making. She'd made short features about sexual assault (*A Red Girl's Reasoning*), indigenous art and cultural appropriation (*Colonial Gaze Sámi Artists' Collective*), and the legacy of trauma and disability (*Hurry Up, You Stupid Cripple*). That October the ImagineNative Film Festival commissioned her to make a documentary short about her family. "[It] was like a year's worth of counseling," she later told CBC.

Elle-Máijá decided to call the film *Bihttoš*, a Sámi word that "essentially means 'rebel,'" she explained. It's also her father's nickname. She set out to map her family's history in painstaking emotional detail. In doing so she learned all she could about her father's time in the Sámi boarding school; the "mythical" love story of her parents' meeting in Australia; and its unraveling when years of trauma could no longer be repressed. "The film was a challenge for me to unpack all this baggage I'd been carrying my whole life," she said. By the time it was finished, she was able to begin healing her relationship with her dad. "If anything, the film helped me find forgiveness," she said, and not only for her: "My parents at the time weren't speaking. Now they've reconciled and they're friends again."

Bihttoš wasn't the end of the story. In some ways it was only the beginning. "We talk about this concept of intergenerational trauma . . . and I knew what it meant," she said. "But I had never fully understood how it really worked within a family." *Bihttoš* gave her an intensely personal education. It made her confront uncomfortable questions about her emotional health. "The boarding school system has so deeply impacted me even though I'm one or two generations removed," she said. Elle-Máijá would like to have children someday, but she sometimes worries that she'll perpetuate a cycle of pain that started before she was born. "How do you become a parent," she said, "without enacting that same sort of damage and trauma that you carry yourself?" Not to mention exposing that child to the potential chaos of climate change.

These types of injustices are rarely acknowledged in mainstream North American culture. And when they are, the results are often mixed. Many indigenous people were thrilled, for instance, that the Hollywood director Alejandro Iñárritu chose to use actual First Nations actors and languages in his historical epic *The Revenant*—and that its star Leonardo DiCaprio used his Best Actor win at the Golden Globes to call for the protection of "indigenous lands from corporate interests."[48] Yet despite the film's careful attention to period details about Native culture, very few of its indigenous characters have speaking roles, many end up dead, and the most prominent female lead is raped by one white man and then saved by another. "The only time we're not helpless in these movies is when we're dead and a white man is learning a lesson from beyond our graves," wrote indigenous author and attorney Gyasi Ross on the *Huffington Post*. "It seems almost a conspiracy how little control, autonomy or voice Native people were given over our own lives in this movie."[49]

Similar critiques were made about a controversial 2012 music video for the British electronic duo Chase & Status, which was filmed on location in Montana's Blackfeet Indian Reservation by the young white director Josh Cole. The video tells the story of a Native teenager who robs a store at gunpoint, overdoses on hard drugs, and wanders his community as a spirit before dropping dead in a snowy field. Cole explained that his goal was to "tell Europe how difficult it is for Native Americans." Elle-Máijá wrote a long and detailed response on her blog: "Josh, I think it is fair to assume that you had good intentions in making this video, but good intentions are not enough. It is critical to fully understand the history of a complex community like Browning [in the Blackfeet Reservation] before swooping in with your cameras and your outsider perspective."

To her, the biggest problem with Cole's video wasn't that it depicted the struggles of a marginalized community, or even that it was directed by a white male. It was that it seemed to offer no historical explanation for the poverty and addiction and violence that are a reality for many indigenous people. "This narrative ignores the complexities of colonialism," she wrote. "It's a narrative about the dying race, the vanishing Indian. And who does this narrative blame for the death of a people? The Indians themselves." She went on: "In telling the story this way, you ignore the reasons behind this young man's addiction and his community's struggles."[50]

Elle-Máijá knows that the only way we can learn—and break free—from the legacy of systemic violence is by first acknowledging it. That's especially true when it comes to climate change. "So often it's indigenous people who are on the frontlines," Elle-Máijá said. "They're feeling firsthand the damage that oil and gas [extraction] can enact on the human body." But in places like the Blood Reserve and Standing Rock, they're also leading many of the battles against it. The members of that resistance see climate change as the result of a political and economic system that's been rigged against them for centuries. Yet their culture is older than that system. "Our people have been in our communities since time immemorial," she said. So in their view the system can be changed. They don't see it as inevitable.

Which is what makes the comments of Silicon Valley leaders like John Zimmer and Mark Zuckerberg so difficult to evaluate. Zimmer spent only a few weeks on the Pine Ridge Reservation, and Zuckerberg spent no time at all among British Columbia's Native peoples. Yet both have claimed to feel a dislike for our current political and economic system—and a conviction that indigenous cultures can help change it. Elle-Máijá shares that conviction. She thinks our planet would be in much better shape if our political and economic leaders listened more seriously to indigenous people. "We have a deep knowledge of the land," she said. "I do think there's a lot to be learned." Yet she's unsure whether "privileged white males like Zimmer and Zuckerberg" are actually interested in doing so: "You can't just pilot into a community for a few days or weeks, then take what you want from it and go back to your life."

ON MY LAST DAY in San Francisco, my search for a healthy breakfast took me to Café St. Jorge, one of the many new coffee shops, cocktail bars, and boutiques catering to the young and affluent tech workers pouring into the Bernal Heights neighborhood. The café's website promised me "organic, natural and traditional fare" served in a setting "that is real and unpretentious." I ordered the chia bowl with house-made almond milk, cinnamon, fresh fruit, nuts, seeds, and agave. With a coffee, my small breakfast came to a cool fifteen dollars—a traveling splurge, I reassured myself after blanching at the bill. The café was packed with stylish, upwardly mobile people typing away on their MacBooks. I ate fast and decided to go for a walk. I had to do some thinking.

I took the side streets north until I crossed Cesar Chavez Street and entered San Francisco's Mission District. Here the subtle push of gentrification that I'd seen in Bernal Heights seemed to have gone into overdrive. Soon I was passing by organic ice cream shops, luxury condos, carefully curated clothing stores, and inexplicably, a "mid-western style perogi bar." Working-class Latino families that had called this area home for generations were being forced out by rents as high as $3,800 for a one-bedroom apartment. "It's a war zone here," one longtime resident and empanada shop owner told the *New York Times*.[51] The Brookings Institution found that income inequality was growing faster in San Francisco than anywhere else in the United States.

I couldn't help but wonder what Zimmer thought of all this. He'd not too long ago scorned his hometown in Connecticut as a place where success is "defined by material objects." In the same interview he'd held up the Pine Ridge reservation—"where they valued connection to the people and the nature around them"—as the inspiration for his ride-share company now valued at $5.5 billion.[52] At the very least, his intentions seemed genuine. In December 2015 Lyft drivers from around the United States traveled to Pine Ridge to help out with an annual Christmas Toy Drive. "I'm lucky to work for a company that supports . . . efforts to empower the Lakota people," said Laura Copeland, the leader of Lyft's driver communications department.[53] But it was obvious that a little bit of charity couldn't fix centuries of systemic violence.

When I was in San Francisco, however, a thirty-nine-year-old coder from Pine Ridge, Payu Harris, claimed to have created a technology that could. Inspired by cryptocurrencies such as Bitcoin, which are operated independently from any centralized bank, Harris teamed up with programmer AnonymousPirate to develop a version specifically for indigenous people. He called it MazaCoin. "I think cryptocurrencies could be the new buffalo," he would later claim. "Once, it was everything for our survival. We used it for food, for clothes, for everything. It was our economy. I think MazaCoin could serve the same purpose."[54] His rationale was that if the Oglala Sioux leadership adopted MazaCoin as Pine Ridge's official currency, then it could keep more of the $220 million that comes through the reservation's casino and other venues inside the actual community.

Harris's plan was always a long shot for a tribe whose members earn on average under $3,000 per year. But MazaCoin caught the attention of Nick Spanos, director of the New York Bitcoin Center. Two weeks after MazaCoin launched, he flew Harris into the city. Investors were pouring billions of dollars into new digital currencies. Much like the sharing economy at large, the technology was seen as a tool that could take away power from large corporate and political entities, give it back to regular people, and rewrite the rules of mass consumption. MazaCoin fit that narrative perfectly. Harris claims that his digital currency would make Pine Ridge less reliant on the whims of federal U.S. funding. "If we're going to be a sovereign nation, we have to act like it," he argues. "Will this currency help rebuild the country and the economy? I believe that it will." By the end of his trip to New York, MazaCoin was valued at $6.8 million.[55]

My thoughts were interrupted by the noisy construction outside Mission Dolores Park, a palm-tree-fringed oasis on the border between the Mission and the historic gay district, the Castro. Mark Zuckerberg and his wife had recently deployed "Pharoah-like construction teams" to turn a building looking onto the park into "a massive $10-million, six-bedroom palace," in the words of *Salon* founder David Talbot.[56] I swear that I caught a glimpse of Zuckerberg as I strolled by. In Facebook's earlier days, Zuckerberg had compared social media to the gift economy of the Kwakwaka'wakw peoples. But any affinity between indigenous cultures and Facebook was becoming harder to imagine. Zuckerberg's political nonprofit, Fwd.Us, had over the last year run ads supporting the Keystone XL pipeline and oil drilling in the Arctic National Wildlife Reserve, two projects vigorously opposed by indigenous communities.[57]

It was getting similarly difficult to see sharing economy leaders like Uber, Airbnb, and Lyft as anything but massive profit-making enterprises. Uber in particular had fought labor unions, underpaid its workers, secretly sabotaged its rivals, and mused in public about digging up dirt on reporters—all weakening its credibility as a purveyor of positive social change. "There's little doubt that Uber is the closest thing we've got today to the living, breathing essence of unrestrained capitalism," argues *Salon*'s Andrew Leonard.[58] As the $68 billion company has expanded across the globe, so has the backlash from unions and regulators. In the opinion of University of Maryland law professor Frank Pasquale, sharing economy firms such as Uber are "acting almost imperialistically to impose American corporate power."[59]

Airbnb has not been immune to such criticism. When San Francisco tried to strictly regulate short-term property rentals, saying they were leading to a serious affordable housing crisis, Airbnb spent more than $8 million to defeat the legislation. It ran—and then later retracted—a series of bus stop ads suggesting that city amenities like bike lanes and libraries would have to be cut back without the hotel taxes it pays. "Rather than inspiring gratitude," the *San Francisco Weekly* wrote, "they mostly seem to be pissing people off."[60] In the *Guardian*, tech writer John Naughton declared that "it's time to discard the rose-tinted spectacles with which we have hitherto viewed these Silicon Valley outfits . . . The economic philosophy that's embedded in this new digital capitalism is neoliberalism red in tooth and claw."[61]

Was that all the sharing economy was? Just a smoother, younger, and cooler version of the same unjust status quo that indigenous communities had been suffering under for centuries? If anybody could prove otherwise, I thought as I headed up 18th Street toward the bare hilltops known as Twin Peaks, it would be Payu Harris, the coder behind MazaCoin. "We've gone through one hundred years of imposed poverty. That's the fight we're having," said a lawyer involved with Harris's company. "What we're trying to do with MazaCoin is just spark something to get us out of this cycle of victimhood."[62] At first it seemed to work. But within days of Harris's visit to the New York Bitcoin Center, wary Pine Ridge leaders openly questioned MazaCoin's viability, investors spooked, and the coin's value fell from $6.8 million to almost nothing. Harris has struggled to revive it ever since.

"The Oglala Sioux of South Dakota, by many measures America's most impoverished Native American tribe," *Newsweek* later concluded, "are a world away from the wealth of Silicon Valley."[63] I was tempted to read that as an epitaph for the socially progressive ideals touted by sharing economy leaders like Zimmer. But a study by Harvard professor Juliet Schor suggested that to do so would be "premature." Over three years, she'd interviewed hundreds of 18-to-34-year-olds involved with the sharing economy. Plenty of them worried "that venture capitalists have transformed a progressive, socially transformative practice—sharing—into amoral and socially destructive profit-seeking." Yet she concluded that "there are many progressives who remain active in this sector. They see enormous potential in both the technologies and the new social arrangements that are being fostered."[64]

I had to remind myself just how new the sharing economy still was. Only a couple of years earlier, few people outside Silicon Valley had ever heard of Lyft, Uber, or Airbnb. Now those companies were at the forefront of an economic shift that could be worth $335 billion. Where that shift would ultimately lead was still very much up for debate. As I crossed the winding curves of Market Street and began trudging up a steep staircase toward the Twin Peaks, I recalled a prescient interview that I'd read with Rebecca Adamson, an indigenous woman of Cherokee descent who founded the organization First Peoples Worldwide and advises the United Nations on rural development. "We have to begin to rethink our economic system," she said back in 2009. "We need an economy that provides for people. It has to be fundamentally, radically brought back into control and harnessed for the well-being of society."

She believed that this process should be guided by the values later cited by Zimmer and Zuckerberg. "An indigenous system is based on prosperity, creation, kinship, and a sense of enough-ness. It is designed for sharing," she said. "Potlatches, give-aways—these involve deliberately accumulating wealth as a person or as a family or as a clan for the sole purpose of giving it away." But here's the difference: if you followed these principles to their conclusion, she argued, as opposed to citing them because they feel good, it'd cause a radical restructuring of our political and economic system. In such a world, it makes no moral sense to drill for oil on sacred indigenous land—or build pipelines through it. That's a model based on heedless short-term profits.

A status quo truly based on sharing operates within ecological limits. It aims to close the gap between rich and poor. It acknowledges historical injustices—and does all it can to address them. But for now we're still stuck inside a system that values "material wealth, rather than human development," as Rebecca Adamson lamented. "What indigenous experience tells us is that an economy [should be] about fairness and equity."[65] Silicon Valley's version of sharing still has a long way to go. The relentless growth strategies of companies like Uber are "fundamentally opposed to most indigenous worldviews," Elle-Máijá Tailfeathers has concluded. And for now, Juliet Schor wrote, "whether [the sharing economy] will devolve to Business-As-Usual or a radically different kind of economic model is unknown."[66] It is still possible to create the type of sharing economy that Adamson described, but only if enough of us demand it.

We can start by seeing the current crop of sharing economy leaders for what they truly are. "Airbnb is a rental broker," reads a 2015 *Grist* story by Sam Bliss. "Uber and Lyft are unregulated cab services." But companies like this "do demonstrate something positive: People are willing to share, even with strangers."[67] For a new generation of 18-to-34-year-olds in particular, this presents an exciting opportunity— and one not requiring a lengthy election or new legislation from a deeply polarized Congress. "If you take a look at any of the serious problems we face as a society, from global climate change to pandemics to developing new energy sources, I would argue that they have to be solved cooperatively," argues University of Vermont professor Josh Farley. "What we need to do is develop models of a cooperative economy that can be scaled up."[68] It was clear to me that Silicon Valley has provided some of the tools to do that.

At last I reached the top of the stairs. I crossed a winding road and made my final ascent to the tip of the northern peak. For the first time, I turned around to see the route that I'd taken up here. The view was totally insane. To the east, I looked out over San Francisco's fog-shrouded financial district to the distant Oakland hills. Beyond them I summoned up an image of the drought-ravaged Californian interior, and beyond that the endless freeways and factories and oil derricks of a society in which indigenous people like Elle-Máijá are subject to systemic violence every day. To the west, I looked out over the Pacific and a cloudless horizon. I thought once again of Adamson's words: "We can do this—we can rebuild the system."[69] I'd come to the conclusion that Silicon Valley isn't yet up for the task. But in the next chapter I'll explain who is.

8

Radical Goes Mainstream

THE POLITICAL REVOLUTION THAT transformed Bernie Sanders from a sideshow candidate into a serious contender for U.S. president was led by young people like Saba Hafeez. Her belief that the structures of our society are profoundly flawed developed years before she knew who Sanders was. And his eventual defeat to Hillary Clinton in the 2016 Democratic primaries made her even more committed to fighting them. Saba is a first-generation American born to Pakistani parents. She was studying English and women's studies at the University of Iowa when she started a student group supporting Sanders's unlikely bid for the White House. Due to young people like her, the Democratic socialist senator from Vermont nearly won a shocking upset against Clinton in Iowa, then went on to challenge some of the basic operating principles of our political system. To Saba, the explanation is simple: "Millennials are seeing that the system is not working. They saw Bernie, and they just clicked."[1]

Saba's political awakening can in some ways be traced to the September 11 terrorist attacks. She was eight years old when the Twin Towers fell, living in Boston with her Pakistani parents and three siblings. "I grew up with my parents always having CNN on, and I never heard [about] Pakistan or any Middle East countries on the news," she said. "And then immediately after 9/11, I started hearing about Pakistan all the time." During her childhood, she and her family went to Pakistan every other summer. It was familiar and full of family. But the country she saw on CNN was foreign and dangerous. "I was intrigued by the representation of Pakistan in mainstream media and then contrasting it to my own experiences," she said.

When Saba was in third grade, her family moved to Sioux City, Iowa. Compared to Boston, the windswept city of 82,000 in America's tallgrass prairie wasn't very culturally diverse. "[It's] very conservative," Saba said. Representative Steve King (R-IA) has called immigrants "deportables," compared same-sex marriage to marrying "your lawnmower," and claimed climate change is "more of a religion than a science." Yet as she grew older, Saba became more and more progressive. There was just too much evidence that the system she lived in was broken. She knew that not everyone in the Middle East was a terrorist. Yet the George W. Bush administration stoked fears of terrorism to justify an endless military intervention that seemed to have more to do with securing new oil supplies than with promoting democracy.

It made Saba question her political leaders, as well as the oil corporations that seemed to have unlimited access to them. "I became very antiwar," she said. "Just the notion of war really bothered me. It sounds very naïve, but at a very young age my biggest wish for the world was peace." Around that time a presidential candidate came along who seemed to offer more hope of achieving it. Saba was in seventh grade when she first learned about Barack Obama. "I didn't really care for him until I heard several of his speeches and I was like 'wow,'" she said. She was drawn to his message of hopeful change. She liked that he came from Muslim ancestry on his dad's side, and he was "saying things I really believe in." She was too young to vote, so she decided to volunteer on his campaign.

Saba Hafeez figured she'd be in politics forever. But seven years later, when she started her undergrad degree at the University of Iowa as a political science major, she began to have doubts. "I was like 'I don't want to be an activist and involved in government,'" she said. The whole idea of being stuck in an office at the State Department for the rest of her life seemed "really dry and like you're not really doing anything." She knew that the only way to create a better future for her generation was for more young people like her to become engaged with civic institutions. "Once they're in the system, that's the best way they can change it," she said. Yet she decided to hedge her bets by changing her college major to English, so that "if I don't pursue politics, at least I'll have a general degree."

But Saba's ambivalence toward political engagement came to an end the night she attended a Democratic meeting that her friend was hosting at her home in Iowa City. "I had kind of not been involved in politics for the past two or three years at college, so I thought 'I'll go check out this meeting and see what happens,'" she recalled. There were about thirty people. They talked spiritedly about the upcoming 2016 presidential election. Saba enjoyed herself. When the meeting was over, her friend came up to her with a proposition: would Saba be interested in applying for a campus organizer job with the liberal group MoveOn.org? "I think you'd be really good at it," the friend said. Saba "didn't really know what I was getting myself into, but I thought, 'Why not?'"

The worldview that she brought to the position was typical of her generation. Like millions of other people her age, she was fed up with an economic system that operated as if making money were life's only worthwhile pursuit. She had grown up witnessing the destructive consequences of this logic. The oil-driven invasion of Iraq was but one example, as was the 2008 financial collapse and the steady accumulation of greenhouse gases in our atmosphere. Saba knew that unless we transformed our means of generating wealth, her generation would suffer the consequences. "Our physical environment is getting damaged, and I think it comes from how closely our system is tied to the corporations," she said. "I'm not saying that relationship needs to be completely dismantled, but I think there needs to be a lot more accountability."

Saba shared the global worldview of many people her age. As someone who had grown up with intimate family connections to two continents, it would have been hard not to. She saw herself first and foremost as an American, but her identity ultimately transcended borders—and so did her perspective on the threats facing her future. Saba knew that the Middle East is much more complex and human than the terrorist training ground depicted in much mainstream media. But political leaders rarely acknowledge that reality. "When candidates are asked what they think is America's biggest threat, a lot of the responses are ISIS and terrorism—things like that," she said. She knew that the more accurate answer was the global threat of climate change. She longed for a leader who "takes the science seriously."

To Saba, that was more important than the party they belonged to. Though she had supported Obama back in 2008 and considered herself to be a progressive, she shared the political independence of many people her age. She could never imagine voting for a Republican like Donald Trump. But she believed that for too long Democrats had been reluctant to stand up to corporate influence. Which is to say that when you really got down to it, she was more interested in social progress than partisan allegiances: "I think Millennials are seeing that the political system is not working in a lot of ways. It's not working to help fulfill the human potential." Often elections came down to two candidates who were more interested in gaining and holding on to power than in transforming society for the better: "We all have choices, but our choices are heavily influenced in unfair and disadvantaging ways."

Those were some of the reasons Saba Hafeez decided in the summer of 2015 to do everything she could to get a seventy-three-year-old Democratic socialist senator from Vermont elected president. Most mainstream observers were shocked at the record numbers of Millennial supporters that Sanders ultimately won over to his campaign. But Saba knew something about people her age that many older people had yet to realize: that after growing up in a broken political and economic system, they badly wanted change. They were hungry for a leader willing to provide it. When that person came along, he gave them a platform to challenge the prevailing structures of our society—and to threaten the vested interests perpetuating them. Sanders helped turn her generation into a potent political force. He didn't conjure this revolution out of nothing. He tapped into one that was already well underway. And though his campaign was eventually defeated, its radical ideals will persist without him.

BERNIE SANDERS ENTERED THE race for president without much fanfare. In April 2015 he simply sent out a short e-mail to his supporters:

"I am writing to inform you that I will be a candidate for President of the United States. I ask for your support." His statement was an indictment of our modern era. It touched directly on the themes that we've been exploring throughout this book. He attacked an economic system that valued "new wealth and income" for "the top 1%" more than societal progress. He argued that America must look outside its borders to confront the "peril of global climate change." He declared that our political system was more beholden to "billionaires" and insiders than to the people it claimed to represent.[2]

The consensus among most observers was Sanders didn't stand a chance against Clinton. "The 73-year-old, second-term senator faces long odds against [her] fund-raising might and name recognition," read a story on Reuters.[3] The *New York Times* agreed that "Mr. Sanders's bid is considered a long shot."[4] CNN described him as an "unlikely candidate for the Democratic nomination."[5] Sanders didn't even have the support of large left-leaning groups like MoveOn.org and Democracy for America—they had been trying to get Senator Elizabeth Warren (D-MA) to enter the race instead. Sanders was undeterred. "People should not underestimate me," the self-described "democratic socialist" told the Associated Press. "The message that has resonated in Vermont is a message that can resonate all over this country."[6]

By the summer it seemed that Sanders's message was resonating with young people all over America. A poll from YouGov and the *Economist* conducted in July 2015 suggested that 44 percent of 18-to-29-year-olds supported him as the Democratic nominee. Clinton still appeared to have a slight lead among Millennials, with 45 percent support.[7] But as the months went on, more and more young people seemed to defect to Sanders. In mid-October an NBC poll suggested this age cohort was twice as likely to support Sanders as Clinton: "[Her] rating among the group aged 19 to 29 has steadily fallen."[8] By early 2016, poll after poll was reaching the same conclusion: a righteously angry old man was killing it with Millennials. "I know I have some work to do, particularly with young people," Clinton admitted.[9]

Clinton was certainly trying. She got Lena Dunham, the young creator of the New York–based TV show *Girls*, to campaign for her. Clinton guest-starred on an episode of *Broad City*. She got a Snapchat account. Yet in cities like Brooklyn, "whose name has become a global buzzword for everything young and cool," *Vice* reported, Sanders was clearly leading among Millennials.[10] It wasn't difficult to understand why. As we saw in Chapter 2, Bradley Johnson moved to Brooklyn to become an artist instead of working in the tar sands because he desired more from life than simply a paycheck. When Sanders railed against "a fossil fuel industry whose greed has put short term profits ahead of climate change,"[11] he tapped into a generational rejection of an economic system that treats money as society's highest pursuit.

Sanders appealed to the global worldview of young people. This was evident in his views on climate change. While Clinton called global warming a "defining challenge" and promised to make America a "clean energy superpower," her position on new fossil fuel projects was sometimes difficult to sort out. She came out against the Keystone XL pipeline, for instance, but also pushed for an expansion of natural gas and was unclear about future oil and gas drilling leases on public land.[12] People like Phil Aroneanu (who, as we saw in Chapter 3, helped lead the successful campaign against Keystone XL) preferred the consistently global outlook of Sanders. The Vermont senator not only attacked Keystone XL, he deemed climate change the "single greatest threat facing our planet" and vowed to keep much of America's oil, coal, and gas underground.[13] In doing so, Sanders was rejecting the idea that the U.S. national interest is separate from the global interest. So it shouldn't be surprising that after leaving 350.org, Phil Aroneanu took a leadership role in the Sanders campaign.

Young people also liked that Sanders had been a political independent for his entire career. Clinton made a big deal out of her connections and experience, the fact she'd been secretary of state, and her ability to get things done. But the flipside was that she was firmly entrenched in a partisan establishment. As we saw in Chapter 4, Millennials like Andrew Frank have become distrustful of our political system because they think it's more concerned with partisan gain than with societal progress. Sanders's disdain for party politics tapped right into that belief. Which helps explain why in Canada, where a surge of young people voted independently to topple Stephen Harper's petrostate, "Sanders is more popular on . . . millennial Facebook feeds than cats and puppies combined," according to *Metro Views*.[14]

Sanders wasn't only rejecting our society—he campaigned on building a new one. Clinton did too, yet her vision of change was slow and incremental. She agreed with Sanders, for instance, that our economic system is too focused on short-term profits. Yet her solution was to tweak corporate law to reward "wealth creation for the long term."[15] As we saw in Chapter 5, though, the economic system that people like Chloe Maxmin desire is radically different from our current one. It's much more akin to the "moral economy" described by Sanders, where social progress is valued just as much as financial returns. "As a world we are rich enough to . . . meet our needs and to protect the planet," he said.[16] After Chloe graduated from Harvard, she decided to intern on the Sanders campaign, seeing it as a "movement for a better future."

The new America that Sanders wanted to build was in many ways more global than Clinton's. The former secretary of state had years of foreign policy experience. She had connections all over the globe. Yet her focus was on the protection of American interests and security—on preventing nuclear material, for instance, from falling "into the wrong hands." Sanders tapped into the global worldview that young people like Morgan Curtis and Erlend Knudsen brought to the Paris climate negotiations in Chapter 6. Not only did Sanders think climate change was a much more threatening issue than terrorism, he looked abroad to countries like Denmark for a new economic model that could better address it. His adherence to the borderless warnings of climate science led Morgan to add her name to a list of activists supporting his campaign.

Sanders didn't just call himself a political independent, he proved it by building a new model of campaign finance. Whereas most of Clinton's political contributions came from large corporate fund-raisers, Sanders's fund-raising, which outpaced his rival's at several points in the campaign, consisted mostly of small donations from regular people. His independence from the political establishment appealed to the type of young tech innovators whom we met in Chapter 7, who built "dozens of websites, tools, and apps" supporting his campaign, *Politico* wrote.[17] But unlike tech leaders such as John Zimmer and Mark Zuckerberg who claimed inspiration from indigenous culture, Sanders hired a young native adviser, Tara Houska, to help him actually put native values into practice. "[He is] the only candidate who has shown a commitment to Indian Country," wrote Gyasi Ross.[18] Elle-Máijá Tailfeathers is among his many indigenous supporters.

All this suggests that Sanders was tapping into a political and economic revolution that young people were leading even before he announced his candidacy for president. The reason he was able to reach so many different types of young people—from Brooklyn hipsters to Harvard activists, and from Muslim feminists to indigenous film-makers—was that he gave voice to a generational anxiety at the heart of this revolution. "[It's] the sense that the [leaders] who are currently in charge of making decisions that affect us are not being as effective as they can be," said Joelle Gamble from a youth-led think tank known as the Roosevelt Institute. In 2016 she led a study of one thousand Millennials across the country and found that what united them was a distrust of the ruling class—a desire, she said, for "reform of who gets to rewrite the rules."[19]

When you get down to it, that's what all the struggles I've described in this book have really been about. Young people know that our political and economic system is fundamentally broken. They've seen the evidence their whole lives. They know that the most damning piece of it is accumulating in our atmosphere. They know that if we don't make profound and immediate changes to our society, the survival of their entire generation could be at risk. And yet they see our leaders fighting against making those changes. They know that our leaders won't have to live with the consequences. Sanders channeled that anger and frustration into a single focused movement. He was the vessel containing the radical values of a new generation. He proved just how powerful they could be.

THE INJUSTICE AT THE heart of the Sanders campaign for president, the one he invoked over and over again, was that corporations are using their immense money and political influence to maximize their profits while leaving everybody else to suffer the consequences. This is particularly true for climate change. "Right now, we have an energy policy that is rigged to boost the profits of big oil companies like Exxon, BP, and Shell at the expense of average Americans," Sanders said. "The wealthiest industry in the history of our planet has bribed politicians into complacency in the face of climate change."[20] Was it hyperbole? A bit. But I knew firsthand how much truth it contained.

I knew because oil lobbyist Tom Corcoran had explained to me how political and economic power really works over coffee at the most exclusive Republican hangout in America. I had been in Washington to interview the lobbyists and politicians we met in chapters 3 and 4. I'd already spoken to Corcoran for an earlier story, and so when I told him I was coming to town, he invited me to spend a Monday morning with him at the Capitol Hill Club. He had served four terms as a Republican congressperson for Illinois in the 1970s and 1980s. His latest job was as the leader of a lobbying group known as the Center for North American Energy Security, which was, he later explained, funded "by all the major oil and pipeline companies."[21]

We met outside a stately white building that for over sixty years had been a "refined and elegant" hangout for presidents, vice presidents, governors, congresspersons, and "influential Republicans everywhere," according to its website. The fossil fuel billionaire David Koch had hosted a party here just a few months earlier.

"How was your trip to Washington?" asked Corcoran, who was in his early seventies when we met. "Come on, let's go inside."

As we walked into the Capitol Hill Club, it was hard to miss the wood-carved elephants—the official GOP mascot—flanking the entrance. Beyond them, in the front lobby, was a large painted portrait of George W. Bush. I followed Corcoran past a shoeshine station, then down one floor to the Auchincloss Grill, which resembled a cross between a sports bar, a Legion hall, and a rich friend's dad's basement den.

What I wanted to learn from Corcoran was how much influence the corporations that he helped represent actually have on Capitol Hill. I wanted to know whether companies like ExxonMobil really are rigging our system in their favor, if they are using their power to remove any restrictions on their profits, and in so doing, if they are blocking our shift to a safer and more stable future.

According to Corcoran, it was all true, but he would never describe it the way I just did. To him, what is good for Exxon is also good for America. So when fossil fuel companies write the rules, it means our society is working exactly as it should. As we sipped our coffees, he led me through an example to show exactly what he meant.

Several years earlier Congress had made one of the first attempts in U.S. history to limit the use of high-polluting fossil fuels. These were the worst of the worst, stuff like tar sands from up in Canada. It did so by proposing something known as a "low carbon fuel standard." First adopted by California, the standard imposed restrictions on road fuels that have a particularly bad contribution to global warming, while encouraging clean energy solutions that don't. If enacted on a national level, it could be equal to taking 30 million cars off the road, according to research once cited by Obama. It could signal "the end of the petroleum age and the beginning of the low-carbon fuel age," the Natural Resources Defense Council said.[22]

Corcoran and his allies quickly realized that such legislation was an unacceptable threat to the business that was making them rich. The intent of the law, after all, was to help create an economy where protecting the planet was valued as much as financial returns. The companies that Corcoran helped represent—oil and gas behemoths like Chevron and Exxon—knew their business model was the exact opposite, that if they were ever held financially accountable for all the greenhouse gases they released into the atmosphere, then they would no longer be profitable. "Once we'd learned about [the law], we worked against it," Corcoran said.[23] Rather than help build a less destructive future, they chose to reap profits instead.

Corcoran was soft-spoken and friendly. He'd served three terms in Congress. He didn't strike me as an immoral person, yet his actions were literally threatening my future. How did he justify them? A story he told me about his upbringing in the Midwest appeared to offer a clue. Corcoran was born in 1939 in the tiny rural community of Ottawa, Illinois. Growing up, he rode a yellow school bus each day past farmers' fields. The oil powering that bus, Corcoran later realized, was the "life-blood" of America—it was what made the country powerful and free. Oil helped "people do what they want," he saw.[24]

That conviction led him from a career in politics into his current role as an oil lobbyist. Under George W. Bush, the United States enacted the 2005 Energy Policy Act to make America less reliant on oil from the Middle East. To accomplish this goal, the act encouraged the full-bore development of tar sands, shale oil, and whatever other heavy oil could possibly be pulled from the ground. The act was designed to make America secure, but in the process it would let multinational oil corporations like Exxon make billions of dollars in extra profits. Corcoran was a true believer. And a few years after the act was passed, he teamed up with the American Petroleum Institute and other oil companies to ensure its aims were implemented.

The group that resulted from this alliance, the Center for North American Energy Security, which Corcoran now led, has an explicitly national perspective on the world. Its primary goal, in his telling, is to make America strong and safe. The best way to do that is by expanding the profits of the oil companies based there. Which is why the "low-carbon fuel standard" proposed by Democratic senators such as California's Henry Waxman was such a threat to Corcoran. The legislation had an explicitly global perspective on the world. It recognized that the short-term energy security and profits obtained by digging up high-polluting oil would make the climate much warmer and would have negative long-term consequences for the entire planet.

Corcoran and his oil company allies fought the low-carbon fuel standard with all the money and influence at their disposal. In Washington, they identified policy makers and congressional staffers who were potentially unsympathetic to climate change legislation. "Then we talked to those people to (a) alert them it exists, (b) explain why it was a mistake, and (c) try to get support to repeal it," Corcoran said. The Center for North American Energy Security issued briefing notes targeting legislators from oil- and gas-producing states such as Texas and Oklahoma, warning that the low-carbon fuel standard would be "a severe self-inflicted wound to our national security and economic recovery."[25] The center reached out to local constituents in those states and got them to add pressure.

The lobbying offensive appeared to work. Soon enough proponents of the low-carbon fuel standard realized that the wider House legislation it was included with would not have enough votes to make it past the committee stage. "So they deleted the low-carbon fuel standard," Corcoran explained, "and then the legislation moved out of committee." The Senate, too, dropped a proposed low-carbon fuel standard after comparable pressure. I couldn't believe how candid Corcoran was being with me. All around us old white dudes were sitting in conversation on plush chairs and couches as a large flat-screen TV on the wall played sports highlights from ESPN. "I'm not suggesting it was only the Center for North American Energy Security" that killed the climate change laws, he said. "But I would say that we were a big part of it."[26]

Corcoran and his allies weren't doing press conferences. They weren't surveying regular people across America to see if they wanted the low-carbon fuel standard "deleted." His group didn't even have a functioning website. "Nothing against the Internet, it just didn't fit our needs," Corcoran explained. "We're not doing public outreach—we leave that to others."[27] To him, it wasn't very important that our political system represent regular people. He thought it should protect the interests of large corporations instead. He believed that what was good for fossil fuel corporations was also good for America. Which was why his lobbying battles took place behind closed doors, where regular people couldn't participate. They took place in exclusive social clubs like the one where we were drinking our coffee now.

The defeat of the low-carbon fuel standard was just the beginning. In the years that followed, oil companies and groups such as Corcoran's attacked dozens of state-level fuel standards across the United States They derailed a historic bipartisan effort to limit America's carbon emissions and create a new economic model that emits far less—the Waxman-Markey cap and trade climate bill of 2010. They went on to spend more than $500 million on lobbying to weaken Obama's Clean Power Plan, and hundreds of millions more to influence the 2016 presidential election.

Corcoran exuded a cool confidence as he described their victories. "We've been successful," he said in his smooth, gentlemanly drawl, leaning back in his chair in the Republican clubhouse where the Koch brothers have a membership.

It was time to leave. Corcoran led me back upstairs and past the portrait of George W. Bush and outside into the frigid winter air of a February morning. We said our goodbyes, and he walked off down the block. I remained outside the Capitol Hill Club for a few minutes trying to wrap my mind around everything I'd heard. I soon realized that the hour I'd spent with this oil lobbyist from Illinois had taught me an important lesson about how power really works in America—and why it's so resistant to change: The profits of companies like Exxon are incompatible with a future that values more than just money. It's in their best interest to align themselves with the national interest rather than the global one. And they're not all that interested in democracy.

So when I first heard Senator Sanders argue that "we have an energy policy that is rigged to boost the profits of big oil companies like Exxon, BP, and Shell at the expense of average Americans," I knew he wasn't exaggerating. The status quo I've described throughout this book—the relentless focus on short-term profits, the explicitly national perspective, and the insider politics—is the primary obstacle to my generation's future survival. Sanders spoke for many people my age when he declared that "enough is enough." I wasn't the only one who agreed that "it's time for a political revolution that takes on the fossil fuel billionaires, accelerates our transition to clean energy, and finally puts people before the profits of polluters."[28] Corcoran had to be defeated.

IN THE SPRING OF 2015, when Saba Hafeez applied for a campus organizer job with MoveOn.org, it was working with another activist group, Democracy for America, to try to induce Senator Elizabeth Warren (D-MA) to run for president. Warren had said several times that she wouldn't, but the two groups were running a $1.25 million campaign to convince her otherwise.[29] They were opening up two offices in Iowa and one in New Hampshire. They believed that Warren—who was smart, passionate, and progressive in the Senate—would challenge vested interests in a way that the establishment insider Hillary Clinton simply could not. Warren's voice "soars above the turgid Washington morass like Yo-Yo Ma playing a cello suite from a hang glider over a sewage plant," MoveOn wrote.[30]

Saba's job was to do the tireless work of gathering signatures from strangers. She ended up being great at it. She and the rest of the Iowa team set up tables around the University of Iowa. "I would just go up to students telling them, 'Hey sign this,' and then give them background info," she said. Many students and faculty already knew about the progressive senator, and "I was really shocked by their enthusiasm." Her team gathered over 365,000 signatures, and Saba was selected to go to Washington to deliver them in person to Senator Warren. But when she arrived, Warren remained adamant that she wasn't running for president. MoveOn and Democracy for America officially ended their campaign. "It doesn't feel like there is an obvious way that we could change her mind," MoveOn's Ben Wikler said.[31]

Saba was faced with a dilemma. After participating on the MoveOn campaign, she wanted to be involved in the 2016 presidential election, but she was unsure who to support. At the time she was becoming more interested in female identity. She added a women's studies minor to her degree. Clinton seemed the obvious choice, since "women in politics and leadership positions is something I really care about." But Saba had been drawn to Warren because the senator wanted to transform America. Warren critiqued the vested interests responsible for gender inequality—as well as two endless Middle East wars, rampant racial injustices, and the overheating of our planet. Clinton was a strong female leader, but Saba believed she was more interested in ruling the country than in changing it. "I am a proud feminist, but that doesn't mean that I will back a candidate based on their gender over their ideas," she explained.

Which is why Saba decided in the summer of 2015 to get Bernie Sanders elected president. Sanders had entered the race only a few months earlier. He was considered an extreme long shot. National polling put him behind Hillary Clinton by about 56 points.[32] His biggest practical issue was money. Among his major policy goals was to challenge an economy that, in his words, made "the rich richer and everyone else poorer."[33] But that type of language wasn't likely to endear him to the CEOs and billionaires whose donations are required to fund a serious bid for president. "In this day and age, you do need a whole lot of money," Sanders admitted.[34]

One reason was that the 2010 Supreme Court ruling in *Citizens United* had removed any limits on election spending. "Liberals warned that hard-to-track political spending by outside interest groups would explode," *Bloomberg* reported. "If anything, the alarms underestimated the decision's effects." The Brennan Center for Justice at New York University later calculated that Senate election spending by outside groups—in the form of political action committees, or super PACs—doubled to $486 million by 2014. And when you added presidential elections, the figure approached $1 billion. Most of this money came from just 195 people and their spouses. It was no exaggeration to say that political power was being created by billionaires.[35]

Political leaders weren't necessarily happy about this situation. During Clinton's early campaigning, she declared that "we need to get this corporate and unchecked money out of politics." Not long after, though, she was meeting with rich potential donors to a Democratic super PAC known as Priorities USA. "Clinton really had no other choice," NBC reported. The Republican National Committee was expected to spend close to $2 billion getting its nominee elected.[36] If she spurned super PACS altogether, it would create a financial disadvantage. So Clinton decided to play by the system's rules. She courted super PACS, she took millions of dollars from Wall Street, and she justified it as a compromise on the road to becoming president.

Sanders chose a much different path. But then, he didn't really have a choice. No billionaire who'd made a fortune from our current economic system was going to support a candidate who wanted to radically change it. And so Sanders decided to ask regular people to finance his campaign. If enough of them gave small amounts, it could eventually equal the spending of a CEO or a corporation. Within six weeks of entering the race, Sanders had raised $6 million in small donations. "Can a candidate . . . who is prepared to take on billionaires—can you win elections?" he asked.[37] So far the answer was no. But by the end of 2015, his crowdsourced fund-raising was exploding—$33 million in small donations compared to Clinton's $37 million. "We are making history," declared Sanders's campaign manager.[38]

The campaign was winning over people like Saba Hafeez. She'd spent her whole life inside a society that seemed to care only about making money. And she'd witnessed the consequences: an oil-driven war in Iraq, a financial collapse, and soaring carbon emissions. As a serious female contender for president, Clinton seemed to challenge this state of affairs, but she was being funded by the corporations and rich people who were perpetuating it. "It's really important for me to have a female candidate, but it's more important to have someone whose values align with my values," Saba said. Sanders wanted to create an economy that worked for the betterment of humankind. And Saba saw no contradiction in the regular people paying for it. "He's playing by a different set of rules," she said.

BY LATE SUMMER OF 2015, many of the people Saba had worked with at MoveOn were now supporting Sanders. "When Bernie announced and it was clear Senator Warren wasn't running, it was the natural thing to do," said one campaign official.[39] Saba decided to add to the momentum by forming a student group at the University of Iowa. She suspected that people of her generation would be naturally drawn to the Vermont senator's message of radical change, that they were less tied to the status quo than their parents and grandparents, and that they had more to gain from transforming it. With a few other students, she launched Hawkeyes for Bernie right before the fall semester began. Its goal was to foment a revolution.

The conventional wisdom was that people Saba's age didn't care about politics—they were self-centered, apathetic, and cynical. Saba knew those stereotypes weren't true: "There's this negative perception like students don't care, which is false." But when Hawkeyes for Bernie booked a large auditorium for its first general meeting in early September, Saba hoped she wouldn't be proven wrong. "I remember being a little bit worried," she said. "I was like 'Oh no, what if we don't get a bunch of students?'" She couldn't make it to the meeting because of a class conflict. But organizers sent her photos of a packed auditorium—close to one hundred students in total. "That was really reassuring," she explained.

As the weeks and months passed, Saba got more and more messages from students wanting to help out. A lot of them were people she figured would never "want to be involved in politics," she recalled. "They were like the typical college kids who go out, go to bars, smoke pot, and you would think they don't care, but once again that's false." Early-summer polling suggested that Millennials supported Clinton over Sanders as the Democratic nominee,[40] but by the fall that trend was starting to reverse. NBC polls found that Clinton's support among 18-to-29-year-olds had "steadily fallen" from 36 percent in August to 26 percent in October.[41] And a survey conducted in early November by Harvard's Institute of Politics confirmed Sanders had become the preferred Democratic nominee among people of Saba's age.[42]

Even more remarkably, it was happening as many media outlets dismissed the Sanders campaign as unrealistic. After reviewing mainstream coverage over the summer of 2015, Rima Regas concluded that

Bernie Sanders's "ability to succeed is always described in doubtful terms." Reporting focused more on his personality or appearance than on what he stood for. "Overall there is a version of a 'wall of silence' built by the media when it comes to serious reporting and analysis of his policies," Regas wrote.[43] *New York Times* public editor Elizabeth Spayd shared his opinion, conceding in early September that her newspaper "hasn't always taken [the Sanders campaign] very seriously. The tone of some stories is regrettably dismissive, even mocking at times."[44]

Yet on sites like Reddit, a groundswell of Millennial support for Sanders was building. During the summer and early fall, Sanders was regularly the most discussed political subject on the sprawling user-generated site. By October a subreddit known as "/r/SandersForPresident" had more than 115,000 subscribers. "Bernie Sanders's Internet fan base has swelled into a digital army, and his supporters on Reddit have been the ground troops," the *New Republic* wrote. "The site has helped draw massive crowds to his rallies and aided his campaign in raising $26 million in the third quarter."[45] To Saba, it wasn't at all surprising. "I feel like that's just democracy in action," she explained. "Individuals are talking about him like crazy on a day-to-day basis, whereas most media [are] just neglecting him."

To his young and digitally connected supporters, Sanders provided a more global view of America's place in the world than Clinton. It was especially evident during the first Democratic debate in October. Asked to name the biggest security threat to the United States, Clinton answered in the explicitly national terms of America's ongoing War on Terror. "It has to be [the] continued threat from the spread of nuclear weapons, nuclear material that can fall into the wrong hands," she said. "I know the terrorists are constantly seeking it." Sanders took a wider perspective: "If we do not address the climate change . . . the planet we'll be leaving our kids and our grandchildren may well not be habitable," he said. *Vox*'s Max Fisher observed that you could interpret this several ways. Sanders was either dodging a question on U.S. foreign policy, "[or] he may be showing us that he's different, that he takes into account larger issues."[46]

During the second Democratic debate, which was held the day after ISIS terrorists killed 130 people in Paris, Sanders stuck to that perspective. "Senator Sanders, you said you wanna rid the planet of ISIS," the moderator John Dickerson said. "In the previous debate you said the greatest threat to national security was climate change. Do you still believe that?" Sanders replied without pause, "Absolutely. In fact, climate change is directly related to the growth of terrorism. And if we do not get our act together and listen to what the scientists say, you're gonna see countries all over the world . . . struggling over limited amounts of water, limited amounts of land to grow their crops. And you're gonna see all kinds of international conflict."[47]

Republicans immediately slammed Sanders. "I would view that assertion as pretty absurd," said Senator Ron Johnson (R-WI), chair of the Homeland Security and Governmental Affairs Committee. Senator John McCain (R-AZ) said Sanders was probably stoned: "There is a ballot initiative in Arizona concerning the substance that he must have been consuming."[48] Sanders's view on climate change and terrorism was in fact fairly mainstream. The Department of Defense, for one, sees the climate as a threat multiplier that could "threaten stability in a number of countries." But sites like *PolitiFact* were skeptical: "We couldn't find any evidence of a 'direct' relationship between climate change and terrorism, though many reports have noted an indirect link."[49] It appeared as though Sanders was oversimplifying a complicated issue.

Yet the broader point he was making was impossible to dispute: over a decade of military interventions in the Middle East had done nothing to make the United States safe from the existential threat of climate change. Saba knew firsthand that the threat America faced from Islamic extremists was exaggerated. She knew how badly the region was misrepresented. And as Republican leaders called for severe restrictions on Muslim immigration in the wake of the Paris attacks, she shook her head in dismay: "It just blows my mind these conversations are still happening." To her, Sanders was the only candidate who acknowledged the true threat to her future. "He's the only one, Democrat or Republican, that takes climate science seriously," she said.

"I think that resonates with a lot of people—at least, a lot of millennials."

It also appeared to be resonating in Iowa. During the lead-up to the state's caucus vote on February 1, 2016, a Quinnipiac University poll suggested that Sanders had a dramatic lead over Clinton among voters who saw climate change as an important issue. Two-thirds of those voters favored the Vermont senator, as opposed to less than one-third for Clinton. "Climate is clearly Sanders's biggest advantage," wrote the *New Republic*'s Rebecca Leber. "His lead shrinks on other key issues." But with polls suggesting a tight race in Iowa, it was poised to be a decisive factor, since "voters who care deeply about climate change could be key to a Sanders upset over Hillary Clinton."[50] They wanted the United States to have a much wider view on the world—after all, the divide between the global interest and the national one was rapidly shrinking.

THE IOWA CAUCUS VOTE holds a special place in American politics. It's the first state that votes for each party's nominee. For that reason the outcome is often perceived as a predictor of how competitive each candidate's campaign for president will be. "The state's discerning political activists can make or break campaigns painstakingly pieced together over years in a single night," CNN explained.[51] As Iowa's election got nearer, young women like Saba seemed to be holding the balance of power among Democratic voters. Polls suggested that women between 18 and 34 favored Sanders over Clinton by 19 points.[52] "As a young female Millennial, I want to see a more ethical system in place," Saba explained.

Sanders had a lot of momentum heading into Iowa. He was speaking to huge rallies across the state. His fund-raising was nearly equal to Clinton's. He was finally getting serious media attention. He was undoubtedly the favorite among Millennials. Yet for any of it to matter, Sanders had to win the Iowa vote, to show that he could be competitive in a long presidential race. "What if Sanders loses Iowa?" wrote Nate Silver on *FiveThirtyEight*. "It's probably over . . . He probably won't be winning other relatively favorable states like Wisconsin, much less more challenging ones like Ohio and Florida. His ceiling wouldn't be high enough to win the nomination." Sanders had tough odds. Though polls showed a tight Iowa race, "Clinton is somewhat more likely—a little better than a 2-to-1 favorite—to come out on top," Silver predicted.[53]

On the night of the caucus vote, Saba Hafeez was a precinct captain at the University of Iowa. She was exhausted. She'd returned from a trip to Pakistan the night before, a more-than-thirty-hour journey, and spent the whole day in classes. Her job was to help check in voters who arrived at the school's postmodern Art Building West, and to help make sure the vote went smoothly. It was a big task. Iowa's caucus is notoriously complex. "You can't just get away with pulling a lever in a curtained polling booth," explained CNN.[54] Instead, people show up to a public meeting that can sometimes take several hours. Registered voters pick a candidate, physically gather with fellow supporters, and cast several rounds of votes. "It's very easy for things to go wrong," Saba said. "There's no structure—it's just a big room, and you're counting with note cards."

Saba got to her registration table early. Clinton's precinct team arrived not long after and put up blue signs all over the building. It was an effective psychological tool. "Everywhere I looked, I saw Hillary supporters," Shane Ryan later wrote in *Paste Magazine*. "I let the panic sweep in— if Sanders supporters are outnumbered here, in a city, in a university town, he'll get killed across the state." But his fears were unfounded. It was soon clear that hundreds of the people who showed up to the precinct were there for Sanders. The precinct chair, a professor with a white goatee and Swiss Alpine–style hat, shouted for Clinton supporters to stay put and for Sanders supporters to convene downstairs. "[He] may as well have said, 'Young people go downstairs, old people stay,' because that was the effect," Ryan wrote.[55]

In the first round of voting, Sanders won a slim majority. But the vote wasn't over. As people cheered and congratulated each other and chanted "Feel the Bern!," Clinton's team ran all over the building convincing undecided voters to join their side. "[They] had their asses in gear," Ryan wrote. "They knew exactly how many they needed to peel off in order to force a tie." Sanders's team realized what was happening, but it was too late. The second round of voting resulted in a draw. In Saba's precinct Sanders was twelve votes shy of victory. A similar story was playing out across the state. Some voting tallies were so close, they were decided by coin tosses. Saba headed home before the final count for Iowa was in. All she wanted to do was go to sleep.

The next morning she awoke to the news: Clinton had beaten Sanders so narrowly in Iowa that it was effectively a tie. Saba was thrilled. To her it felt like a victory, not only for Sanders but for her generation. In the crucial Iowa primary, people her age had forced America's political system to take their worldview seriously. "Hell yes," she said. "For this guy to pop up and tie with Clinton . . . it's a big deal." Many observers agreed. "The close contest in Iowa confirms that Sanders's anti-establishment message has real muscle and appeal," wrote the *Washington Post*.[56] The BBC reported that "the outcome marks a significant achievement for Mr. Sanders, who was polling in single digits in Iowa six months ago."[57] *Mashable* declared Sanders "the true champion."[58] The *Guardian*'s Lucia Graves speculated that the Iowa vote "will have repercussions on Democrats for years to come."[59]

Others weren't so sure. To mount a serious campaign for the Democratic nomination, Sanders would need huge numbers of young people to come out to vote for him in every state. After Iowa, that appeared to happen in New Hampshire, where he easily beat Clinton. But his early victories were followed by a big loss in Nevada, causing *Washington Post* columnist Philip Bump to declare that "young voters are failing Bernie Sanders." In all three states they had voted in numbers lower than their share of the population. "This is why campaigns that need younger voters in order to win often don't," Bump wrote. "We've noted repeatedly that young people simply don't turn out to vote as much as older voters."[60] But his dismissal of young voters was premature.

As the months went on, the campaign between Sanders and Clinton settled into a reliable pattern. Sanders would win a stunning upset in a state like Michigan, then face painful defeats in states like Ohio and Florida. By early April, Clinton was so far ahead that it seemed virtually impossible for Sanders to win the nomination. Yet his support kept growing. He held massive rallies across the United States. He matched Clinton's fund-raising. And perhaps most significantly, he attracted record numbers of young voters. An analysis from Tufts University showed that voter turnout among people of Saba's age was surpassing the previous record set by Obama in 2008. In the under-thirty demographic, Sanders was beating Clinton by a more than 2–1 margin. "The energy that young voters have kept up throughout the primary has been incredible," said the lead researcher. "It's been amazing."[61]

Much of that had to do with Sanders's perceived political independence. He'd didn't belong to a Democratic establishment that for decades had grown more and more accepting of our status quo. Though he ran for president as a Democrat, he'd never been registered to the party. Throughout his campaign, he scorned the entire political spectrum: Republicans were a "right-wing extremist party," while Democrats refused to confront "big-money interests." Sanders's unapologetic radicalism—his plans to break up the big Wall Street banks, for instance, and to ban all U.S. fracking—appealed to young people who were sick of voting for a particular party instead of for their ideals. "I just don't believe in settling for a candidate," Saba explained.

As young people turned out in record numbers, their political influence could no longer be ignored. CNN was not alone in arguing that "the Vermont senator is poised to leave behind a durable legacy: A generation of liberal voters enthralled by his populist message—and a Democratic Party whose ideological center has shifted left during the 2016 election."[62] Saba saw in the campaign a crucial lesson for her generation. By operating outside the partisan system, Sanders demonstrated to millions of young people—not just in America, but around the world—that politics didn't have to be one compromise after another. They could aspire toward transformative change instead. The Millennials who worked on his campaign were becoming more effective at achieving it. "They have gained sophistication in almost every area of politics, especially new organizing and fundraising techniques," the *Guardian* reported.[63] Saba believed the experience would have an impact far beyond the Sanders campaign. "The students I've been surrounded by . . . they've seen how the system works," she said. She was confident that "we'll find ways to change it."

IN THE SPRING OF 2016, I drove down to Seattle with my partner, Kara, and several friends to see Sanders speak at Safeco Field. Our car broke down just outside the city. Had Kara not graciously agreed to stay behind with the stoner tow-truck driver while the rest of us hopped into a cab, I would've missed the rally. It was an unusually warm evening when we finally arrived at Safeco Field. It had been the hottest March in recorded history, and the ten months before it had also set heat records. "I continue to be shocked by what we are seeing," said the Penn State University climate scientist Michael Mann. "[It's] a reminder of how perilously close we now are to permanently crossing into dangerous territory."[64]

The Arctic was melting. Wildfires were burning out of control in Indonesia. India was suffering its worst drought in a generation. The Great Barrier Reef was bleaching white. And here on this warm evening, I was standing in line with fifteen thousand people hoping to radically transform our society. I couldn't help noticing how normal everybody looked. Apart from the dude wearing a tie-dye robe and walking a goat while chanting socialist slogans, the crowd was almost boringly regular. All around me were the same students and hipsters and retirees and parents and children you'd expect to see on most city streetcorners across America. "Socialists come in all stripes," my friend joked.

As I waited in the line, which snaked dozens of blocks through Seattle's downtown waterfront, I kept asking myself what we were doing here. By this point in the primary race, the Vermont senator's odds of beating Clinton were extremely formidable. "The challenges facing Sanders are enormous," wrote John Cassidy in the *New Yorker*. He trailed Clinton by more than two hundred delegates. His percentage of superdelegates—party insiders who hold huge sway over the nomination—was minuscule. *Predictwise*, a site that aggregates data from political polling and other sources, predicted that Sanders's chances of becoming the Democratic nominee were only 8 percent.[65] It's true that he'd faced tough odds every step of the way. The crowd here in Seattle had to know they were getting tougher every day. And still thousands of regular people had chosen to spend a warm Friday evening here anyway.

When Sanders strode out onto Safeco Field and began to address the crowd, the true import of what we were all doing here finally began to make sense.

You could see it most tangibly in the massive amounts of money still flooding into his campaign. In the month leading up to this Seattle rally, Sanders had taken in over $44 million from his supporters, according to the Federal Election Commission, which was $15 million more than Clinton had raised over the same time period. Sanders's fund-raising was all the more impressive for the fact that most of it came from regular people. His campaign claimed that the $109 million it had raised since the beginning of 2016 came from donors each giving on average $27. "This money is just bubbling up from everywhere," senior fellow at the Center for Responsive Politics Bob Biersack explained.[66] It allowed Sanders to wage a long and serious campaign independent of large corporations.

In doing so, he had challenged one of the basic operating principles of modern politics: that the only way to succeed is to win over rich elites. "Sanders' model represents a break from what political consultants consider the traditional way of fundraising," *Vox* argued. "Compile a Rolodex of wealthy donors, then tap them and their friends for the maximum $2,700 contribution."[67] Even if he'd wanted to take this route, Sanders's self-identification as a "Democratic socialist" who wanted to radically restructure corporate America effectively ruled it out. So instead he'd built out a huge network of small donors all across the country. By spring his e-mail list included the names, addresses, and credit card numbers of more than 2.5 million supporters. "The Sanders camp knows that, long after the Democratic primary is over, this is the key part of the digital inheritance it is leaving for the political left," *Politico* reported.[68]

But that digital inheritance came with an ideological one as well. The reason so many people donated to the Sanders campaign in the first place is that they were fed up with our business leaders. The senator's young supporters in particular knew that the relentless drive for financial returns is one of the main reasons that greenhouse gases are rapidly accumulating in the atmosphere and that it threatens their future survival on this planet. But they also knew that a better future is possible, one where our economy works within nature's limits instead of exceeding them. By giving to the campaign, they were helping to build it. "We don't represent Wall Street, corporate America, or the billionaire class," he declared to the Seattle crowd.

But the Sanders campaign had been about more than a critique of our economy. He also sought to expand the worldview of people living within it. At every chance he got, the Vermont senator took big-picture perspectives on challenges transcending America's borders: global inequality, the struggles of indigenous peoples, criminal justice, and climate change. "This is a new kind of election," Bill McKibben explained on *Politico*. "The Sanders campaign has been about issues, issues, issues. I mean, the guy gives 90-minute speeches every day that are entirely about actual things that need to change. It seems weird in an American political context, which is normally about posturing and spin, but for many of us it's refreshing."[69]

Sanders intended to keep it that way. Even though Clinton was likely to win the nomination, the millions of supporters and donors that he mobilized during his campaign would give him leverage within the Democratic Party. And when he was given the chance to pick six advisers to help write the party's platform, he made sure they reflected his global worldview. Among them were the black scholar Cornel West, the pro-Palestine activist James Zogby, the indigenous activist Deborah Parker, and McKibben, people who "could potentially help to transform U.S. progressive politics for years to come," *Salon* predicted.[70] When the party platform was being drafted, Clinton's own advisers supported plans to reform Wall Street and raise the minimum wage to $15, but they voted down proposals to institute a tax on carbon emissions and ban fracking. "The Clinton campaign was ready to acknowledge serious problems" like climate change, McKibben wrote. "But when it came to specific policy changes they often balked."[71]

Sanders's advisers, for their part, proposed a moratorium on all new fossil fuel extraction on federal lands, explicitly recognizing that a narrow definition of America's national self-interest is insufficient to deal with global threats like climate change. In doing so, they were channeling my generation's rejection of the idea that our world is composed of selfish and competing nations. They were channeling our belief that national borders are a veneer, and that to deal with threats like climate change, we have to transcend them. "We have a moral responsibility to leave this planet healthy for future generations," Sanders told the Safeco crowd. The fact that this global worldview was being considered and debated by the Democratic Party—one of the leading institutions of American politics—was hugely significant. "Just by being aired, these ideas can gain currency and support among lawmakers," wrote *Vox*.[72] By the time of the Democratic convention in July, Clinton had become more open to some of them, supporting in principle a price on carbon emissions and a climate change impact test for new oil pipelines.[73]

It wasn't as firm a commitment to change as activists like McKibben had wanted. But the fact such policies were being discussed at all was a testament to the political independence of Sanders and his many young supporters. As the odds that he would win the nomination became slimmer and slimmer, many prominent Democrats suggested Sanders should drop out of the race and endorse Clinton's bid for president. A few weeks before the Seattle rally, President Obama told a meeting of Democratic donors in Texas that it would be in the best interest of the party for Sanders to step down. As Sanders's long-shot campaign continued on, Democrats became more explicit. "It's actually harmful" for him to stay in the race, said Senator Dianne Feinstein (D-CA). It "slows the takeoff of [Clinton's] general-election campaign," said Senator Sherrod Brown (D-OH).[74] Those calls were echoed in the media. "Sanders is not yet irrelevant," argued Stuart Rothenburg in the *Washington Post*. "But he is moving in that direction.

The longer he delays endorsing Clinton, the pettier and smaller he seems."[75]

But Sanders's young supporters thought those calls were completely missing the point. A huge part of the Vermont senator's appeal was that he didn't play by the established rules of partisan politics. He let his ideals guide him instead, and in so doing, his campaign transcended the particulars of the 2016 presidential election. It became something bigger. Winnie Wong, creator of the "Feel the Bern" hashtag, called him "both a conduit and a tactic" for a social movement that was in some ways independent of electoral politics.[76] His bid for the Democratic nomination was the pretext that millions of people—particularly of my generation—needed to make a collective demand for radical social change. He was the symbol of a new way of engaging politically, much as Occupy Wall Street had been several years earlier. Maryland state senator Jamie Raskin pointed out that "the Sanders movement brought Occupy Wall Street into Democratic Party presidential politics. [Sanders] occupied the Democratic primaries."[77]

Perhaps it's more accurate to say that Sanders's young supporters occupied them. A Tufts University study found that by June more people under 30 had voted for Sanders than for Clinton and Trump combined. "It's hard to overemphasize how completely and utterly [Sanders] domi-nated the youth vote to this point," reported the *Washington Post.*[78] The young people who voted for him were sick of political leaders who cared more about their careers and their parties than about the long-term threats facing society. They wanted someone who would take their future seriously. By voting in record numbers for Sanders, my generation had debunked the stereotype that Millennials are apathetic and cynical when it comes to politics. We'd created a massive social movement infused with our unique values. We'd shown the power of our idealism. We were proving, in the words of Sanders, that we "want a say in the future of our nation."

And that, after all, is why fifteen thousand people had gathered here tonight in Seattle. "We can change the status quo," Sanders practically shouted into the microphone. The roars of cheering and applause that erupted around me were staggering. Hesitating for only a second, I added my voice to them. Outside the world was burning up. The planetary changes that we were inflicting were existentially terrifying—and everyone my age could potentially live to see their full doomsday impact in our lifetimes. We had no choice but to fight this injustice and all the political and economic leaders who perpetuated it. For years the prospect of doing so had intimidated me. I felt daunted by it. But right now I felt different. Surrounded by thousands of people who shared my generation's values in the floodlit bleachers of Safeco Field, I truly felt like a better future was possible. I felt like that future wasn't very radical at all. I felt like it was the only option we had left. And tonight I felt like it was within our reach.

Afterword

SO ARE WE SCREWED?

The only word I could use to describe the expression on my face and all the other people around me on U.S. election night in November 2016 was *shocked*. Several dozen of us had gathered in Vancouver to watch the results. Even as the night began, Donald Trump was still a joke. *Free shots if he wins*, we all laughed. By the time Trump made his victory speech I felt like I was in a parallel universe. At Bernie Sanders's rally in March my generation's worldview felt unstoppable. Now we had to deal with a bigoted 70-year-old white man who called climate change a "hoax," referred to oil as America's "lifeblood," and vowed to "cancel" the Paris treaty. If there was ever a time to despair for the future, it was now. Yet when I thought back on all the people my age I'd met while writing this book I couldn't help but feel a strange flicker of hope. I realized that the lessons contained in their stories could be drawn from to prevent Trump from totally screwing us over—and to build a safer, more equitable, and less destructive world.

I know that the very first step toward creating it is contained in Peter's story. His decision more than a decade ago to reject mainstream society was more powerful than even he had realized. Each day that he spends out on Denman Island, he's confronting everything Trump stands for: a system that privileges money over morals, the national interest over the global one, and political partisanship over his generation's survival. Peter hasn't yet been successful in resisting that system's inertia, but by dedicating his life to questioning its logic, he's shown that it doesn't have to be inevitable. He's shown that our current way of life is based not on inviolable laws but on our collective values.

And when our values start to change, our world changes along with them. I'd gotten my first glimpse of how profound those changes can be when I spoke with Bradley Johnson. His decision to become an artist in Brooklyn instead of a tar sands worker in Fort McMurray might not seem like a big deal, but he was rejecting an economic system that pursues short-term profits with little regard for the consequences. When millions of other people his age came to the same conclusion, it caused an employment crisis in North America's oil and gas industry, put $100 billion worth of new projects at risk, and called into question the basic operating principles of capitalism. This happened because people my age decided there is more to life than making the most money possible. It wasn't the result of some carefully coordinated effort. It was the by-product of a generational values shift.

It took someone like Phil Aroneanu to grasp the untapped potential of this shift—and what could be achieved by channeling it toward a specific, society-transforming goal. That realization was the result of years of hard work. It began when he decided that his global identity superseded his national one and he set out with six other Middlebury grads and their adviser Bill McKibben to build a planet-spanning network of young people imbued with that worldview. The true power of what they created was revealed when they aimed that network against the Keystone XL pipeline, transformed the project from a national debate about a piece of steel into a global referendum on climate change, and ultimately convinced President Obama to reject it. It proved what could be achieved when a new generation's worldview went into battle against an older one's.

Influencing a world leader's position on climate change was one thing. But it wasn't until I met Andrew Frank that I realized how much power my generation had to actually choose our leaders in the first place. For years, that hadn't been obvious to many of us. When Andrew chose to take a stand against Canada's Conservative government—and lost his progressive activist job in the process—he in effect joined millions of other young people in declaring his independence from partisan politics.

But the question of how my generation could meaningfully participate in a system that we had rejected wasn't answered until several years later, when a surge of young voters like Andrew cast their ballots strategically to end the ten-year petrostate of Prime Minister Stephen Harper. Canada's election showed that when the conditions are right, people my age can be a potent electoral force—and that leaders who ignore our unique worldview do so increasingly at their peril.

What the young people at the center of these generational shifts shared in common was a rejection of mainstream society. They'd questioned its operating principles, threatened its ability to make profits, influenced its political leaders, and removed them from office completely. But if my generation was truly going to be less screwed, we couldn't only abandon the status quo—we had to build a better one to replace it. What Chloe Maxmin showed me is that the values of this new system already exist within millions of young people, and when they're given the proper outlet, they can propel rapid and immediate change. This is what allowed the small fossil fuel divestment campaigns that student organizers like Chloe started in the fall of 2012 to within three years spread to more than four hundred universities and influence trillions of dollars worth of economic activity.

It was the same dynamic that, in the final month of 2015, helped end more than three decades of diplomatic stalemate on climate change. For as long as people of my generation had been alive, world leaders had failed to set aside their national differences and fight together to ensure a safe future on this planet. At the COP21 climate talks, the generational injustice of this situation became impossible to ignore: older leaders were pushing for a weak agreement whose consequences they wouldn't have to live with. At first the outcries of young people like Erlend Knudsen and Morgan Curtis seemed drowned out by the power politics that dominate each year's round of talks. But my generation's sense of shared planetary fate, our belief that the gap between the national interest and the global one is shrinking, in the end seemed to have a profound impact on key negotiators. Though the final Paris treaty contained many flaws, it was also an important victory for our worldview.

Of course, the treaty was just a framework for a new global status quo—it didn't have the power to simply will one into existence. That job requires plenty of money and innovation, two resources that feel limitless these days in a place like Silicon Valley. Its leaders seem genuine in their desire to create a more equitable and less destructive world. The young tech executives at the helm of the sharing economy in particular, as well as the millions of people my age responsible for its explosive growth, have the power to create that world. If the expressed ideals of this $335 billion sector become reality, we have the potential to rewrite the rules of mass consumption, accelerate our transition to renewable energy, and help lift billions of people out of poverty. But for now that's a big *if*.

Leaders like Mark Zuckerberg and Lyft co-founder John Zimmer may claim to take inspiration from indigenous culture. But I learned from young people like Elle-Máijá Tailfeathers that the progressive society promised by Silicon Valley requires more than simply improving our technology. To actually create a just and livable future on this planet, we have to take a long, hard look at systemic injustices and do everything we can to address them. Around the world indigenous peoples are still struggling to overcome a centuries-old legacy of colonial violence. These are people often feeling the worst impacts of climate change and of the fossil fuel extraction that is causing it. And until tech companies like Facebook and Lyft can meaningfully address the injustices that Elle-Máijá has spent much of her adult life confronting, it will be hard to take Silicon Valley's promise of social progress seriously.

A more convincing version of that promise came from Bernie Sanders. He campaigned for the Democratic nomination on the set of values that had been growing in tandem with my generation. He called for an economic system that improved society and the planet, brought an awareness of global issues to a national election, and put his political ideals above his partisan affiliations. Sanders channeled the desire for transformative change that many people my age so desperately yearn for. It was the primary reason that millions of young supporters like Saba Hafeez rallied behind him—and turned what began as a fringe candidacy for the 2016 Democratic nomination into a passionate social movement whose repercussions will be felt for years. Sanders's success came not from creating a Millennial revolution but rather from tapping into one that was already well underway.

That was the primary lesson I had to repeat to myself on election night as I threw back beer after beer and thought anxiously about the future. On the surface, the world looks very bad right now. We are hurtling toward an absolutely terrifying ecological abyss, and nobody in charge seems to want to do anything about it. But in the hearts and minds of millions of people my age, a new vision of the future is taking hold. It's full of infinitely more hope and possibility than the one our political and economic leaders tell us is inevitable. That future won't come easily. We are going to have to fight for it every step of the way. The victories I've explored throughout this book (and the young idealistic leaders behind them) are just the beginning. None of it is enough to avoid the planetary catastrophe that someone like Trump seems determined to create. But the lessons we can learn from their stories take us ever closer to a world that does.

Which is why, as my partner and I left the election night party in stunned silence, I finally found myself ready to answer the question that had started this entire journey—the question at the heart of my generation: Are we screwed? I had intentionally put off answering it for years. I'd danced around it. I'd evaded its implications. But with an aging climate change denier now in the White House, it finally had come time for me to face it. The Vancouver sky began to spit rain. A Pacific wind howled down the empty nighttime streets. I took a deep breath and turned over the question one more time: *Are we screwed?* I said the first word that came to my mind: *No.* Was this how I actually felt? I asked myself the question again and again, and still it was the only answer I could give. *No*, I thought, *we are not screwed.*

How to Not Screw Up
the Climate

A GUIDE FOR DAILY LIVING

You know that climate change is a big deal. You're aware that a primary cause of it is our outdated way of doing politics and economics. You badly want to create a better system. But it all seems so daunting. Is it even possible for someone like you—with loads of other issues and responsibilities demanding your attention—to make a difference? And if so, where do you even start?

By asking that question you already have started. Caring enough about climate change to want to do something about it is the first and most important step toward a livable future on this planet. What you should do next, though, is stop worrying about the fact that in a million small ways your daily existence is contributing to climate change. Be strategic in your concern. Nobody can live a perfectly sustainable life within the structures of our current society. Or as Bill McKibben has noted, "Changing the system, not perfecting our own lives, is the point. 'Hypocrisy' is the price of admission in this battle."[1] As an individual, you have more leverage than you might think to win it. Hopefully by the end of this resource guide, you'll get a better idea of how.

READ

Begin by educating yourself. Though there are endless books you can read about climate change, most of them are disempowering and boring and not worth your time. For a variety of reasons, however, the five books I've listed below definitely are worth your time, and they're as good a starting place as I can think of—besides reading my book and getting all your friends to buy it!—to gain a high-level understanding of the causes, impacts, and solutions to our current planetary crisis.

1. Elizabeth Kolbert, *The Sixth Extinction: An Unnatural History*. New York: Henry Holt, 2014. For learning in precise, and gripping, scientific detail how we humans are destroying everything of biological value on this planet.

2. Naomi Klein, *This Changes Everything: Capitalism vs. the Climate*. New York: Simon & Schuster, 2014. For appreciating the extent to which our crisis is really about a system of global capitalism that cares more about making money than about your future.

3. McKenzie Funk, *Windfall: The Booming Business of Global Warming*. New York: Penguin, 2014. For going inside the minds of businesspeople so driven by the bottom line that they're hoping to profit from the damage caused by climate change.

4. Jane Mayer, *Dark Money: The Hidden History of the Billionaires Behind the Rise of the Radical Right*. New York: Doubleday, 2016. For confirming in exhaustively reported detail that fossil fuel billionaires are indeed attempting to manipulate our political system in their favour.

5. Jeremy Rifkin, *The Zero Marginal Cost Society: The Internet of Things, the Collaborative Commons, and the Eclipse of Capitalism*. New York: St. Martin's, 2015. For sketching out a plausible—though sometimes breathless—vision of the future where we build a society that doesn't so badly damage Mother Nature.

For solid daily news coverage of climate change, I would start by reading one or several of the following: the *Guardian, Vox, Grist, Quartz*, and the *New York Times*. In general, a good way to evaluate the quality of an outlet's coverage—besides the amount of stories it does—is to look at how it frames the issue. Any outlet giving serious airtime to deniers of climate science is obviously not a great source of information. But also consider the following biases: Does the outlet continually diminish solutions as fringe or impractical? Does it portray the climate as primarily a left-wing issue? Does it rely on the same pundits over and over? Does it make climate change feel hopelessly complicated? Does it make you feel disempowered most of the time? A yes answer to any of those questions means you should probably be looking for climate news elsewhere.

CONSUME

Attempting to take responsibility for the climate impacts of everything you consume in an average day is a recipe for mental breakdown. At worst it will lead you to a psychiatric unit—which is what happened to an Australian seventeen-year-old who became so anxious about his carbon footprint that he refused to drink water.[2] Add to that the fact that many so-called eco-friendly companies or products are in fact nothing more than attempts by the same corporations who got us into this mess to greenwash their image. (Remember BP's "Beyond Petroleum" campaign?) In my opinion, there are more effective ways to leverage your concern about climate change than in the consumer marketplace. But here are a few areas where you can actually have a direct impact.

1. *Meat.* Eat less of it. Meat production is one of the biggest single contributors to climate change. A worldwide shift toward low-meat diets, one academic study estimated, could reduce the costs of fixing global warming by 50 percent.[3]
2. *Compost.* When you send food waste to a landfill, it can't decompose properly. The result is methane, a greenhouse gas 72 times more potent than CO_2. Composting all the food waste sent to U.S. landfills would be like taking millions of cars off the road.[4]
3. *Canvas bags.* Switching from plastic to canvas bags won't make a huge reduction in emissions. But using a reusable bag

communicates to neighbors and friends and strangers that you care about the climate. And a values shift grows faster when it's visible.

TRANSPORTATION

This is another tricky one. Ideally, we'd all be getting around on electrified mass transit powered by solar panels and wind turbines. But in many parts of North America you simply need a vehicle to get by. Even in high-density cities like Seattle and San Francisco and New York, it's not always possible to, say, do your weekly grocery trip via the city bus. Though this is a favorite argument of right-wing pundits for not shifting off fossil fuels—"Why, even Al Gore needs to drive and fly"—don't let the fact that we live in a system with suboptimal choices dissuade you from demanding a better one. Unless you can afford an electric car, I suggest you use your transportation choices as an opportunity to think systematically. Sure, you need to drive to work today, but as you do it, consider what improvements to your neighborhood, transit system, city—whatever—would make you less reliant on fossil fuels. Change begins with imagining a different future.

ENGAGE POLITICALLY

Yes, I know what you're thinking: politics sucks. It's slow and unsexy and maddening. But no matter how disillusioned you may be, especially with Donald Trump in power, it remains the most effective means of achieving changes to our society. It's also where you as an individual have disproportionate leverage. Often all it takes to get a new law passed or blocked is an outspoken group of citizens organized behind a clear set of values. For some reason, the political right seems to understand this better than the left—the NRA, the Tea Party, anyone?—but with progressive victories like 2015's Keystone XL pipeline rejection, that's starting to change. How you participate in the political process is entirely up to you, and the outcomes you can expect vary widely by which level of government you engage with.

1. *Municipal.* This is the easiest political arena to have your voice heard. In cities, climate solutions are implemented block by block. It's where transit plans are made. And increasingly, thanks to organizations like the C40 Cities Climate Leadership Group, it's where new social experiments can quickly become global norms.
2. *State/provincial/subnational.* This is like the neglected middle child of the political system. But as national climate politics grow more and more polarized, state legislatures have become the places where globally significant laws, like California's cap and trade emissions plan, get implemented, tested, and in some cases, scaled to the federal level.
3. *National.* The high-profile nature of national politics is both a curse and blessing for those seeking change. It means complex policy debates quickly become ideological battles. But it's also an arena where new political values—particularly radical ones, as we saw with Bernie Sanders in 2016—can quickly take hold across the country.

Whether you're pushing for more transit in your neighborhood, a state-level carbon price, or a national commitment to keep all new fossil fuels in the ground, the addition of your voice will make a meaningful difference. Finding out where to most effectively use it requires a bit of research and awareness, though. Start by paying attention to upcoming civic meetings in your neighborhood. Chat with those smiling Greenpeace volunteers who want you to sign their petition. Reach out to civil society organizations like the Sierra Club. Register to vote. If you are in college (or have recently been), there's almost certainly someone in your social media who tracks this stuff compulsively and would love to pump you with information. Once you've signaled to your social circles and the wider world that you're interested in making progressive change, I guarantee the opportunities will present themselves.

Far-reaching reform often begins outside the political system. And sometimes, as we saw with the $5 trillion divestment movement that arose on U.S. college campuses in 2012, it skips the system entirely. The reason protest is so powerful and worth your time is that it challenges our society's prevailing values. It often reveals them to be more arbitrary and open to negotiation than they initially appeared. Engaging in protest enables you to transcend the particulars of your own existence and give yourself something bigger to live for. It's a good way to make friends! So by all means attend demonstrations, sign up for e-mail updates from groups like 350.org, join a local divestment chapter, and share your beliefs openly and freely on social media—and don't be afraid to defend them. Above all else, be conscious of the fact that every major cultural shift in history began in the hearts and minds of regular people just like you.

CAREERS

Contrary to what the political right has been saying reflexively for decades, there are tons and tons of jobs in a less environmentally destructive economy. The United Nations predicts that in the next twenty years more than 60 million new ones will be created by our shift off fossil fuels.[5] One of the most effective ways you can build this economy is by deciding to work in it. Demand is booming right now for urban growers, solar cell technicians, sustainable designers, water quality technicians—basically any job you can think of that reduces humankind's impact on the planet. This is where our economy is clearly heading. Unfortunately academia has been slow to catch up. Degree programs relevant to the low-carbon future—teaching stuff like smart grid engineering and green building—are not as widespread as they should be and mostly exist now at the graduate level. But search, and you will find them.

However, you can have an equally important impact on climate change by simply deciding not to work for industries that perpetuate it.

Remember that in order to keep existing, companies like Exxon need new young workers. They need to replace all the older people who are retiring. And the fact that increasing numbers of Millennials are shunning careers in oil and gas is terrifying to the industry. It's putting hundreds of millions of dollars worth of new projects at risk. So as you begin a new career—or contemplate the one you already have—think seriously about its contribution to our political and economic status quo. Is the work you're doing making the world a better or worse place? Answer the question honestly, because the future of our planet and all of us who live here depends on it. It depends on people just like you and me. And with a bit of imagination and courage and dedication, it doesn't have to be totally screwed.

Acknowledgments

It's often assumed that in order to write a book you have to be extraordinarily gifted. What you actually need is lots and lots of time and a community of smart and patient people willing to call bullshit on your bad ideas and help you make the good ones better. My transition from clueless journalism school graduate to the writer of the book now in your hands began with all the brilliant people I worked with at the *Tyee* in Vancouver—including Monte Paulsen, Chris Wood, Michelle Hoar, Robyn Smith, Sarah Berman, Phillip Smith, Mitch Anderson, Crawford Kilian, Andrew Nikiforuk, and the countless other talented writers and editors and supporters of independent media who came through its doors over the years. I'm grateful to the *Tyee*'s founder David Beers, under whose mentorship and guidance the idea for "Are We Screwed?" first developed—and to my agent Trena White for helping me turn that idea into a book proposal. I'm indebted to the entire team at Bloomsbury—especially my editor, Anton Mueller, who led me through the chaos of writing my first draft with insight, empathy and humor— for making this book much better than I ever could have hoped. Props also to my awesome production editor, Jenna Dutton. So many others contributed to *Are We Screwed?* that I could not possibly name all of them. Thanks in particular to all the people whose stories are featured in its pages. Thanks to all my friends. Thanks to my mom, Diana Salomaa, and my brother, Nigel, for all their support. Thanks to my dad, who will never get to read this book but who I think of every day. And thanks most of all to my partner, Kara Hornland. There is really no way to express all the love and intelligence and awareness she contributed to this project. It would not exist without her.

Notes

INTRODUCTION: TIME IS TICKING DOWN

1   Eric Holthaus, "James Hansen's Bombshell Climate Warning Is Now Part of the Scientific Canon," *Slate*, March 22, 2016, http://www.slate.com/blogs/ the_slatest/2016/03/22/james_hansen_sea_level_rise_climate_warning_ passes_peer_review.html.

2   Gavin O'Toole, "Leading Companies Invest $674 Billion in Potentially Worthless Fossil Fuels," *Guardian*, April 9, 2013, https://www.theguardian .com/sustainable-business/companies-invest-worthless-fossil-fuels.

3   Isaac Arnsdorf, "US Fossil Fuel Lobby Outspent Green Groups 22 Times to Blunt Obama Climate Plan," *Sydney Morning Herald*, August 6, 2015, http://www.smh.com.au/environment/climate-change/us-fossil-fuel-lobby- outspent-green-groups-22-times-to-blunt-obama-climate-plan-20150805- gislg1.html.

4   Reihan Salam, "The Koch Brothers Were Supposed to Buy the 2016 Election," *Slate*, May 18, 2016, http://www.slate.com/articles/news_and_ politics/politics/2016/05/the_koch_brothers_were_supposed_to_buy_ the_2016_election_what_happened.html.

1. ALONE ON A LITTLE ISLAND

1   Shaonie Bhattacharya, "European Heatwave Caused 35,000 Deaths," *New Scientist*, October 10, 2003, https://www.newscientist.com/article/dn4259- european-heatwave-caused-35000-deaths/.

2   Dr. George Kling and Dr. Donald Wuebbles, "Confronting Climate Change in the Great Lakes Region Impacts on Our Communities and

Ecosystems: 2005 Update," *Union of Concerned Scientists and the Ecological Society of America*, November 2005, http://www.ucsusa.org/sites/default/files/legacy/assets/documents/global_warming/gl-exec-summary-update-05-doc.pdf.

3   Andrew Weaver, "The Science of Climate Change," *Geoscience Canada* 30, no. 3 (September 2003): 91.

4   Neela Banerjee, Lisa Song, and David Hasemyer, "Exxon's Own Research Confirmed Fossil Fuels' Role in Global Warming Decades Ago," *InsideClimateNews*, September 16, 2015, https://insideclimatenews.org/news/15092015/Exxons-own-research-confirmed-fossil-fuels-role-in-global-warming.

5   Greenpeace, "Koch Industries: Secretly Funding the Climate Denial Machine," *Greenpeace.org*, accessed August 5, 2016, http://www.greenpeace.org/usa/global-warming/climate-deniers/koch-industries/.

6   Damien Cave, "The United States of Oil," *Salon*, November 19, 2001, http://www.salon.com/2001/11/19/bush_oil/.

7   Faiz Shakir, "Bush Ignores Science, Claims 'There Is a Debate' over the Cause of Global Warming," *ThinkProgress*, June 26, 2006, http://thinkprogress.org/politics/2006/06/26/5997/bush-debate-climate/.

8   Peter Janes, interview by author, December 12, 2013. All quotations from Peter come from this interview unless otherwise cited.

9   Graham Readfearn, "Mourning Loomis Reef—The Heart of the Great Barrier Reef's Coral Bleaching Disaster," *Guardian*, April 21, 2016, https://www.theguardian.com/environment/planet-oz/2016/apr/21/mourning-loomis-reef-the-heart-of-the-great-barrier-reefs-coral-bleaching-disaster.

10   Oil Change International, "Fossil Fuel Funding to Congress: Industry Influence in the U.S.," *Priceofoil*, accessed August 5, 2016, http://priceofoil.org/fossil-fuel-industry-influence-in-the-u-s/.

11   Gavin O'Toole, "Leading Companies Invest $674 Billion in Potentially Worthless Fossil Fuels," *Guardian*, April 9, 2013, https://www.theguardian.com/sustainable-business/companies-invest-worthless-fossil-fuels.

12   Ben Block, "A Look Back at James Hansen's Seminal Testimony on Climate," *Grist*, June 16, 2008, http://grist.org/article/a-climate-hero-the-early-years/.

13   Robinson Meyer, "The Struggle of Clear Climate Communication," *Atlantic*, March 23, 2016, http://www.theatlantic.com/science/archive/2016/03/the-struggle-of-clear-climate-communication/474987/.

14 Andrew Revkin, "A Rocky First Review for a Climate Paper Warning of a Stormy Coastal Crisis," *New York Times*, July 15, 2015, http://dotearth .blogs.nytimes.com/2015/07/25/a-rocky-first-review-for-a-climate-paper-warning-of-a-stormy-coastal-crisis/.

15 Eric Holthaus, "James Hansen's Bombshell Climate Warning Is Now Part of the Scientific Canon," *Slate*, March 22, 2016, http://www.slate.com/blogs/the_slatest/2016/03/22/james_hansen_sea_level_rise_climatewarning_passes_peer_review.html.

16 Meyer, "Struggle of Clear Climate Communication."

17 Chris Mooney, "We Had All Better Hope These Scientists Are Wrong about the Planet's Future," *Washington Post*, March 22, 2016, https:// www.washingtonpost.com/news/energy-environment/wp/2016/03/22/we-had-all-better-hope-these-scientists-are-wrong-about-the-planets-future/? utm_term=.376319c39c31.

18 Eric Holthaus, "Earth's Most Famous Climate Scientist Issues Bombshell Sea Level Warning," *Slate*, July 20, 2015, http://www.slate.com/blogs/the_slatest/2015/07/20/sea_level_study_james_hansen_issues_dire_climate_warning.html.

19 Libby Nelson, "The US Won't Reach Peak Millennial Until 2036," *Vox*, April 26, 2016, http://www.vox.com/2016/4/26/11512608/millennials-baby-boomers-how-many.

20 Holthaus, "Earth's Most Famous."

21 Oliver Milman, "Climate Guru James Hansen Warns of Much Worse than Expected Sea Level Rise," *Guardian*, March 22, 2016, https://www .theguardian.com/science/2016/mar/22/sea-level-rise-james-hansen-climate-change-scientist.

22 Andrew Freedman, "Global Warming Policies We Set Today Will Determine the Next 10,000 Years," *Mashable*, February 8, 2016, http:// mashable.com/2016/02/08/global-warming-implications-study/#bYZmC CD2aZqf.

23 Eric Holthaus, "Our Planet's Temperature Just Reached a Terrifying Milestone," *Slate*, March 12, 2016, http://www.slate.com/blogs/future_tense/2016/03/01/february_2016_s_shocking_global_warming_temperature_record.html.

24 Robin Mckie, "February Was the Warmest Month in Recorded History, Climate Experts Say," *Guardian*, March 20, 2016, https://www.theguardian .com/environment/2016/mar/20/february-was-the-warmest-month-in-recorded-history-climate-experts-say.

25   Chris Mooney, "Poll: Millennials Are No More Convinced about Global
     Warming than Their Parents," *Washington Post*, April 30, 2015, https://
     www.washingtonpost.com/news/energy-environment/wp/2015/04/30/
     poll-millennials-are-no-more-convinced-about-global-warming-than-their-
     parents/?utm_term=.3dc2b0197316.

26   Lisa Hymas, "Gen Y and Gen X Get it Right on the Environment; Old
     Folks Don't," *Grist*, November 7, 2011, http://grist.org/climate-energy/
     2011-11-07-gen-y-and-gen-x-get-it-right-on-the-environment-old-folks-
     dont/.

27   Bruce Stokes, Richard Wike, and Jill Carle, "Global Concern about
     Climate Change, Broad Support for Limiting Emissions," *Pew Research
     Center*, November 5, 2015.

28   Harvard University Institute of Politics (IOP), "Survey of Young Americans'
     Attitudes toward Politics and Public Service," 27th ed., March 18 to
     April 1, 2015, http://iop.harvard.edu/sites/default/files_new/IOPSpring
     15%20PollTopline.pdf.

29   Stokes, Wike, and Carle, "Global Concern about Climate."

30   Geoff Dembicki, "On Climate Change, the Generation Gap Is Widening,"
     Tyee, March 16, 2015, http://thetyee.ca/News/2015/03/16/Climate-Change-
     Generation-Gap/.

31   Wendy Koch, "Poll Finds Generation Gap on Energy Issues as Millennials
     Voice Climate Concerns," *National Geographic*, October 30, 2014, http://
     energyblog.nationalgeographic.com/2014/10/30/poll-finds-generation-gap-
     on-energy-issues-as-millennials-voice-climate-concerns/.

32   David Roberts, "Millennials Love Clean Energy, Fear Climate Change, and
     Don't Vote. This Campaign Wants to Change That," *Vox*, April 30, 2016,
     http://www.vox.com/2016/4/30/11535004/millennials-climate-votes.

33   Harvard IOP, "Survey of Young."

34   "Millennials & Climate Action," *NextGen Climate*, May 2015, https://
     nextgenclimate.global.ssl.fastly.net/wp-content/uploads/2016/01/1.7.16-
     PNA-NGC-Millennial-Deck-FIN1.pdf.

35   "Research Findings from Battleground-State Millennials on Climate,"
     Hart Research Associates, September 8, 2015, https://nextgenclimate
     .global.ssl.fastly.net/wp-content/uploads/2015/09/ME11528c-NextGen-Press-
     08Sept153.pdf.

36   Ibid.

37 Jamison Foser, "50 Million Millennials Can't Be Wrong (But Will They Vote?)," *NextGen Climate*, April 29, 2016, https://nextgenclimate.org/blog/elections/50-million-millennials-will-they-vote/.

38 David Weinberger, "Millennials Are Committed to a Multidimensional Approach to Saving the Environment," *Roosevelt Institute*, April 9, 2012, http://rooseveltinstitute.org/millennials-are-committed-multidimensional-approach-saving-environment/.

39 Wendell Berry, "Manifesto: The Mad Farmer Liberation Front," in *The Country of Marriage* (New York: Harcourt Brace Jovanovich, 1973).

40 Joy Poliquin, "Off the Beaten Track," *Ring*, September 19, 2002, http://ring.uvic.ca/02sep19/summer.html.

41 Chris Turner, "On Strawberry Hill," *Walrus,* September 12, 2007, http://thewalrus.ca/2007-09-society/.

42 Jim Bohlen, *Making Waves: The Origins and Future of Greenpeace* (Montreal: Black Rose Books, 2000).

43 Emily Eakin, "The Civilization Kit," *New Yorker*, December 23 and 30, 2013, http://www.newyorker.com/magazine/2013/12/23/the-civilization-kit.

44 Holthaus, "Earth's Most Famous Climate Scientist."

45 Brian Merchant, "If We Release a Small Fraction of Arctic Carbon, 'We're Fucked': Climatologist," *Motherboard*, August 1, 2014, http://motherboard.vice.com/read/if-we-release-a-small-fraction-of-arctic-carbon-were-fucked-climatologist.

46 Geoff Dembicki, "'What Good Is It to Save the Planet If Humanity Suffers?': Exxon CEO," *Tyee*, May 30, 2013, http://thetyee.ca/Blogs/TheHook/2013/05/30/exxon-mobil-resolution-climate-tillerson/.

47 "The Degrowth Paradigm," *CBC Radio*, December 10, 2013, http://www.cbc.ca/radio/ideas/the-degrowth-paradigm-1.2458191.

48 Nicky Woolf, "'America Is Not a Planet': Republicans Resist Climate Change Action at Debate," *Guardian*, September 17, 2015, https://www.theguardian.com/us-news/2015/sep/17/marco-rubio-chris-christie-climate-change-republican-debate.

49 Robert Stavins, "Divestment Is No Substitute for Real Action on Climate Change," *Yale 360 Environment*, March 20, 2014, http://e360.yale.edu/feature/counterpoint_robert_stavins_divestment_no_substitute_for_real_action_on_climate/2749/.

2. CAPITALISM'S WORST NIGHTMARE

1   Bradley Johnson, interview by author, August 17, 2015. All quotations from Bradley come from this interview unless otherwise cited.

2   Carol Linnitt, "PHOTOS: Famed Photographer Alex MacLean's New Photos of Canada's Oilsands Are Shocking," *DeSmog Canada*, July 2, 2014,http://www.desmog.ca/2014/07/02/photos-famed-photographer-alex-maclean-s-new-photos-canada-s-oilsands-are-shocking.

3   David Biello, "How Much Will Tar Sands Oil Add to Global Warming?" *Scientific American*, January 23, 2013, http://www.scientificamerican.com/article/tar-sands-and-keystone-xl-pipeline-impact-on-global-warming/.

4   Ria Voorhar and Lauri Myllyvirta, *Point of No Return: The Massive Climate Threats We Must Avoid* (Amsterdam: Greenpeace International, 2013).

5   Alberta Venture, "The 50 Greatest Albertans," *Alberta Venture*, December 1, 2005, http://albertaventure.com/2005/12/the-50-greatest-albertans/.

6   "Washing Machine Helped Unlock Oilsands," *Business Edge News Magazine*, September 18, 2002, http://www.businessedge.ca/archives/article.cfm/washing-machine-helped-unlock-oilsands-1031.

7   Mary Clark Sheppard, *Oil Sands Scientist: The Letters of Karl A. Clark 1920–1949* (Edmonton: University of Alberta Press, 1989), p. 61.

8   Mary Clark Sheppard, "Daughter of Oil Sands Pioneer Reflects on Her Father's Legacy," *Alberta Oil*, May 1, 2009, http://www.albertaoilmagazine.com/2009/05/rooted-in-nature/.

9   Sheppard, *Oil Sands Scientist.*

10 Alastair Sweeny, *Black Bonanza: Canada's Oil Sands and the Race to Secure North America's Energy Future* (Mississauga: John Wiley & Sons Canada, 2010), p. 103.

11 Sheppard, "Daughter of Oil Sands Pioneer."

12 Andrew Nikiforuk, *Tar Sands: Dirty Oil and the Future of a Continent* (Vancouver: Greystone Books, 2010), p. 103.

13 Biello, "How Much Will Tar Sands."

14 Sheppard, "Daughter of Oil Sands Pioneer."

15 "Karl A. Clark," *Canadian Petroleum Hall of Fame,* accessed August 9, 2016, http://www.canadianpetroleumhalloffame.ca/karl-clark.html.

16 Sheppard, "Daughter of Oil Sands Pioneer."

17 Guy Chazen, "'Terrifying' Oil Skills Shortage Delays Projects and Raises Risks," *Financial Times*, July 16, 2014, http://www.ft.com/cms/s/0/cf831e0c-006f-11e4-a3f2-00144feab7de.html#axzz4Grxyt5mz.

18 John Kemp, "Mass Layoffs Complicate Oil Industry's Long-Term Plans: Kemp," *Reuters*, February 16, 2015, http://www.reuters.com/article/us-oil-employment-graduates-kemp-idUSKBN0LK0TR20150216.

19 Jim Fearon, during webinar "Oil & Gas Global Salary Guide 2015—United States," *Hays North America*, February 22, 2015, https://www.youtube.com/watch?v=fGLXL_sHsn4.

20 Jim Fearon, during webinar "Oil & Gas Global Salary Guide 2015—Canada," *Hays North America*, February 22, 2015, https://www.youtube.com/watch?v—Hm3uXzhfUo.

21 Neil Gascoigne, during webinar "Oil & Gas Global Salary Guide 2016—Canada," *Hays North America*, February 4, 2016, https://www.youtube.com/watch?v=7hCielIvv90.

22 "A Turbulent Year for the Global Oil and Gas Industry Could Result in Exacerbated Skills Shortages When Growth Returns," *Hays Oil & Gas Salary Guide 2016*, January 18, 2016, http://www.hays.dk/press-releases/hays-oil-gas-salary-guide-2016-1561198.

23 Bradley Olson, Edward Klump, and Jack Kaskey, "Dearth of Skilled Workers Imperils $100 Billion Projects," *Bloomberg*, March 7, 2013, http://www.bloomberg.com/news/articles/2013-03-07/dearth-of-skilled-workers-imperils-100-billion-projects.

24 Jared Head, "The Rise of the Millennials Will Either Make or Break the Oil and Gas Industry," *OilGrowth*, May 30, 2015, http://www.oilgrowth.com/the-rise-of-the-millennials-will-either-make-or-break-the-oil-gas-industry/.

25 Jason Rubli, "What Do Millennials Think about Oil and Gas?" *Molten Group RSS*, April 14, 2015, post has been removed from site, http://www.molten-group.com/en-us/uncategorized/what-do-millennials-think-about-oil-and-gas/.

26 Andrew Topf, "Canada's Oil Patch Bracing for 'Retirement Tsunami,'" *OilPrice*, June 27, 2014, http://oilprice.com/Energy/energy-general/Canadas-Oil-Patch-Bracing-for-Retirement-Tsunami.html.

27 "Millennials at Work: Reshaping the Workplace," *PricewaterhouseCoopers*, 2011, accessed August 9, 2016, https://www.pwc.com/gx/en/managing-tomorrows-people/future-of-work/assets/reshaping-the-workplace.pdf.

28   American Petroleum Institute, "API Energy and Jobs Tomorrow," *805 Innovations*, April 8, 2015, http://www.slideshare.net/ColbyCox1/american-petroleum-industry-marketing-campaign.

29   Ilya Skripnikov, "Oil and Gas, the Millennial Perspective," *Molten*, June 2, 2014, post has been removed from site.

30   Meagan Clark, "Wall Street Pay Raises for Juniors a Sign of Millennials' Declining Interest in Banking," *International Business Times*, August 27, 2014, http://www.ibtimes.com/wall-street-pay-raises-juniors-sign-millennials-declining-interest-banking-1671060.

31   Morley Winograd and Dr. Michael Hais, "Millennials and the Future of Corporate America," *Governance Studies at Brookings* (May 2014), page 7, accessed August 9, 2016, https://www.brookings.edu/wp-content/uploads/2016/06/Brookings_Winogradfinal.pdf.

32   DTTL Global Brand and Communications, "Mind the Gaps: The 2015 Deloitte Millennial Survey," *Deloitte*, 2015, accessed August 9, 2016, https://www2.deloitte.com/content/dam/Deloitte/global/Documents/About-Deloitte/gx-wef-2015-millennial-survey-executivesummary.pdf.

33   DTTL Global Brand and Communications, "The Millennial Survey 2014," *Deloitte*, 2014, accessed August 9, 2016, http://www2.deloitte.com/al/en/pages/about-deloitte/articles/2014-millennial-survey-positive-impact.html.

34   Robin Scher, "New Poll Shows a Majority of Young Americans Oppose Capitalism," *Alternet*, April 30, 2016, http://www.alternet.org/economy/new-poll-shows-majority-young-americans-oppose-capitalism.

35   Max Ehrenfreund, "A Majority of Millennials Now Reject Capitalism, Poll Shows," *Washington Post*, April 26, 2016, https://www.washingtonpost.com/news/wonk/wp/2016/04/26/a-majority-of-millennials-now-reject-capitalism-poll-shows/.

36   Tim Marcin, "Hard Times In 'Boomtown, USA': The Rise and Fall of Oil in Williston, North Dakota," *International Business Times*, December 23, 2015, http://www.ibtimes.com/hard-times-boomtown-usa-rise-fall-oil-williston-north-dakota-2224834.

37   Bobby Magill, "U.S. 'Likely Culprit' of Global Spike in Methane Emissions over Last Decade," *Guardian*, February 17, 2016, https://www.theguardian.com/environment/2016/feb/17/us-likely-culprit-of-global-spike-in-methane-emissions-over-last-decade.

38   Voorhar and Myllyvirta, *Point of No Return*.

39   John Cotter and Jennifer Graham, "Almost 30,000 Under Mandatory Order to Flee Fort McMurray Fire," *National Observer*, May 3, 2016, http://www.nationalobserver.com/2016/05/03/news/almost-30000-under-mandatory-order-flee-fort-mcmurray-fire.

40   Martin Lukacs, "The Arsonists of Fort McMurray Have a Name," *Guardian*, May 12, 2016, https://www.theguardian.com/environment/true-north/2016/may/12/the-arsonists-of-fort-mcmurray-have-a-name.

41   Mike De Souza, "Justin Trudeau Criticizes Elizabeth May's Fort McMurray Climate Connection," *National Observer*, May 4, 2016, http://www.nationalobserver.com/2016/05/04/news/fort-mcmurray-fires-related-global-climate-crisis-says-elizabeth-may.

42   Eric Holthaus, "We Need to Talk about Climate Change," *Slate*, May 6, 2016, http://www.slate.com/articles/health_and_science/science/2016/05/the_mcmurray_fire_is_worse_because_of_climate_change_and_we_need_to_talk.html.

43   Blair King, "On Forest Fires Climate Activist Aren't Just Insensitive, They Are Also Wrong," *A Chemist in Langley*, May 4, 2016, https://achemistinlangley.wordpress.com/2016/05/04/on-forest-fires-climate-activist-arent-just-insensitive-they-are-also-wrong/.

44   Michael Platt, "Middle-Finger Salute to Fort McMurray Climate Tweeters," *Calgary Sun*, May 4, 2016, http://www.calgarysun.com/2016/05/04/middle-finger-salute-to-fort-mac-climate-tweeters.

45   Kevin Libin, "Kevin Libin: Oil Didn't Cause the Fort McMurray Fire—It Helped Save People's Lives," *National Post*, May 5, 2016, http://business.financialpost.com/fp-comment/kevin-libin-oil-didnt-cause-the-fort-mcmurray-fire-it-helped-save-peoples-lives.

46   Ibid.

47   Gary Mason, "Used by Many and Loved by Few, Fort McMurray Deserves Only Our Support," *Globe and Mail*, May 4, 2016, http://www.theglobeandmail.com/news/alberta/fort-mcmurrays-impact-was-felt-in-struggling-provinces-across-canada/article29864978/.

48   Lorrie Goldstein, "Stupid, Stupid, Stupid," *Calgary Sun*, May 7, 2016, http://www.torontosun.com/2016/05/07/stupid-stupid-stupid.

49   Jeff Lee, "Western Premiers Call for More Health Care Dollars, Immigration, Free Trade," *Vancouver Sun*, May 6, 2016, http://vancouversun.com/news/politics/western-premiers-call-for-more-health-care-dollars-immigration-free-trade.

50   Nicholas Ellan, "Yes, It's Okay To Talk about Climate Change Right
     Now," *Nicholasellan.ca*, May 4, 2016, http://www.nicholasellan.ca/2016/
     05/04/yes-its-okay-to-talk-about-climate-change-right-now/.

51   Holthaus, "We Need to Talk."

52   Elizabeth Kolbert, "Fort McMurray and the Fires of Climate Change,"
     New Yorker, May 5, 2016, accessed August 9, 2016, http://www
     .newyorker.com/news/daily-comment/fort-mcmurray-and-the-fires-of-climate-
     change.

3. CITIZENS OF PLANET EARTH

1   Phil Aroneanu, interview by author, February 17, 2016. All quotations
     from Aroneanu come from this interview unless otherwise cited.

2   Allyse Heartwell, interview by author, March 18, 2016. All quotations
     from Allyse come from this interview unless otherwise cited.

3   Katharine Mieszkowski, "The Oil Is Going, the Oil Is Going!" *Salon*,
     March 22, 2006, http://www.salon.com/2006/03/22/peakoil/.

4   Allyse Heartwell, "Things to Lose," *aheartwell.blogspot.ca*, June 30, 2013,
     http://aheartwell.blogspot.ca/2013/06/things-to-lose.html.

5   Charlene Porter, "Young U.S. Adults Bring New World View to National
     Problems," *Philadelphia News*, September 27, 2013, http://www
     .zogbyanalytics.com/news/335-young-u-s-adults-bring-new-world-view-to-
     national-problems.

6   Pew Research Center, "Millennials in Adulthood," *Pew Social Trends*,
     March 7, 2014, http://www.pewsocialtrends.org/2014/03/07/millennials-
     in-adulthood/.

7   Haley Cohen and Howard Dean, "The First Global Generation,"
     Huffington Post, April 2, 2013, http://www.huffingtonpost.com/haley-
     cohen/global-generation_b_3000065.html?utm_hp_ref=tw.

8   Gayle Macdonald, "Youth Anxiety on the Rise Amid Changing Climate,"
     Globe and Mail, May 1, 2014, http://www.theglobeandmail.com/life/
     health-and-fitness/health/youth-anxiety-on-the-rise-amid-changing-
     climate/article18372258/.

9   BrainPOP, "Kids Fear Global Warming More than Terrorism, Car Crashes,
     and Cancer, According to National Earth Day Survey," *PRNewswire*,
     April 20, 2007, http://www.prnewswire.com/news-releases/kids-fear-global-

warming-more-than-terrorism-car-crashes-and-cancer-according-to-national-earth-day-survey-58684647.html.

10 John Zogby, "Enter the First Globals," *Forbes*, July 1, 2013, http://www .zogbyanalytics.com/news/312-enter-the-first-globals.

11 Lynn Vavreck, "Younger Americans Are Less Patriotic. At Least, in Some Ways," *New York Times*, July 4, 2014, http://www.nytimes.com/2014/07/05/ upshot/younger-americans-are-less-patriotic-at-least-in-some-ways.html.

12 Bruce Stokes, Richard Wike, and Jill Carle, "Global Concern about Climate Change, Broad Support for Limiting Emissions," *Pew Research Center*, November 5, 2015.

13 Geoff Dembicki, "Gulf Disaster Raises Alarms about Alberta to Texas Pipeline," *Tyee*, June 21, 2010, http://thetyee.ca/News/2010/06/21/Alberta ToTexasPipeline/.

14 Geoff Dembicki, "On Both Sides of Border, Indigenous Groups Oppose Keystone," *Tyee*, October 5, 2011, http://thetyee.ca/News/2011/10/05/ Keystone-Indigenous-Opposition/.

15 Ibid.

16 Ibid.

17 Ibid.

18 Ibid.

19 Matthew Nisbet, "Nature's Prophet: Bill McKibben as Journalist, Public Intellectual and Activist," Joan Shorenstein Center on the Press, Politics and Public Policy, March 2013, http://scholar.harvard.edu/files/matthewnisbet/ files/d-78-nisbet1.pdf.

20 Ibid.

21 Will Bates, "24 Hours That Shifted the World," 350.org, October 25, 2012, http://350.org/24-hours-shifted-world/.

22 Brittney Martin, "Al Gore: 2015 Paris Conference Will Spur Global Climate Change Policies," *Dallas Morning News*, March 14, 2015, http:// trailblazersblog.dallasnews.com/2015/03/al-gore-2015-paris-conference-will-spur-global-climate-change-policies.html/.

23 Evan Mackinder, "Pro-Environment Groups Outmatched, Outspent in Battle Over Climate Change Legislation," *OpenSecrets*, August 23, 2010, http://www.opensecrets.org/news/2010/08/pro-environment-groups-were-outmatc/.

24 Nisbet, "Nature's Prophet."

25 James Hansen, "Silence Is Deadly," June 3, 2011, http://www.columbia .edu/~jeh1/mailings/2011/20110603_SilenceIsDeadly.pdf.

26   Andrew Leach, "On the Potential for Oilsands to Add 200ppm of CO_2 to the Atmosphere," *Rescuing the Frog*, June 4, 2011, http://andrewleach.ca/oilsands/on-the-potential-for-oilsands-to-add-200ppm-of-co2-to-the-atmosphere/.

27   Hansen, "Silence Is Deadly."

28   Maude Barlow et al., "Environmental Leaders Call for Civil Disobedience to Stop the Keystone XL Pipeline," *Common Dreams*, June 23, 2011, http://www.commondreams.org/views/2011/06/23/environmental-leaders-call-civil-disobedience-stop-keystone-xl-pipeline.

29   Timothy Gardner, "U.S. Green Groups Write Obama to Oppose Oil Pipeline," *Reuters*, August 24, 2011, http://www.reuters.com/article/us-usa-keystone-protest-idUSTRE77N8DF20110824.

30   Ben Adler, "The Inside Story of How the Keystone Fight Was Won," *Grist*, November 6, 2015, http://grist.org/climate-energy/the-inside-story-of-how-the-keystone-fight-was-won/.

31   Darren Samuelsohn and Darren Goode, "Why GOP Embraced Keystone," *Politico*, December 20, 2011, http://www.politico.com/story/2011/12/why-gop-embraced-keystone-070722.

32   Adler, "Inside Story."

33   David Roberts, "A Chat with the Sierra Club's Michael Brune about Civil Disobedience," *Grist*, January 28, 2013, http://grist.org/climate-energy/a-chat-with-the-sierra-clubs-michael-brune-about-civil-disobedience/.

34   Bryan Walsh, "Greens Are Justifiably Mad about the Oil Sands Pipeline. But Sitting Out 2012 Elections Would Be Insane," *Time*, August 26, 2011, http://science.time.com/2011/08/26/greens-are-justifiably-mad-about-the-oil-sands-pipeline-but-sitting-out-2012-elections-would-be-insane/.

35   David Roberts, "The Virtues of Being Unreasonable on Keystone," *Grist*, February 19, 2013, http://grist.org/climate-energy/the-virtues-of-being-unreasonable-on-keystone/.

36   Bryan Walsh, "Obama's Energy Strategy: All of the Above—and a Lot of Oil," *Time*, March 22, 2012, http://science.time.com/2012/03/22/obamas-energy-strategy-all-of-the-above-and-a-lot-of-oil/.

37   Adler, "Inside Story."

38   Wen Stephenson, "Nearly 400 Arrested at XL Dissent—the Largest White House Civil Disobedience Action in a Generation," *Nation*, March 7, 2014, https://www.thenation.com/article/nearly-400-arrested-xl-dissent-largest-white-house-civil-disobedience-action-generati/.

39 Joel Gehrke, "Obama Kills Keystone Pipeline to Preserve America's 'Global Leadership' on Climate Change," *National Review*, November 6, 2015,http://www.nationalreview.com/article/426706/symbolic-obama-kills-keystone-act-global-leadership-joel-gehrke.

40 Rebecca Penty, "How a CEO Reacts When Robert Redford Pegs Him a Villain," *Bloomberg*, February 19, 2002, http://www.bloomberg.com/news/articles/2014-02-19/how-a-ceo-reacts-when-robert-redford-pegs-him-a-villain.

41 Geoff Dembicki, "Alberta's Hired Gun in Washington," *Tyee*, March 29, 2011, http://thetyee.ca/News/2011/03/29/AlbertasHiredGun/.

42 Ibid.

43 Ibid.

44 Geoff Dembicki, "Climate Group Says Washington's Oil Sands War Is 'David vs. Goliath,'" *Tyee*, March 28, 2011, http://thetyee.ca/News/2011/03/28/DavidVsGoliath/.

45 Penty, "How a CEO Reacts."

46 Ibid.

47 Geoff Dembicki, "War Cry of the Oil Sands Lobby: 'Us Against the World,'" *Tyee*, March 30, 2011, http://thetyee.ca/News/2011/03/30/UsAgainstTheWorld/.

48 Stefanie Spear, "Breaking: 400 Youths Arrested at White House Protesting Keystone XL Pipeline," *EcoWatch*, March 2, 2014, http://www.ecowatch.com/breaking-400-youths-arrested-at-white-house-protesting-keystone-xl-pip-1881869939.html.

49 Geoff Dembicki, "Oil Sands Lobbying Without End, Vows American Petroleum Institute," *Tyee*, April 6, 2011, http://thetyee.ca/News/2011/04/06/LobbyingWithoutEnds/.

50 Canadian Press, "TransCanada CEO Russ Girling: 'Rhetoric Won Out Over Reason,'" *Maclean's*, November 6, 2015, http://www.macleans.ca/politics/ottawa/transcanada-cco-russ-girling-rhetoric-won-out-over-reason/.

51 Phil Aroneanu, "Moving on From 350.org . . ." *blog.philaroneanu.com*, 2016, accessed August 10, 2016, http://blog.philaroneanu.com/post/134882029226/moving-on-from-350org.

4. BEYOND LEFT AND RIGHT

1   Stephen Marche, "The Closing of the Canadian Mind," *New York Times*, August 14, 2015, http://www.nytimes.com/2015/08/16/opinion/sunday/the-closing-of-the-canadian-mind.html.

2   Campbell Clark, "For Harper, All Trade Roads Now Lead to China," *Globe and Mail*, February 5, 2012, http://www.theglobeandmail.com/news/politics/for-harper-all-trade-roads-now-lead-to-china/article544163/.

3   Andrew Frank, interview by author, October 16, 2015. All quotations from Andrew come from this interview unless otherwise cited.

4   Geoff Dembicki, "At Ground Zero for Next Huge Enviro War: Hartley Bay," *Tyee*, September 13, 2010, http://thetyee.ca/News/2010/09/13/Hartley BayEnviroWar/.

5   ForestEthics and Mustel, "ForestEthics: Opposition to B.C. Oil Tankers on the Rise," *MarketWired*, May 26, 2010, http://www.marketwired.com/press-release/forestethics-opposition-to-bc-oil-tankers-on-the-rise-1266656.htm.

6   "New Survey Indicates 75% of British Columbians Want to Ban Oil Tankers on North Coast," DogwoodInitiative.org, April 1, 2011, https://dogwoodinitiative.org/phone-survey-results/.

7   Geoff Dembicki, "Native Leader to Harper: 'We Will Be the Wall That Enbridge Cannot Break Through,'" *Tyee*, December 1, 2011, http://thetyee.ca/Blogs/TheHook/Environment/2011/12/01/native-harper-enbridge-wall/.

8   Carolynne Wheeler, "Chinese 'Frustrated' by Northern Gateway Regulatory Delays," *Globe and Mail*, February 9, 2012, http://www.theglobeandmail.com/report-on-business/industry-news/energy-and-resources/chinese-frustrated-by-northern-gateway-regulatory-delays/article 545314/.

9   Jessica Dorfmann, "The Power of Young Voters: Canada's Historic Election," *Harvard International Review*, November 4, 2015, http://hir.harvard.edu/power-young-voters-canadas-historic-election/.

10 David Roberts, "Millennials Love Clean Energy, Fear Climate Change, and Don't Vote. This Campaign Wants to Change That," *Vox*, April 30, 2016, http://www.vox.com/2016/4/30/11535004/millennials-climate-votes.

11 Derek Thompson, "The Liberal Millennial Revolution," *Atlantic*, February 29, 2016, http://www.theatlantic.com/politics/archive/2016/02/the-liberal-millennial-revolution/470826/.

12 "The Youth Vote in 2012," Center for Information and Research on Civic Learning and Engagement, May 10, 2013, http://civicyouth.org/wp-content/uploads/2013/05/CIRCLE_2013FS_outhVoting2012FINAL.pdf.

13 Julia Glum, "Youth Voter Turnout For 2014 Midterm Election Lowest in 40 Years: Report," *International Business Times*, July 22, 2015, http://www.ibtimes.com/youth-voter-turnout-2014-midterm-election-lowest-40-years-report-2019813.

14 George Arnett and Pablo Gutierrez, "UK Election 2015: Can Young Voters Make a Difference?" *Guardian*, February 24, 2015, http://www.theguardian.com/politics/datablog/2015/feb/24/uk-election-2015-can-young-voters-make-a-difference.

15 "How Britain Voted in 2015," *Ipsos Mori*, August 26, 2015, https://www.ipsos-mori.com/researchpublications/researcharchive/3575/How-Britain-voted-in-2015.aspx.

16 Marc Mayrand, "Declining Voter Turnout: Can We Reverse the Trend?" *Elections Canada*, February 6, 2012, http://www.elections.ca/content.aspx?section=med&document=feb1712&dir=spe&lang=e.

17 "A Deep Dive into Party Affiliation," *Pew Research Center*, April 7, 2015, http://www.people-press.org/2015/04/07/a-deep-dive-into-party-affiliation/.

18 Arnett and Gutierrez, "UK Election 2015."

19 Geoff Dembicki, "Young Voters Could Defeat Harper, So Why Don't They?" *Tyee*, April 6, 2015, http://thetyee.ca/News/2015/04/06/Young-Voters-Could-Defeat-Harper/.

20 Hunter Walker, "Harvard Poll Shows Millennials Have 'Historically Low' Levels of Trust in Government," *Business Insider*, April 29, 2014, http://www.businessinsider.com/poll-millenials-have-historically-low-levels-of-trust-in-government-2014-4.

21 DTTL Global Brand and Communications, "The Millennial Survey 2014," *Deloitte*, 2014, accessed August 9, 2016, http://www2.deloitte.com/al/en/pages/about-deloitte/articles/2014-millennial-survey-positive-impact.html.

22 Russell Berman, "What's the Answer to Political Polarization in the U.S.?" *Atlantic*, March 8, 2016, http://www.theatlantic.com/politics/archive/2016/03/whats-the-answer-to-political-polarization/470163/.

23　C. Andris et al., "The Rise of Partisanship and Super-Cooperators in the U.S. House of Representatives," *PLOS ONE* 10, no. 4 (2015), accessed August 11, 2016, http://journals.plos.org/plosone/article?id=10.1371/journal.pone.0123507.

24　Michael Hiltzik, "Five Years After Citizens United Ruling, Big Money Reigns," *Los Angeles Times*, January 24, 2015, http://www.latimes.com/business/hiltzik/la-fi-hiltzik-20150125-column.html.

25　Jay Newton-Small, "Interview: John McCain on Ukraine, Syria, Barack Obama, Chris Christie," *Time*, March 2, 2014, http://time.com/11165/john-mccain-barack-obama-syria-ukraine/#ixzz2voLJebtY.

26　Jeffrey Kluger, "Senator Throws Snowball! Climate Change Disproven!" *Time*, February 27, 2015, http://time.com/3725994/inhofe-snowball-climate/.

27　David Roberts, "Obama Can't Change Polarization on Climate Change," *Grist*, February 12, 2013, http://grist.org/politics/obama-cant-change-polarization-on-climate-change/.

28　"The Fossil Fuel Industry Spent More than Seven-Hundred Million Dollars During 2014's Midterm Elections," *ThinkProgress*, December 23, 2014, https://thinkprogress.org/the-fossil-fuel-industry-spent-more-than-seven-hundred-million-dollars-during-2014s-midterm-85cf181503a7#.iupqaut3f

29　Justin Farrell, "Corporate Funding and Ideological Polarization about Climate Change," *Proceedings of the National Academy of Sciences* 113, no. 1 (2016), accessed August 11, 2016, http://www.pnas.org/content/113/1/92.abstract.

30　Pew Research Center, "Millennials in Adulthood," *Pew Social Trends*, March 7, 2014, http://www.pewsocialtrends.org/2014/03/07/millennials-in-adulthood/.

31　Yong Jung Cho, Waleed Shahid, Devontae Torriente, and Sara Blazevic, "Here's Why We're Committing Civil Disobedience: Millennials Can No Longer Be Silent about Our Broken System," *Salon*, November 2, 2015, http://www.salon.com/2015/11/02/heres_why_were_committing_civil_disobedience_millennials_can_no_longer_be_silent_about_our_broken_system/.

32　Geoff Dembicki, "Gary Doer's Startling Embrace of the Oil Sands," *Tyee*, April 4, 2011, http://thetyee.ca/News/2011/04/04/GaryDoer/.

33　Jim Snyder, "Keystone Pipeline Causes Rift Between Gary Doer and One-Time Allies," *Bloomberg*, January 16, 2014, http://business.financial-post.com/news/energy/gary-doer-keystone-xl-pipeline?__lsa=c287-2aa9.

34 Dembicki, "Gary Doer's Startling Embrace."

35 Ibid.

36 Snyder, "Keystone Pipeline."

37 Paul Koring, "Canada Accuses EPA of 'Distortion and Omission' in Keystone XL Assessment," *Globe and Mail*, February 11, 2015, http://www.theglobeandmail.com/news/world/canada-accuses-epa-of-distortion-on-keystone-pipeline/article22914580/.

38 Geoff Dembicki, "TransCanada to Ambassador Doer: 'Thank you,'" *Tyee*, November 26, 2012, http://thetyee.ca/Blogs/TheHook/Federal-Politics/2012/11/26/keystone-xl-transcanada-doer-emails/.

39 Snyder, "Keystone Pipeline."

40 Dembicki, "Gary Doer's Startling Embrace."

41 Mychaylo Prystupa, "Ambassador Doer Says Obama Risks Surge in Oil Trains by Rejecting Keystone XL," *Vancouver Observer*, January 22, 2015, http://www.vancouverobserver.com/news/ambassador-doer-says-obama-risks-surge-oil-trains-rejecting-keystone-xl.

42 Governments of Manitoba and California, "Memorandum of Understanding," December 2006, https://www.gov.mb.ca/asset_library/en/premier/mou_california.pdf.

43 Canadian Press, "Greenhouse Gas Targets Difficult But Doable, Says Doer," *Hamilton Spectator*, February 3, 2010, http://www.thespec.com/news-story/2187360-greenhouse-gas-targets-difficult-but-doable-says-doer/.

44 Eric Andrew-Gee, "Our Tar Sands Man in Washington," *Maisonneuve*, January 16, 2012, https://maisonneuve.org/article/2012/01/16/our-tar-sands-man-washington/.

45 Ibid.

46 Andrew Nikiforuk, "Oh, Canada," *Foreign Policy*, June 24, 2013, http://foreignpolicy.com/2013/06/24/oh-canada/.

47 Crawford Kilian, "'Environmentalists, Other Radical Groups,' Threaten Pipeline: Joe Oliver," *Tyee*, January 9, 2012, http://thetyee.ca/Blogs/TheHook/Environment/2012/01/09/Environmentalists_other_radical_groups/.

48 Jason Feteke, "Harper in China: PM Attacks 'Foreign Money' Behind Oil Sands Protest, Refuses to Trade Human Rights," *Postmedia News*, February 10, 2012, http://news.nationalpost.com/news/canada/stephen-harper-pushes-for-responsible-oil-and-gas-trade-in-china-speech.

49   Andrew Frank, "A Whistleblower's Open Letter to the Citizens of Canada,"
      Voices-Voix, January 22, 2012, http://voices-voix.ca/en/news/whistleblowers-
      open-letter-citizens-canada.

50   Andrew Frank, "Affidavit," *Voices-Voix*, accessed August 11, 2016, http://
      voices-voix.ca/sites/voices-voix.ca/files/andrew_frank_sworn_affidavit
      .pdf.

51   Ibid.

52   Frank, "Whistleblower's Open Letter."

53   Canadian Press, "Affidavit Accuses PMO of Threatening Environmental
      Group," *CTV News*, January 24, 2012, http://www.ctvnews.ca/affidavit-
      accuses-pmo-of-threatening-environmental-group-1.758063.

54   "PMO Accused of Threatening Environmental Group," *CBC News*,
      January   24,   2012,   http://www.cbc.ca/news/canada/pmo-accused-of-
      threatening-environmental-group-1.1294632.

55   Nathan   Vanderklippe   and   Shawn   McCarthy,   "Environmentalist's
      Departure Sheds Light on Tension Felt by Green Groups," *Globe and
      Mail*, January 24, 2012, http://www.theglobeandmail.com/news/politics/
      environmentalists-departure-sheds-light-on-tension-felt-by-green-groups/
      article546410/.

56   "PMO Accused," *CBC News*.

57   Ross McMillan, "Tides Canada: Let's Have Open, Honest Debate about
      Our Energy Future," *Tyee*, January 31, 2012, http://thetyee.ca/Opinion/
      2012/01/31/Tides-Canada-Joe-Oliver/.

58   Andrew Frank, "The #EnemyGate Scandal," *Rabble,* February 3, 2012,
      http://rabble.ca/blogs/bloggers/andrew-frank/2012/02/enemygate-scandal.

59   Canadian Press, "Higher Youth Turnout Could Change Tone, Outcome of
      Elections," *CBC News,* March 22, 2014, http://www.cbc.ca/news/canada/
      higher-youth-turnout-could-change-tone-outcome-of-elections-1.2582855.

60   Mayrand, "Declining Voter Turnout."

61   Michael Adams and Maryantonett Flumian, "Many Canadians Aren't
      Voting. Have They Stopped Caring about Democracy," *Globe and Mail*,
      January 26, 2015, http://www.theglobeandmail.com/opinion/the-young-are-
      quitting-politics-and-thats-a-danger-to-our-democracy/article22633913/.

62   "Samara Canada Releases a Myth-Busting Report on Youth Apathy,"
      Samara Canada, September 10, 2015, http://www.samaracanada.com/
      samarablog/blog-post/samara-main-blog/2015/09/10/samara-canada-releases-
      a-myth-busting-on-youth-apathy.

63 Ashley Csanady, "Millennials Are in Many Ways More Political Than Older Canadians, Study Finds," *National Post*, September 9, 2015, http://news.nationalpost.com/news/canada/canadian-politics/to-call-this-generation-apathetic-i-think-is-a-disservice-millennials-totally-care-about-politics.

64 Geoff Dembicki, "Young Voters Could Defeat Harper, So Why Don't They?" *Tyee*, April 6, 2015, http://thetyee.ca/News/2015/04/06/Young-Voters-Could-Defeat-Harper/.

65 Ibid.

66 Andrew Frank, "11 Ridings Where Progressive British Columbians Should Vote Liberal to Defeat Harper," *Huffington Post*, October 9, 2015, http://www.huffingtonpost.ca/andrew-frank/bc-voters-canada-election-liberal-harper_b_8272076.html.

67 Leadnow, "The Vote Together Campaign," *Vote Together*, accessed August 12, 2016, https://www.votetogether.ca/pages/about/.

68 Eric Andrew-Gee, "The 'Big Experiment' of Voting Strategically This Election," *Globe and Mail*, October 11, 2015, http://www.theglobeandmail.com/news/politics/elections/the-big-experiment-of-voting-strategically-this-election/article26767617/.

69 Ibid.

70 Brigette DePape, "Why the Youth Vote Is Going Viral," *Huffington Post*, October 16, 2015, http://www.huffingtonpost.ca/the-council-of-canadians/youth-vote-is-going-viral_b_8312832.html.

71 Andy Blatchford, "Justin Trudeau in Victory Speech: 'We Beat Fear with Hope, We Beat Cynicism with Hard Work,'" *National Post*, October 20, 2015, accessed August 12, 2016, http://news.nationalpost.com/news/canada/canadian-politics/justin-trudeau-in-victory-speech-we-beat-fear-with-hope-we-beat-cynicism-with-hard-work.

72 Dorfmann, "Power of Young Voters."

73 David Coletto, "Canada's New Electoral Powerhouse?" *Abacus Data and the Canadian Alliance of Student Associations*, April 19, 2016, http://abacusdata.ca/the-next-canada-politics-political-engagement-and-priorities-of-canadas-next-electoral-powerhouse-young-canadians/.

74 Zi-Ann Lum, "Edward Snowden Warns Canadians to Be 'Extraordinarily Cautious' over Anti-Terror Bill," *Huffington Post*, February 3, 2015, http://www.huffingtonpost.ca/2015/02/03/edward-snowden-ucc-canada-surveillance_n_6601812.html.

75 Bruce Anderson and David Coletto, "Canadian Politics: A Generational Divide?" *Abacus Data*, July 27, 2015, http://abacusdata.ca/canadian-politics-a-generational-divide/.

76 Geoff Dembicki, "Why Are Young Workers Shunning the Oilsands?" *Tyee*, March 23, 2015, http://thetyee.ca/News/2015/03/23/Young-Workers-Shunning-Oilsands/.

77 Geoff Dembicki, "On Climate Change, the Generation Gap Is Widening," *Tyee*, March 16, 2015, http://thetyee.ca/News/2015/03/23/Young-Workers-Shunning-Oilsands/http://thetyee.ca/News/2015/03/16/Climate-Change-Generation-Gap/.

78 "Vote Compass: Economy and Environment Rate as Top Issues," *CBC News*, September 10, 2015, http://www.cbc.ca/m/touch/politics/story/1.3222945.

79 Robin Levinson King, "How the Parties Stack Up on Youth Issues," *Toronto Star*, October 8, 2015, https://www.thestar.com/news/federal-election/2015/10/08/how-the-parties-stack-up-on-youth-issues.html.

80 Canadian Press, "Higher Youth Turnout."

81 Brigette DePape and Tamo Campos, "Brigette DePape and Tamo Campos: Talkin' bout Our Generation," *Georgia Straight*, January 21, 2015, http://www.straight.com/news/811086/brigette-depape-and-tamo-campos-talkin-bout-our-generation.

82 Geoff Dembicki, "Among Millennials, No Political Party Has a Commanding Lead," *Tyee*, April 27, 2015, http://thetyee.ca/News/2015/04/27/Millennials-No-Political-Party-Leads/.

83 Anderson and Coletto, "Canadian Politics."

84 Mario Canseco, "Change, Leader Appeal Propelled Liberals in British Columbia," *Insights West*, October 22, 2015, http://www.insightswest.com/news/change-leader-appeal-propelled-liberals-in-british-columbia/.

85 Tom Flanagan, "The Conservative Campaign," *Samara Canada*, November 18, 2015, http://www.samaracanada.com/samarablog/blog-post/samara-main-blog/2015/11/18/the-conservative-campaign.

86 Dorfmann, "Power of Young Voters."

87 Peter O'Neil, "Justin Trudeau Won't Be Pinned Down on B.C. Oil Tanker Ban Timing," *Vancouver Sun*, June 21, 2016, http://vancouversun.com/news/local-news/justin-trudeau-wont-be-pinned-down-on-b-c-oil-tanker-ban-timing.

88 Mychaylo Prystupa, "Trudeau Orders Oil Tanker Ban That Could Kill Northern Gateway," *National Observer*, November 13, 2015, http://www

.nationalobserver.com/2015/11/13/news/trudeau-orders-oil-tanker-ban-could-kill-northern-gateway.

5. WHY WALL STREET IS CHANGING

1 Chloe Maxmin, interview by author, February 26, 2016. All quotations from Chloe come from this interview unless otherwise cited.

2 Chloe Maxmin, "The Shopping Bag Heard Round the World," *Changemakers*, accessed August 12, 2016, https://www.changemakers.com/competition/staplesyv/entries/shopping-bag-heard-round-world.

3 Ibid.

4 Deborah Sayer, "Nobleboro Teen Hailed as Environmental Hero," *Portland Press Herald*, October 6, 2010, http://www.pressherald.com/2010/10/06/an-environmental-hero_2010-10-06/.

5 Gaby Berkman, "ACE Alumna Profile: Chloe," *Alliance for Climate Education*, January 26, 2012, https://acespace.org/blog/ace-alumna-profile-chloe.

6 Bill McKibben, "Global Warming's Terrifying New Math," *Rolling Stone*, July 19, 2012, http://www.rollingstone.com/politics/news/global-warmings-terrifying-new-math-20120719.

7 Ibid.

8 Morgan Simon, "Shareholder Resolution Filing at Swarthmore College," *Responsible Endowments Coalition*, Fall 2008, accessed August 12, 2016, http://endowmentethics.dreamhosters.com/swarthmore-college.

9 Ibid.

10 Responsible Endowments Coalition, *Everything You Need to Know to Bring Responsible Investment to Your College or University*, Version 5.0, July 2012, accessed August 12, 2016, http://community-wealth.org/sites/clone.community-wealth.org/files/downloads/tool-rec-student-handbook-endowments_0.pdf.

11 James Leaton, "Unburnable Carbon—Are the World's Financial Markets Carrying a Carbon Bubble?" 2011, accessed August 12, 2016, *Carbon Tracker Initiative*, http://www.carbontracker.org/wp-content/uploads/2014/09/Unburnable-Carbon-Full-rev2-1.pdf.

12 McKibben, "Global Warming's Terrifying New Math."

13 Joe Romm, "McKibben Must-Read: 'Global Warming's Terrifying New Math,'" *ThinkProgress*, July 23, 2012, https://thinkprogress.org/mckibben-must-read-global-warmings-terrifying-new-math-62f4e812e8c8#.opn4ja9l4.

14 Chloe Maxmin, "Fossil Fuel Divestment Is Simple Yet Compelling Logic. It's Time Harvard Understood," *Blue and Green Tomorrow*, May 29, 2014, http://blueandgreentomorrow.com/features/fossil-fuel-divestment-is-simple-yet-compelling-logic-its-time-harvard-understood/.

15 Frankfurt School of Finance and Management, "Global Trends in Renewable Energy Investment 2015," *Frankfurt School-UNEP Centre/Bloomberg New Energy Finance*, 2015, accessed August 12, 2016, http://fs-unep-centre.org/sites/default/files/attachments/key_findings.pdf.

16 David Roberts, "College Students Are Making Global Warming a Moral Issue. Here's Why That Scares People," *Vox*, April 29, 2015, http://www.vox.com/2015/4/29/8512853/fossil-fuel-divestment.

17 Geoff Dembicki, "How Millennials Are Changing Wall Street," *Tyee*, May 5, 2014, http://thetyee.ca/News/2014/05/05/Millennials-Changing-Wall-Street/.

18 Audrey Choi, "Sustainable Investing: Imperative and Opportunity," *Morgan Stanley*, February 2014, https://www.morganstanley.com/sustainableinvesting/pdf/Sustainable_Investing_Imperative_Opportunity.pdf.

19 David Banks, "Big Investors and the Young Nudge Morgan Stanley Toward Sustainable Investing," *Bloomberg*, November 21, 2013, http://www.bloomberg.com/news/articles/2013-11-21/big-investors-and-the-young-nudge-morgan-stanley-toward-sustainable-investing.

20 Chris Cillizza, "Millennials Don't Trust Anyone. That's a Big Deal," *Washington Post*, April 30, 2015, https://www.washingtonpost.com/news/the-fix/wp/2015/04/30/millennials-dont-trust-anyone-what-else-is-new/.

21 Dembicki, "How Millennials."

22 Ibid.

23 "From the Margins to the Mainstream Assessment of the Impact Investment Sector and Opportunities to Engage Mainstream Investors," World Economic Forum and Deloitte Touche Tohmatsu, September 2013, http://www3.weforum.org/docs/WEF_II_FromMarginsMainstream_Report_2013.pdf.

24 Institute for Sustainable Investing, "Sustainable Reality: Understanding the Performance of Sustainable Investment Strategies," *Morgan Stanley*, March 2015, accessed August 12, 2016, https://www.morganstanley.com/sustainableinvesting/pdf/sustainable-reality.pdf.

25 Ibid.

26 Institute for Sustainable Investing, "A Changing Climate: The Fossil Fuel Debate," *Morgan Stanley*, February 12, 2016, http://www.morganstanley .com/pub/content/dam/msdotcom/articles/fossil-fuels/A-Changing%20 Climate_The%20Fossil_Fuel_Debate.pdf.

27 Maxmin, "Fossil Fuel Divestment Is Simple."

28 Eric Russell, "Groups Raise Alarm Over Possible Tar Sands Pipeline," *Portland Press Herald*, June 19, 2012, http://www.pressherald.com/ 2012/06/19/opposition-to-possible-tar-sands-pipeline-comes-as-expected/.

29 Tony Iallornardo, "Tar Sands Giants Sneaky New Playbook Revealed," *National Wildlife Federation*, July 6, 2012, http://blog.nwf.org/2012/07/ tar-sands-giants-sneaky-new-playbook-revealed/.

30 Jim Murphy, "Big Oil's Plans for Tar Sands in New England," *National Wildlife Federation*, May 21, 2012, http://blog.nwf.org/2012/05/big- oils-big-plans-for-tar-sands-in-new-england/.

31 Eric Lipton and Clifford Krauss, "Fossil Fuel Industry Ads Dominate TV Campaign," *New York Times*, September 13, 2012, http://www.nytimes .com/2012/09/14/us/politics/fossil-fuel-industry-opens-wallet-to-defeat- obama.html?pagewanted=all.

32 Nicky Woolf, "Cornel West Warns of 'Planetary Selma' at Harvard Fossil Fuel Divestment Protest," *The Guardian*, April 17, 2015, https://www .theguardian.com/environment/2015/apr/17/harvard-divestment-protest- civil-rights-moment.

33 Chloe Maxmin, "Harvard Students Call for Fossil Fuel Divestment," *First Here Then Everywhere*, November 17, 2012, https://firstheretheneverywhere .org/2012/11/17/harvard-students-call-for-fossil-fuel-divestment/.

34 Justin Gillis, "To Stop Climate Change, Students Aim at College Portfolios," *New York Times*, December 4, 2012, http://www.nytimes .com/2012/12/05/business/energy-environment/to-fight-climate-change-college- students-take-aim-at-the-endowment-portfolio.html.

35 David Keith, "The Fossil Fuel Divestment Movement Can Succeed Where Politics Failed," *Boston Review*, December 23, 2013, https://bostonreview .net/blog/david-keith-fossil-fuel-university-endowment-divestment.

36 Geoffrey Morgan, "The Energy Industry Ignores the Fossil Fuel Divestiture Movement at Its Own Peril," *Alberta Oil*, December 4, 2013, http://www .albertaoilmagazine.com/2013/12/universities-divest-fossil-fuel-holdings/.

37 Hannah Borowsky, Chloe Maxmin, and Ben Franta, "Harvard Students Meet with Trustees to Discuss Divestment," *Go Fossil Free*,

February 2, 2013, http://gofossilfree.org/harvard-students-meet-with-trustees-to-discuss-divestment/.

38 Drew Faust, "Fossil Fuel Divestment Statement," Harvard Office of the President, October 3, 2013, http://www.harvard.edu/president/news/2013/fossil-fuel-divestment-statement.

39 Chloe Maxmin, Hannah Borowsky, and StudentNation, "The Time to Divest: A Response to Harvard President Drew Faust," *Nation*, October 15, 2013, https://www.thenation.com/article/time-divest-response-harvard-president-drew-faust/.

40 Steven Mufson, "Stanford Becomes the Most Prominent University Yet to Divest from Coal," *Washington Post*, May 6, 2014, https://www.washingtonpost.com/news/wonk/wp/2014/05/06/stanford-becomes-the-most-prominent-university-yet-to-divest-from-coal/.

41 Joe Romm, "Exclusive: Harvard President Faust Says Fossil Fuel Companies Are Not Blocking Clean Energy," *ThinkProgress*, March 4, 2014, https://thinkprogress.org/exclusive-harvard-president-faust-says-fossil-fuel-companies-are-not-blocking-clean-energy-17a1257dca7d#.79pfdivko.

42 Robert Stavins, "Divestment Is No Substitute for Real Action on Climate Change," *Yale 360 Environment*, March 20, 2014, http://e360.yale.edu/feature/counterpoint_robert_stavins_divestment_no_substitute_for_real_action_on_climate/2749/.

43 Martha Hall Findlay and Jean Charest, "Fossil Fuels Divestment Movement: Good Intention, Bad Idea," *Globe and Mail*, February 2, 2015, http://www.theglobeandmail.com/opinion/fossil-fuels-divestment-movement-good-intention-bad-idea/article22743277/.

44 Suzy Thompson, "Is It Time to Stop Ignoring the Fossil Fuel Divestment Campaign?" *Alberta Oil*, January 12, 2015, http://www.albertaoilmagazine.com/2015/01/tipping-point/.

45 Nathaniel Bullard, "Fossil Fuel Divestment: A \$5 Trillion Challenge," *Bloomberg New Energy Finance*, August 23, 2014, http://about.bnef.com/content/uploads/sites/4/2014/08/BNEF_DOC_2014-08-25-Fossil-Fuel-Divestment.pdf.

46 "ESG Keys: Fossil Fuel Disinvestment," *UBS Global Research*, September 30, 2014, http://www.thegreenenterprise.com/wp-content/uploads/2013/11/UBS-Fossil-Fuel-Disinvestment-Is-it-the-answer-No-distributed-Power-Is-Sept30-2014.pdf.

47 Suzanne Goldenberg, "Harvard Prepares to Fight Fossil Fuel Divestment Case in Court," *Guardian*, February 19, 2015, https://www.theguardian.com/

environment/2015/feb/19/harvard-prepares-to-fight-fossil-fuel-divestment-case-in-court.

48 Theodore Delwiceh and Mariel Klein, "Judge Dismisses Divestment Lawsuit," *Crimson*, March 23, 2015, http://www.thecrimson.com/article/2015/3/24/judge-dismisses-divestment-lawsuit/.

49 Jennifer Reingold, "The Devastating Impact of Falling Oil Prices, in One Chart," *Fortune*, December 15, 2015, http://fortune.com/2015/12/15/oil-prices-impact-energy-industry/.

50 Merran Smith and Dan Woynillowicz, "The Clock Is Ticking for Canada to Capitalize on Renewable Energy," *Globe and Mail*, February 29, 2016, http://www.theglobeandmail.com/report-on-business/rob-commentary/the-clock-is-ticking-for-canadian-renewable-energy-developers-to-capitalize/article28941818/.

51 Emma Howard, "Harvard Divestment Campaigners Gear Up for a Week of Action," *Guardian*, April 13, 2015, https://www.theguardian.com/environment/2015/apr/13/harvard-divestment-campaigners-gear-up-for-a-week-of-action.

52 John Lauerman, "Harvard Names Former Oil Executive Hollister Financial Head," *Bloomberg*, April 23, 2015, http://www.bloomberg.com/news/articles/2015-04-23/harvard-names-former-oil-executive-hollister-financial-head.

53 Chloe Maxmin, "How Divest Harvard Has Already Won," *NuMundo*, June 12, 2015, https://blog.numundo.org/2015/06/12/how-divest-harvard-has-already-won/.

54 Reed Landberg, "Oxford University Limits Its Fossil Fuel Investments," *Bloomberg*, May 18, 2015, http://www.bloomberg.com/news/articles/2015-05-18/oxford-university-to-avoid-making-investments-in-coal-oil-sands.

55 Benjamin Hulac, "Norway's Plan to Divest Massive $900B Fund from Coal Could Hit U.S. Companies," *E&E*, June 8, 2015, http://www.eenews.net/stories/1060019806/print.

56 Damian Carrington, "Norway Confirms $900bn Sovereign Wealth Fund's Major Coal Divestment," *Guardian*, June 5, 2015, https://www.theguardian.com/environment/2015/jun/05/norways-pension-fund-to-divest-8bn-from-coal-a-new-analysis-shows.

57 Alex Nussbaum, "Fossil-Fuel Divestment Tops $3.4 Trillion Mark, Activists Say," *Bloomberg*, December 2, 2015, http://www.bloomberg.com/news/articles/2015-12-02/fossil-fuel-divestment-tops-3-4-trillion-mark-activists-say.

58 "ESG Keys: Fossil Fuel Disinvestment," *UBS Global Research.*

59 Chloe Maxmin, "In 2016, No More Human-As-Usual," *Nation,* January 22, 2016, https://www.thenation.com/article/in-2016-no-more-human-as-usual/.

60 Geoff Dembicki, "Civilization in 2025: Cleaner, Richer, Decentralized?" *Tyee,* April 14, 2014, http://thetyee.ca/News/2014/04/14/Civilization-2025/.

61 Ibid.

62 "Renewable Electricity Futures Study," *National Renewable Energy Laboratory,* January 21, 2016, http://www.nrel.gov/analysis/re_futures/.

63 Tim Dickinson, "The Koch Brothers' Dirty War on Solar Power," *Rolling Stone,* February 11, 2016, http://www.rollingstone.com/politics/news/the-koch-brothers-dirty-war-on-solar-power-20160211.

64 Arthur Nelson, "BP Lobbied Against EU Support for Clean Energy to Favour Gas, Documents Reveal," *Guardian,* August 20, 2015, https://www.theguardian.com/environment/2015/aug/20/bp-lobbied-against-eu-support-clean-energy-favour-gas-documents-reveal.

65 "How to Lose Half a Trillion Euros," *Economist,* October 12, 2013, http://www.economist.com/news/briefing/21587782-europes-electricity-providers-face-existential-threat-how-lose-half-trillion-euros.

66 Zachary Davies Boren and Lauri Myllyvirta, "2015: The Year Global Coal Consumption Fell Off a Cliff," *Greenpeace,* November 9, 2015, http://energydesk.greenpeace.org/2015/11/09/2015-the-year-global-coal-consumption-fell-off-a-cliff/.

67 Geoff Dembicki, "The End of Coal," *Foreign Policy,* December 10, 2015, http://foreignpolicy.com/2015/12/10/the-end-of-coal-paris-climate-summit-cop21-china/.

68 Ibid.

69 Charles Mann, "Solar or Coal? India's Decision May Decide the Fate of the Planet," *Wired,* December 23, 2015, http://www.wired.co.uk/article/india-climate-change-solar-coal.

70 Tom Randall, "Fossil Fuels Just Lost the Race Against Renewables," *Bloomberg,* April 14, 2015, http://www.bloomberg.com/news/articles/2015-04-14/fossil-fuels-just-lost-the-race-against-renewables.

71 Stephen Letts, "Global Energy Emissions Plateau Despite Economic Growth, International Energy Agency Data Shows," *ABC,* March 16, 2016,http://www.abc.net.au/news/2016-03-17/global-energy-emissions-have-decoupled-from-economic-growth-iea/7252980.

6. STAYING ALIVE IN PARIS

1 Erlend Knudsen, interview by author, December 9, 2015. All quotations from Erlend come from this interview unless otherwise cited.

2 Renee Lewis, "As UN Says World to Warm by 3 Degrees, Scientists Explain What That Means," *Al Jazeera*, September 23, 2015, http://america .aljazeera.com/articles/2015/9/23/climate-change-effects-from-a-3-c-world .html.

3 Makereta Komai, "Marshall Islands Youth Shares His Hopes for COP21," *SPREP*, December 2, 2015, https://www.sprep.org/climate-change/marshall-islands-youth-shares-his-hopes-for-cop21.

4 Morgan Curtis, "About Us," *Climate Journey*, accessed August 13, 2016, http://climatejourney.org/about/us/.

5 Morgan Curtis, interview by author, December 9, 2015. All quotations from Morgan come from this interview unless otherwise cited.

6 Chloe Maxmin, "Morgan Curtis of Climate Journey," *First Here, Then Everywhere*, accessed August 13, 2016, https://hrsthereneverywhere .org/morgan-curtis/.

7 Anna Fiorentino, "Dartmouth Engineer Bikes on a 'Climate Journey' to UN Conference," *Dartmouth Engineer Magazine*, April 2015, accessed August 13, 2016, http://engineering.dartmouth.edu/magazine/dartmouth-engineer-bikes-on-a-climate-journey-to-un-conference.

8 Amy Goodman, "'I'm Scared for My Future': Student Disrupts Speech by U.S. Climate Envoy Todd Stern in Durban," *Democracy Now*, December 8, 2011, http://www.democracynow.org/2011/12/8/im_scared_for_my_future_student.

9 Ed King, "Stern Discipline: The US Climate Envoy Walking a Fine Line," *Climate Home*, November 13, 2015, http://www.climatechangenews .com/2015/11/13/stern-discipline-the-us-climate-envoy-walking-a-fine-line/.

10 Morgan Curtis, "What It's Like to Be a Youth Delegate at the U.N. Climate Summit in Paris," *Mashable*, December 6, 2015, http://mashable .com/2015/12/06/paris-climate-summit-youth/#m.obss_SQOq6.

11 Jennifer Anikst, "Questions for David Burstein," *Rotman Management Magazine*, Fall 2015, accessed August 13, 2016, http://www.rotman .utoronto.ca/Connect/Rotman-MAG/Idea-Exchange/David-Burstein.

12   Curtis, "What It's Like."

13   Jonathan Chait, "The Sunniest Climate-Change Story You've Ever Read," *New York Magazine*, September 7, 2015, http://nymag.com/daily/intelligencer/2015/09/sunniest-climate-change-story-ever-read.html.

14   Katherine Bagley, "Paris Climate March Is Canceled over Security Concerns," *Inside Climate News*, November 19, 2015, https://insideclimatenews.org/news/19112015/french-police-cancel-paris-climate-rallies.

15   Mikey Smith, "Is Justin Trudeau the Sexiest Politician in the World?", *Mirror*, October 20, 2015, http://www.mirror.co.uk/news/uk-news/justin-trudeau-sexiest-politician-world-6666495.

16   Bruce Campion-Smith, "Barack Obama Lays Out Red Carpet for Justin Trudeau in Reset of Relations," *Toronto Star*, November 19, 2015, https://www.thestar.com/news/canada/2015/11/19/trudeau-will-bring-energy-and-reform-to-canada-obama-says.html.

17   Geoff Dembicki, "In Paris, Trudeau 'Here to Help,' But Quiet on New Emissions Targets," *Tyee*, December 1, 2015, http://thetyee.ca/News/2015/12/01/Paris-Trudeau-No-New-Emissions-Targets/.

18   Morgan Curtis, "As COP21 Enters Final Week, Civil Society Escalates Message," *New Internationalist*, December 7, 2015, https://newint.org/blog/2015/12/07/civil-society-escalates-cop21-message/.

19   "Copenhagen Climate Summit: Live," *Telegraph*, December 7, 2009, http://www.telegraph.co.uk/news/earth/copenhagen-climate-change-confe/6728106/Copenhagen-climate-summit-live.html.

20   Fiona Harvey, "UN Chief Challenges World to Agree Tougher Target for Climate Change," *Guardian*, June 1, 2011, https://www.theguardian.com/environment/2011/jun/01/climate-change-target-christiana-figueres.

21   Reuters, "Climate Change Could Push 100 Million into Poverty by 2030: WorldBank,"*Newsweek*,November8,2015,http://www.newsweek.com/climate-change-push-people-poverty-world-bank-392024.

22   "Youth 'Climate Ambassador' Captures the Stage at Copenhagen Conference," *UNICEF*, December 9, 2009, http://www.unicef.org/infoby country/denmark_52046.html.

23   Raquel Rosenberg and Dyanna Jaye, "A Future under Negotiation," *Huffington Post*, December 1, 2015, http://www.huffingtonpost.com/raquel-rosenberg/a-future-under-negotiatio_b_8684612.html.

24   Maryam Omidi, "Threatened Maldives Urges Joint Action at Climate Talks," *Reuters*, November 9, 2009, http://www.reuters.com/article/us-climate-maldives-idUSTRE5A83R020091109.

25   Kyla Mandel, "Meet the Climate Scientists Travelling by Bike and Foot from the Poles to Paris," *DesmogUK*, December 12, 2015, http://www .desmog.uk/2015/11/12/meet-climate-scientists-travelling-bike-and-foot-poles-paris.

26   Emma Howard, "Running for Climate Change: 'I Was Very Much on the Edge Physically and Mentally,'" *Guardian*, November 10, 2015, https:// www.theguardian.com/environment/2015/nov/10/through-snowstorms-and-deserts-the-climate-scientists-running-from-the-poles-to-paris.

27   Ibid.

28   Mandel, "Meet the Climate Scientists."

29   "Global Consultation at Bonn: Climate Action by Most Vulnerable Could Soar to New Levels," Climate Vulnerable Forum, June 4, 2015, http://www .thecvf.org/global-consultation-at-bonn-climate-action-by-most-vulnerable-could-soar-to-new-levels/.

30   Sohara Mehroze, "Harnessing Power of Youth for Climate Action," *Climate Tracker*, February 23, 2016, http://climatetracker.org/harnessing-power-of-youth-for-climate-action/.

31   Joeri Rogelj et al., "Energy System Transformations for Limiting End-of-Century Warming to Below 1.5 °C," *Nature Climate Change* 5 (2015): 519–27.

32   "World's Vulnerable Open Gateway to Climate Safe Future at Paris," *Climate Vulnerable Forum*, November 30, 2015, http://www.thecvf.org/ worlds-vulnerable-open-gateway-to-climate-safe-future-at-paris/.

33   Morgan Curtis, "Youth Stand with Vulnerable to Demand Climate Justice," *New Internationalist*, December 3, 2015, https://newint.org/ features/web-exclusive/2015/12/03/youth-join-vulnerable-countries-to-demand-climate-justice/.

34   Ibid.

35   Ibid.

36   Ibid.

37   Samisoni Pareti, "Young i-Kiribati Woman Features in COP21 Speech," *SPREP*, December 7, 2015, https://www.sprep.org/climate-change/young-i-kiribati-woman-features-in-cop21-speech.

38   Ari Shapiro, "For the Marshall Islands, the Climate Goal Is '1.5 to Stay Alive,'" *NPR*, December 9, 2015, http://www.npr.org/sections/parallels/ 2015/12/09/459053208/for-the-marshall-islands-the-climate-goal-is-1-5-to-stay-alive.

39 Karl Mathiesen and Fiona Harvey, "Climate Coalition Breaks Cover in Paris to Push for Binding and Ambitious Deal," *Guardian*, December 8, 2015, https://www.theguardian.com/environment/2015/dec/08/coalition-paris-push-for-binding-ambitious-climate-change-deal.

40 Ed King, "Foie Gras, Oysters and a Climate Deal: How the Paris Pact Was Won," *Climate Home*, December 14, 2015, http://www.climatechange news.com/2015/12/14/foie-gras-oysters-and-a-climate-deal-how-the-paris-pact-was-won/.

41 Ed King and Megan Darby, "COP21: US Joins 'Coalition of High Ambition' at Paris Talks," *Climate Home*, December 9, 2015, http://www .climatechangenews.com/2015/12/09/cop21-live-climate-talks-intensify-in-paris/.

42 Alex Pashley, "Brazil Backs 'High Ambition Coalition' to Break Paris Deadlock," *Climate Home*, December 11, 2015, http://www .climatechangenews.com/2015/12/11/brazil-backs-high-ambition-coalition-to-break-paris-deadlock/.

43 Selina Leem, "Marshall Islands 18-year-old Thanks UN for Climate Pact," *Climate Home*, December 14, 2015, http://www.climatechangenews .com/2015/12/14/marshall-islands-18-year-old-thanks-un-for-climate-pact/.

44 Bill McKibben, "World Leaders Adopt 1.5 C Goal—And We're Damn Well Going to Hold Them to It," *Grist*, December 12, 2015, http://grist .org/climate-energy/world-leaders-adopt-1-5-c-goal-and-were-damn-well-going-to-hold-them-to-it/.

45 Ibid.

46 Chloe Maxmin, "In 2016, No More Human-As-Usual," *Nation*, January 22, 2016, https://www.thenation.com/article/in-2016-no-more-human-as-usual/.

47 Andrew Freedman, "The Hottest Year," *Mashable*, January 20, 2016, http://mashable.com/2016/01/20/2015-hottest-year-record/#_OpDFFm Makqs.

48 Bobby Magill, "Study Sees Possible Decline in Global CO_2 Emissions," *Climate Central*, December 7, 2015, http://www.climatecentral.org/news/study-sees-possible-decline-in-emissions-19775.

49 Morgan Curtis, "In Final Hours Thoughts Turn to Look at What 'Winning' Looks Like in Paris," *New Internationalist*, December 11, 2015, https://newint.org/blog/2015/12/11/avaaz-petitioning-for-a-poor-climate-agreement/.

7. THE TRUE MEANING OF SHARING

1   Elle-Máijá Tailfeathers, interview by author, January 12, 2016. All quota-
    tions from Elle-Máijá come from this interview unless otherwise cited.

2   Lisa Charleyboy, "Filming Your Family's Past," *CBC Radio*, August 4,
    2015,http://www.cbc.ca/radio/newfire/what-does-it-mean-to-come-of-age-
    1.3172991/filming-your-family-s-past-1.3173202.

3   Ibid.

4   Jason Tanz, "How Airbnb and Lyft Finally Got Americans to Trust Each
    Other," *Wired*, April 23, 2014, http://www.wired.com/2014/04/trust-in-
    the-share-economy/.

5   Whitney Pastorek, "How One Young Car Sharing Entrepreneur Keeps
    Disrupting How We Get Around," *Fast Company*, October 31, 2013,
    http://www.fastcoexist.com/3020788/change-generation/how-one-young-
    car-sharing-entrepreneur-keeps-disrupting-how-we-get-around.

6   Andrew McConnell, "The Politics of the Sharing Economy: Is It
    Republican, Democratic, Libertarian, or Green?" *Rented*, January 27,
    2016, http://www.rented.com/vacation-rental-best-practices-blog/politics-
    sharing-economy/?hsFormKey=29414c94939b4f9b880b4d16b8267ed0.

7   Jeremy Rifkin, "How Developing Nations Can Leapfrog Developed
    Countries with the Sharing Economy," *Huffington Post*, November 2,
    2015, http://www.huffingtonpost.com/jeremy-rifkin/developing-nations-
    sharing-economy_b_8419960.html.

8   Andrew Leonard, "Why Uber Must Be Stopped," *Salon*, August 31, 2014,
    http://www.salon.com/2014/08/31/why_uber_must_be_stopped/.

9   Noam Scheiber, "Silicon Valley Is Ruining 'Sharing' for Everybody," *New
    Republic*, August 13, 2014, https://newrepublic.com/article/119072/silicon-
    valleys-sharing-economy-airbnb-lyft-are-selling-big-lie.

10 Juliet Schor, "Debating the Sharing Economy," *Great Transition Initiative*,
    October 2014, http://www.greattransition.org/images/GTI_publications/
    Schor_Debating_the_Sharing_Economy.pdf.

11 Tim Rayner, "The Family History of Facebook: How Social Media Will
    Change the World," *Philosophy for Change*, September 27, 2012, https://
    philosophyforchange.wordpress.com/2012/09/27/the-family-history-of-
    facebook-why-social-media-will-change-the-world/.

12 John Tierny, "Tips from the Potlatch, Where Giving Knows No Slump," *New York Times*, December 15, 2008, http://www.nytimes.com/2008/12/16/science/16tierney.html.

13 Rayner, "Family History."

14 Pastorek, "How One Young Car Sharing Entrepreneur."

15 Tanz, "How Airbnb and Lyft."

16 "The Sharing Economy—Sizing the Revenue Opportunity," *PricewaterhouseCoopers*, 2014, accessed August 13, 2016, http://www.pwc.co.uk/issues/megatrends/collisions/sharingeconomy/the-sharing-economy-sizing-the-revenue-opportunity.html.

17 "CALinnovates' Comments Regarding the 'Sharing' Economy: Issues Facing Platforms, Participants, and Regulators A Federal Trade Commission Workshop," *CAL Innovates*, June 20, 2015, http://www.calinnovates.org/calinnovates-comments-regarding-the-sharing-economy-issues-facing-platforms-participants-and-regulators-a-federal-trade-commission-workshop/.

18 "Millennials Are More on Board with the Sharing Economy," *eMarketer*, October 13, 2015, http://www.emarketer.com/Article/Millennials-More-On-Board-with-Sharing-Economy/1013098.

19 Jennifer Rossa and Anne Riley, "These Charts Show How the Sharing Economy Is Different," *Bloomberg*, June 15, 2015, http://www.bloomberg.com/news/articles/2015-06-15/these-charts-show-how-the-sharing-economy-is-different.

20 John Burbank, "The Rise of the 'Sharing Economy,'" *Huffington Post*, June 5, 2014, http://www.huffingtonpost.com/john-burbank/the-rise-of-the-sharing-e_b_5454710.html.

21 Neal Gorenflo, "The New Sharing Economy," *Shareable*, December 24, 2010, http://www.shareable.net/blog/the-new-sharing-economy.

22 Alison Griswold, "Hillary Clinton Is Skeptical about the 'Sharing Economy,'" *Slate*, July 13, 2015, http://www.slate.com/blogs/moneybox/2015/07/13/hillary_clinton_economy_speech_i_ll_crack_down_on_sharing_economy_exploitation.html.

23 Gregory Ferenstein, "The Unusual Politics of Silicon Valley, Explained," *Vox*, November 6, 2015, http://www.vox.com/2015/9/29/9411117/silicon-valley-politics-charts.

24 Anthony Caole, "The 'New' Sharing Economy," *Three Star Enterprises*, September 26, 2013, http://www.3starak.com/home/blog.

25 Tracy Sherlock, "Aboriginal Leader Calls for Indigenous Initiatives," *Vancouver Sun*, May 14, 2015, http://www.pressreader.com/canada/the-vancouver-sun/20150514/281608124009888.

26 Geoff Dembicki, "Finding Hope in the 'Sharing Economy,'" *Tyee*, February 17, 2014, http://thetyee.ca/Opinion/2014/02/17/Sharing-Economy-Hope/.

27 Ibid.

28 Tyler Hamilton, "Hotels, Airbnb Battle for Green Cred," *Corporate Knights*, September 21, 2015, http://www.corporateknights.com/channels/built-environment/hotels-airbnb-battle-for-green-cred-14428152/.

29 Dominique Mosbergen, "Most Millennials Won't Own a Car in 5 Years, Says Lyft Co-Founder John Zimmer," *Huffington Post*, July 7, 2015, http://www.huffingtonpost.com/2015/07/08/millennials-car-ownership-rideshare-services_n_7750246.html.

30 Derek Thompson and Jordan Weissman, "The Cheapest Generation," *Atlantic*, September, 2012, http://www.theatlantic.com/magazine/archive/2012/09/the-cheapest-generation/309060/.

31 Derek Thompson, "Millennials: Not So Cheap, after All," *Atlantic*, April 21, 2015, http://www.theatlantic.com/business/archive/2015/04/millennials-not-so-cheap-after-all/391026/.

32 Greg Migliore, "After Further Review, Millennials Like Cars after All," *Autoblog*, January 27, 2015, http://www.autoblog.com/2015/01/27/millennials-like-cars-after-all-mtv-study/.

33 Joe Cortwright, "Young People Are Buying Fewer Cars," *CityObservatory*, April 22, 2015, http://cityobservatory.org/young-people-are-buying-fewer-cars/.

34 Tony Dutzik, Jeff Inglis, and Phineas Baxandall, "Millennials in Motion: Changing Travel Habits of Young Americans and the Implications for Public Policy," United States Public Interest Research Group, 2014, accessed August 13, 2016, http://www.uspirg.org/sites/pirg/files/reports/Millennials%20in%20Motion%20USPIRG.pdf.

35 Peter Viechnicki, Abhijit Khuperkar, Tiffany Dovey Fishman, and William D. Eggers, "Carsharing," Deloitte University Press, May 18, 2015, http://dupress.com/articles/smart-mobility-trends-carsharing-market/.

36 Norihiko Shirouzu, "Millennials Are Shifting Car Ownership Model; Ask Toyota," *Reuters*, February 2, 2016, http://www.reuters.com/article/us-autos-toyota-millennials-idUSKCN0VI295.

37 Kathleen Burke, "The Auto Industry Will Change More in Next Five Years Than Prior 50, Says GM's President," *MarketWatch*, June 12, 2016, http://www.marketwatch.com/story/why-gms-president-says-you-wont-be-driving-its-cars-2016-06-01.

38 Dembicki, "Finding Hope."

39 Rifkin, "How Developing Nations."

40 Christopher Bateman, "A Colossal Fracking Mess," *Vanity Fair*, June 2010, accessed August 15, 2016, http://www.vanityfair.com/news/2010/06/fracking-in-pennsylvania-201006.

41 "2006 Community Profiles," *Statistics Canada*, 2006, accessed August 15, 2016, http://www12.statcan.ca/census-recensement/2006/dp-pd/prof/92-591/details/page.cfm?Lang=E&Geo1=CSD&Code1=4803802&Geo2=PR&Code2=48&Data=Count&SearchText=blood&SearchType=Begins&SearchPR=01&B1=All&Custom=.

42 Abrahm Lustgarten, "Land Grab Cheats North Dakota Tribes Out of $1 Billion, Suits Allege," *ProPublica*, February 23, 2013, https://www.propublica.org/article/land-grab-cheats-north-dakota-tribes-out-of-1-billion-suits-allege.

43 Elle-Máijá Tailfeathers, "Fractured Land," *Briar Patch Magazine*, February 28, 2012, https://briarpatchmagazine.com/articles/view/fractured-land.

44 "Human Rights Crisis," *Amnesty International Canada*, accessed August 15, 2016, http://www.amnesty.ca/our-work/campaigns/no-more-stolen-sisters/human-rights-crisis.

45 A. C. Shilton, "The Human Cost of Keystone XL," *Pacific Standard*, May 14, 2015, https://psmag.com/the-human-cost-of-keystone-xl-231e04adf683#.yom4s64ki.

46 "Frack Off: Elle-Máijá Tailfeathers-Blood Indian Tribe," *School of Media Studies*, New School, October 16, 2014, https://www.youtube.com/watch?v=6ENPM-9vJxQ.

47 Charleyboy, "Filming Your Family's Past."

48 "DiCaprio Wins at Golden Globes, Urges Recognition of Indigenous People and Lands," *CBC News*, January 11, 2016, http://www.cbc.ca/news/canada/saskatchewan/dicaprio-golden-globes-recognition-1.3398212.

49 Gyasi Ross, "The Revenant Is Ultimately the Same Old White Savior Stuff for Native People," *Huffington Post*, January 18, 2016, http://www.huffingtonpost.com/gyasi-/revenant-review-native-people_b_9005464.html.

50 "'Alive' or Better Off Dead?" *Elle-Maija-Tailfeathers.com*, December 10, 2013, http://elle-maija-tailfeathers.com/?p=107.

51 Kimberly Truong, "Historically Latino District in San Francisco on Track to Lose Half Its Latino Population," *Mashable*, October 30, 2015, http://mashable.com/2015/10/30/san-francisco-mission-latino-population/#WnUKzz4RQEqE.

52 Pastorek, "How One Young Car Sharing Entrepreneur."

53 Heather Stenberger, "#LyftCheyenneRiver: CRYP Prepares to Welcome Lyft Drivers This December," *Lakota Youth*, October 19, 2015, http://www.lakotayouth.org/2015/10/lyftcheyenneriver-cryp-prepares-to-welcome-lyft-drivers-this-december/.

54 Bianca Consunji and Evan Engel, "No Country for Cryptocurrency," *Mashable*, September 18, 2014, http://mashable.com/2014/09/18/mazacoin-bitcoin-native-americans/#_OpDFFmMakqs.

55 Ibid.

56 Tim Redmond, "Don't Be a Stanford Asshole," *48 Hills*, January 26, 2015, http://48hills.org/2015/01/26/dont-stanford-asshole/#permanently-moved.

57 Andy Kroll, "Electric Car Guru Elon Musk Ditches Mark Zuckerberg's FWD.us Group," *Mother Jones*, May 13, 2013, http://www.motherjones.com/mojo/2013/05/elon-musk-mark-zuckerberg-fwd-us-immigration.

58 Leonard, "Why Uber Must Be Stopped."

59 Antony Funnell, "The Threat Uber Poses to Competition and Productive Capitalism," *ABC*, September 2, 2015, http://www.abc.net.au/radio-national/programs/futuretense/the-threat-uber-poses-to-competition-and-productive-capitalism/6743580.

60 Julia Carrie Wong, "Airbnb Apologizes for Passive Aggressive Ads on Muni Shelters," *San Francisco Weekly*, October 21, 2015, http://archives.sfweekly.com/thesnitch/2015/10/21/passive-aggressive-pro-airbnb-ads-appear-on-muni-shleters.

61 John Naughton, "Big, Bad Tech: How America's Digital Capitalists Are Taking Us All for a Ride," *Guardian*, November 23, 2014, https://www.theguardian.com/commentisfree/2014/nov/23/uber-dig-dirt-big-tech-digital-capitalists.

62 Adrianne Jeffries, "Native American Tribes Adopt Bitcoin-like Currency, Prepare to Battle US Government," *Verge*, March 5, 2015, http://www.theverge.com/2014/3/5/5469510/native-americans-assert-their-independence-through-cryptocurrency-mazacoin.

63 Lynnley Browning, "Oglala Sioux Hope Bitcoin Alternative, Mazacoin, Will Change Economic Woes," *Newsweek*, August 14, 2014, http://www.newsweek.com/2014/08/22/tribe-brought-you-custers-last-stand-sitting-bulls-bitcoin-264440.html.

64 Juliet Schor, "The Sharing Economy: Reports from Stage One," *Connected Consumption and Connected Economy Project—MacArthur Foundation*, November 2015, accessed August 15, 2016, https://www.bc.edu/content/dam/files/schools/cas_sites/sociology/pdf/TheSharingEconomy.pdf.

65 Sarah van Gelder and Rebecca Adamson, "Age-Old Wisdom for the New Economy," *Yes! Magazine*, July 7, 2009, http://www.yesmagazine.org/issues/the-new-economy/age-old-wisdom-for-the-new-economy.

66 Schor, "Sharing Economy,"

67 Sam Bliss, "The Sharing Economy Is Bullsh!t. Here's How We Can Take It Back, *Grist*, March 9, 2015, http://grist.org/politics/the-sharing-economy-is-bullsht-heres-how-we-can-take-it-back/.

68 Ibid.

69 Gelder and Adamson, "Age-Old Wisdom."

8. RADICAL GOES MAINSTREAM

1   Saba Hafeez, interview by author, March 15, 2016. All quotations from Saba come from this interview unless otherwise cited.

2   Bernie Sanders, "Bernie Sanders: 'I Will be a Candidate for President,'" *Bernie 2016*, April 30, 2015, https://berniesanders.com/press-release/bernie-sanders-i-will-be-a-candidate-for-president/.

3   Emily Stephenson, "Liberal U.S. Senator Sanders to Challenge Clinton in 2016 Race," *Reuters*, April 30, 2015, http://www.reuters.com/article/us-usa-election-sanders-idUSKBN0NL1HA20150430.

4   Alan Rappeport, "Bernie Sanders, Long-Serving Independent, Enters Presidential Race," *New York Times*, April 29, 2015, http://www.nytimes.com/2015/04/30/us/politics/bernie-sanders-campaign-for-president.html.

5   Dan Merica, "Bernie Sanders Is Running for President," *CNN*, April 30, 2015, http://www.cnn.com/2015/04/29/politics/bernie-sanders-announces-presidential-run/.

6   Ibid.

7   Adam Gabbatt, "Millennials 'Heart' Bernie Sanders: Why the Young and Hip Are #FeelingtheBern," *Guardian*, August 20, 2015, https://www.theguardian.com/us-news/2015/aug/20/bernie-sanders-millennials-young-voters.

8   Ed Adamcyzk, "Sanders Leads Clinton Among Millennials, Poll Finds," *UPI*, October 16, 2015, http://www.upi.com/Top_News/US/2015/10/16/Sanders-leads-Clinton-among-millennials-poll-finds/3071445008835/.

9   Eric Bradner and Dan Merica, "Young Voters Abandon Hillary Clinton for Bernie Sanders," *CNN*, February 10, 2016, http://www.cnn.com/2016/02/10/politics/hillary-clinton-new-hampshire-primary/.

10 Liz Fields, "'We Will Not Be Tricked': Why Millennials Really Love Bernie Sanders," *Vice*, November 2, 2015, https://news.vice.com/article/we-will-not-be-tricked-why-millennials-really-love-bernie-sanders.

11 Bernie Sanders, "The Urgency of a Moral Economy: Reflections on the 25th Anniversary of Centesimus Annus," *Bernie 2016*, April 15, 2016, https://berniesanders.com/urgency-moral-economy-reflections-anniversary-centesimus-annus/.

12 David Roberts, "Hillary Clinton's Climate and Energy Policies, Explained," *Vox*, July 29, 2016, http://www.vox.com/2016/5/9/11548354/hillary-clintons-climate-and-energy-policies-explained.

13 "Combating Climate Change to Save the Planet," *Bernie 2016,* accessed August 16, 2016, https://berniesanders.com/issues/climate-change/.

14 Rosemary Westwood, "To Yearn for Bernie Sanders Is to Be the Quintessential Young Canadian Lefty," *Metro Views*, April 11, 2016, http://www.metronews.ca/views/metro-views/2016/04/11/to-yearn-for-bern-is-to-be-the-quintessential-canadian-lefty.html.

15 Myles Udland, "HILLARY: Corporate America Is Obsessed with 'Quarterly Capitalism—Here's How I'd Change That," *Business Insider*, April 1, 2016, http://www.businessinsider.com/hillary-clinton-quarterly-capitalism-2016-4.

16 Sanders, "Urgency of a Moral Economy."

17 Darren Samuelsohn, "Bernie's Army of Coders," *Politico*, February 18, 2016, http://www.politico.com/magazine/story/2016/02/bernie-sanders-army-of-coders-2016-213647.

18 Gyasi Ross, "The Only Presidential Candidate That Makes Indian Country a Priority: Native People Feeling the Bern," *Indian Country Today*, March 18, 2016, http://indiancountrytodaymedianetwork.com/2016/03/18/only-presidential-candidate-makes-indian-country-priority-native-people-feeling-bern.

19 Elias Isquith, "Something Bold Needs to Happen": An In-depth Look at Millennial America," *Salon*, February 20, 2016, http://www.salon.com/2016/02/20/something_bold_needs_to_happen_an_in_depth_look_at_millennial_america/.

20 Sanders, "Combating Climate Change."

21 Geoff Dembicki, "Killing Clean Energy Laws," *CorpWatch*, May 5, 2011, accessed August 16, 2016, http://www.corpwatch.org/article.php?id=15645.

22 Kate Galbraith, "California Weighs Low-Carbon Fuel Standard," *New York Times*, April 23, 2009, http://green.blogs.nytimes.com//2009/04/23/california-weighs-low-carbon-fuel-standard/.

23 Geoff Dembicki, "The Battle to Block Low Carbon Fuel Standards," *Tyee*, March 17, 2011, http://thetyee.ca/News/2011/03/17/LowCarbonFuelFight/.

24 Dembicki, "Killing Clean Energy Laws."

25 Ibid.

26 Ibid.

27 Ibid.

28 Sanders, "Combating Climate Change."

29 Scott Malone, "Liberals Work to Lure Elizabeth Warren into White House Race," *Reuters*, February 13, 2015, http://www.reuters.com/article/us-usa-politics-newhampshire-warren-idUSKBN0LH27L20150213.

30 Ben Wikler, "Yes, We Need Elizabeth Warren in the Senate. And She Should Also Run for President," *Huffington Post*, March 19, 2015, http://www.huffingtonpost.com/ben-wikler/yes-we-need-elizabeth-warren-in-the-senate-and-she-should-also-run-for-president_b_6896892.html.

31 Dan Merica, "Run Warren, Done: Liberal Effort to Draft Warren Disbands," *CNN*, June 2, 2015, http://www.cnn.com/2015/06/02/politics/elizabeth-warren-election-2016-democrats/.

32 Harper Neidig, "One Year into His Campaign, a Look at Sanders's Ascent in the Polls," *Hill*, April 30, 2016, http://thehill.com/campaign-polls/278260-one-year-into-his-campaign-a-look-at-sanderss-remarkable-rise-through-the.

33 Bernie Sanders, "Bernie's Announcment," *Bernie 2016*, May 26, 2015, https://berniesanders.com/bernies-announcement/.

34 Merica, "Bernie Sanders."

35 Paul Barrett, "Five Ways the Supreme Court Transformed Campaign Finance," *Bloomberg*, January 14, 2015, http://www.bloomberg.com/news/articles/2015-01-14/the-effect-of-citizens-united-supreme-court-ruling-on-campaign-finance.

36 Perry Bacon Jr., "Why Hillary Clinton Embraced Big Money in Politics," *NBC News*, May 7, 2015, http://www.nbcnews.com/meet-the-press/why-hillary-flip-flopped-big-money-politics-n355276.

37 Gregory Krieg, "Bernie Sanders Raised $6 Million from Small Donors in the First Six Weeks of His Campaign," *Mic*, June 12, 2015, https://mic.com/articles/120587/bernie-sanders-raised-6-million-from-small-donors-in-the-first-six-weeks-of-his-campaign#.FxUvBE7jw.

38 John Wagner, "Bernie Sanders Raises More than $33 Million in Latest Fundraising Quarter," *Washington Post*, January 2, 2016, https://www .washingtonpost.com/news/post-politics/wp/2016/01/02/bernie-sanders-raises-more-than-33-million-in-latest-fundraising-quarter/.

39 Eric Garcia, "Bernie Sanders's Team Is Embracing Former Elizabeth Warren Backers," *Atlantic*, August 19, 2015, http://www.theatlantic.com/ politics/archive/2015/08/bernie-sanderss-team-is-embracing-former-elizabeth-warren-backers/446484/.

40 Gabbatt, "Millennials 'Heart' Bernie Sanders."

41 Adamcyzk, "Sanders Leads Clinton."

42 "Harvard IOP Fall 2015 Poll," *Harvard Institute of Politics*, December 10, 2015, http://iop.harvard.edu/survey/details/harvard-iop-fall-2015-poll.

43 Rima Regas, "Bernie Bias: The Mainstream Media Undermines Sanders at Every Turn," *Alternet*, September 2, 2015, http://www.alternet.org/election-2016/bernie-bias-mainstream-media-undermines-sanders-every-turn.

44 Elizabeth Spayd, "Has the *Times* Dismissed Bernie Sanders?" *New York Times*, September 9, 2015, http://publiceditor.blogs.nytimes.com/2015/ 09/09/has-the-times-dismissed-bernie-sanders/.

45 Suzy Khimm, "Can Bernie Sanders's Reddit Army Get Organized?" *New Republic*, October 23, 2015, https://newrepublic.com/article/123199/can-bernie-sanderss-reddit-army-get-organized.

46 Max Fisher, "What They Said vs What They Really Meant: Democratic Candidates on 'America's Greatest Threat," *Vox*, October 14, 2015, http:// www.vox.com/2015/10/14/9528769/democratic-debate-national-security-threat.

47 "Democractic Debate Transcript: Clinton, Sanders, O'Malley in Iowa," *CBS News*, November 14, 2015, http://www.cbsnews.com/news/ democratic-debate-transcript-clinton-sanders-omalley-in-iowa/.

48 Devin Henry, "GOP Senators Rip Sanders for Linking Global Terror, Climate Change," *Hill*, November 17, 2015, http://thehill.com/policy/ energy-environment/260465-gop-senators-rip-sanders-for-linking-terror-climate.

49 Linda Qiu, "Fact-checking Bernie Sanders' Comments on Climate Change and Terrorism," *PolitiFact*, November 16, 2015, http://www.politifact .com/truth-o-meter/statements/2015/nov/16/bernie-s/fact-checking-bernie-sanders-comments-climate-chan/.

50 Rebecca Leber, "Bernie Sanders Might Want to Thank Climate Change Voters if He Wins Tonight," *New Republic*, February 1, 2016, https://

newrepublic.com/minutes/128871/bernie-sanders-might-want-thank-climate-change-voters-wins-tonight.

51   Stephen Collinson, "The Iowa Caucuses, Explained," *CNN*, February 2, 2016, http://www.cnn.com/2016/01/29/politics/iowa-caucuses-explainer/.

52   Nick Allen and Ruth Sherlock, "Clinton Faces Losing Iowa to Sanders Thanks to Young Women," *Telegraph*, January 31, 2016, http://www.telegraph.co.uk/news/worldnews/northamerica/usa/12132135/Clinton-faces-losing-Iowa-to-Sanders-thanks-to-young-women.html.

53   Nate Silver, "What Happens If Bernie Sanders Wins Iowa," *FiveThirtyEight*, January 29, 2016, http://fivethirtyeight.com/features/what-happens-if-bernie-sanders-wins-iowa/.

54   Collinson, "Iowa Caucuses, Explained."

55   Shane Ryan, "Caucus Night, or How Iowa Failed the Nation and Redeemed It Again," *Paste Magazine*, February 2, 2016, https://www.pastemagazine.com/articles/2016/02/post-251.html.

56   Anne Gearan and John Wagner, "Clinton Declares Narrow Iowa Victory Even as Final Tally Counted in Deadheat with Sanders," *Washington Post*, February 2, 2016, https://www.washingtonpost.com/politics/clinton-and-sanders-dead-even-after-iowa-voting-are-poised-for-a-long-slog/2016/02/02/ac52ff8a-c8fd-11e5-88ff-e2d1b4289c2f_story.html.

57   Anthony Zurcher, "US Election: Winners and Losers after Iowa Vote," *BBC*, February 2, 2016, http://www.bbc.com/news/election-us-2016-35462570.

58   Juana Summer and Megan Specia, "Hillary Clinton Barely Won, But Bernie Sanders Is the True Champion," *Mashable*, February 2, 2016, http://mashable.com/2016/02/02/sanders-tie-with-clinton-in-iowa/#S6f2GGMmaqqH.

59   Lucia Graves, "Iowa Proved Bernie Sanders Can Win—And That Hillary Clinton Is Beatable," *Guardian*, February 2, 2016, https://www.theguardian.com/commentisfree/2016/feb/02/iowa-caucus-bernie-sanders-can-win-hillary-clinton-beatable.

60   Philip Bump, "Young Voters Are Failing Bernie Sanders, Just as They've Failed So Many Before," *Washington Post*, February 22, 2016, https://www.washingtonpost.com/news/the-fix/wp/2016/02/22/younger-votes-didnt-come-through-for-bernie-sanders-because-they-almost-never-do/.

61   Jeff Stein, "Sanders Is Beating Obama's 2008 Youth Vote Record. And the Primary's Not Even Over," *Vox*, June 2, 2016, http://www.vox.com/2016/6/2/11818320/bernie-sanders-barack-obama-2008.

62 M. J. Lee, "How Bernie Sanders Has Changed the Democratic Party," *CNN*, May 9, 2016, http://www.cnn.com/2016/05/09/politics/bernie-sanders-democratic-party/.

63 Jill Abramson, "Sanders Is Bad on Detail, But He Has What Hillary Lacks: The Spirit of Protest," *Guardian*, April 9, 2016, accessed August 19, 2016, https://www.theguardian.com/commentisfree/2016/apr/09/hillary-clinton-winning-bernie-sanders-supporters-campaign-jill-abramson.

64 Damian Carrington, "March Temperature Smashes 100-year Global Record," *Guardian*, April 15, 2016, https://www.theguardian.com/environment/2016/apr/15/march-temperature-smashes-100-year-global-record.

65 John Cassidy, "Can Bernie Sanders Really Win the Nomination," *New Yorker*, March 27, 2016, http://www.newyorker.com/news/john-cassidy/can-bernie-sanders-really-win-the-nomination.

66 Jeff Stein, "Bernie Sanders's Campaign Is Still Raising Far More Money Than Hillary Clinton's," *Vox*, March 23, 2016, http://www.vox.com/2016/3/23/11286028/sanders-fundraising-beating-clinton.

67 Ibid.

68 Shane Goldmacher, "Bernie's Legacy: One of the Most Valuable Donor Lists Ever," *Politico*, June 6, 2016, http://www.politico.com/story/2016/06/bernie-sanders-actblue-donor-lists-223964.

69 Bill McKibben, "The Clinton Campaign Is Obstructing Change to the Democratic Platform," *Politico*, June 27, 2016, http://www.politico.com/magazine/story/2016/06/hillary-clinton-2016-democratic-platform-213993.

70 Ben Norton, "Sanders' Impressive Activist DNC Platform Committee Could Help Transform U.S. Progressive Politics," *Salon*, May 24, 2016, http://www.salon.com/2016/05/24/sanders_impressive_activist_dnc_platform_committee_could_help_transform_u_s_progressive_politics/.

71 McKibben, "Clinton Campaign."

72 Jeff Stein, "Bernie Sanders's Fight Over the Democratic Convention's Platform, Explained," *Vox*, June 28, 2016, http://www.vox.com/2016/6/28/12039638/bernie-sanders-convention-fight.

73 Phil McKenna, "Democrats Embrace Price on Carbon While Clinton Steers Clear of Carbon Tax," *InsideClimate News*, July 15, 2016, https://insideclimatenews.org/news/14072016/democratic-party-embrace-carbon-price-tax-hillary-clinton-bernie-sanders.

74 Callum Borchers, "No, the Pressure on Bernie Sanders to Drop Out Isn't a Media Creation," *Washington Post*, May 25, 2016, https://www

.washingtonpost.com/news/the-fix/wp/2016/05/25/no-pressure-on-bernie-sanders-to-drop-out-isnt-a-media-creation/.

75 Stuart Rothenburg, "How Bernie Sanders Missed His Moment," *Washington Post*, June 30, 2016, https://www.washingtonpost.com/news/powerpost/wp/2016/06/30/how-bernie-sanders-missed-his-moment/.

76 Abramson, "Sanders Is Bad on Detail,"

77 Jonathan Mahler and Yamiche Alcindor, "Bernie Sanders Makes a Campaign Mark. Now, Can He Make a Legacy?" *New York Times*, May 23, 2016, http://www.nytimes.com/2016/05/23/us/politics/bernie-sanders-campaign-legacy.html.

78 Aaron Blake, "More Young People Voted for Bernie Sanders Than Trump and Clinton Combined—By a Lot," *Washington Post*, June 20, 2016, https://www.washingtonpost.com/news/the-fix/wp/2016/06/20/more-young-people-voted-for-bernie-sanders-than-trump-and-clinton-combined-by-a-lot/.

HOW TO NOT SCREW UP THE CLIMATE: A GUIDE FOR DAILY LIVING

1   Bill McKibben, "Embarrassing Photos of Me, Thanks to My Right-Wing Stalkers," *New York Times*, August 5, 2016, http://www.nytimes.com/2016/08/07/opinion/sunday/embarrassing-photos-of-me-thanks-to-my-right-wing-stalkers.html

2   Bonnie Malkin, "Psychiatrists Discover First Case of Climate Change Delusion," *Telegraph*, July 11, 2008, http://www.telegraph.co.uk/news/earth/earthnews/3346988/Psychiatrists-discover-first-case-of-climate-change-delusion.html.

3   Annick de Witt, "People Still Don't Get the Link Between Meat Consumption and Climate Change," *Scientific American*, April 11, 2016, http://blogs.scientificamerican.com/guest-blog/people-still-don-t-get-the-link-between-meat-consumption-and-climate-change/.

4   "Composting and Climate Change," *Turning Earth*, accessed August 20, 2016, http://turningearthllc.com/what-we-do-2/compost-and-soil-amendments/composting-and-climate-change/.

5   Associated Press, "UN Green Economy Report: Millions of Jobs Can Be Created Protecting Environment," *Huffington Post*, May 31, 2012, http://www.huffingtonpost.ca/2012/05/31/un-green-economy-jobs-report_n_1558681.html.

Index

A Note on the Author

Geoff Dembicki has contributed to the *New York Times*, *Foreign Policy*, *Vice*, *Salon*, the *Atlantic*, the *Toronto Star*, and *The Tyee*, the independent online publication where the idea for this book began as a series called "Are We Screwed?" He's received media fellowships from the Asia-Pacific Foundation of Canada and the New York–based Solutions Journalism Network. Geoff lives in Vancouver, British Columbia. He was born in 1986.